Greek Islands

Limnos

Lesbos

Chios

dros

Tinos

MyKonos

Delos

ros

Naxos

Paros

Folegandros

Santorini

TURKEY

(Asia Minor)

Samos

Patmos

Kalymnos

Kos

Astypalaia

Rhodes

Karpathos

Kassos

rete

Cyprus

THE FOODS OF THE
GREEK ISLANDS

THE FOODS OF THE

COOKING AND CULTURE AT

GREEK ISLANDS

THE CROSSROADS OF THE MEDITERRANEAN

AGLAIA KREMEZI

INCLUDING RECIPES FROM NEW YORK'S ACCLAIMED MOLYVOS RESTAURANT
OWNERS, THE LIVANOS FAMILY; EXECUTIVE CHEF, JIM BOTSACOS

PHOTOGRAPHS BY AGLAIA KREMEZI

HOUGHTON MIFFLIN COMPANY

BOSTON NEW YORK

For information about permission to reproduce selections from
this book, write to Permissions, Houghton Mifflin Company,
215 Park Avenue South, New York, New York 10003.

Portions of this book have previously been published in the
Proceedings of The Oxford Symposium on Food and Cookery
(1994, 1995, 1996) and in the following magazines: *Gourmet*,
Slow (*the Slow Food Quarterly*), *Saveur* and *New Choices*.

Library of Congress Cataloging-in-Publication Data
Kremezi, Aglaia
    The foods of the Greek islands : cooking and culture at the
crossroads of the Mediterranean, including recipes by New York's
acclaimed Molyvos restaurant / Aglaia Kremezi ; photographs
by Aglaia Kremezi.
        p. cm.
ISBN 0-395-98211-1
        1. Cookery, Greek. 2. Molyvos (Restaurant) I. Botsacos, Jim.
II. Title
TX723.5.G8 K655   2000
641.59495—dc21   00-061324

Book design by Anne Chalmers
Cover photograph: Shrimp Baked in Tomato Sauce with Feta
        (*Garides Saganaki*), page 76
Food styling by Rori Spinelli
Prop styling by Betty Alfenito
Printed in the United States of America

RRD   10   9   8   7   6   5   4

ACKNOWLEDGMENTS

I can't thank my editor, Rux Martin, enough for embracing my work with such enthusiasm and devotion. Working with Rux for the first time was a truly enriching experience. I am similarly indebted to Sarah Jane Freymann, my dear friend and agent, who is a constant source of inspiration for me. Many thanks also to assistant managing editor Lori Galvin-Frost and designer Anne Chalmers.

My cooking is based on the foods that my mother, Frossoula Kremezi, prepared every day in our house. Tireless, well organized, intelligent and discreet, my mother has provided me with the best model in life that a woman could dream of. I owe a lot to my grandmother Anna Patiniotis, as well as to my aunt Katina Patiniotis, both great cooks.

I collected the material for this book over the course of many years. Although I keep extensive notes, I worry that I may miss thanking some of the generous people who helped me discover the foods of their region, by sharing their recipes, letting me read their mother's or grandmother's kitchen ledgers or simply by mentioning an old dish.

I would like to start by thanking the hardworking Vasso Kritaki and Yannis Mandalas on Chios, as well as Eleni Prochori on Syros, because they are among the very few Greek public servants who understand the importance of preserving the traditional recipes and use the re- sources of their regional governments to try and record them. I am really grateful to Achilleas Dimitropoulos for sharing with me his vast knowledge concerning the variety and the ways of cooking fish and seafood; also to Giorgos and Maria Koutsoumbis for uncovering the secrets of the cooking of Lesbos; and, on the same island, Christina and Dimitris Panteleimonitis, for their immense help and hospitality. I learned a lot from Viktoria Athanasiadou and her friends Evridiki Kalogeraki, Katina Xirouhaki, Virginia Bertaki and all the women of the Cultural Center of the Diocese of Chania, Crete, who invited me to taste the best foods of their region, cooking and sharing recipes with me. Many thanks to Kalliopi Delios from Avgonima, Chios, one of the most accomplished cooks I know, and, on the same island, Thomas Karamouslis, who shared so many stories and recipes. I am also grateful to the family of Yannis Choremis, who let me read his late mother's extensive kitchen notes; thanks to Katina Kritouli, from Pitios; Marionga Bobari, from Chios Town; and especially to Stefanos Kovas, an inspired chef devoted to the traditions of that island. Frosso Podotas, Kali and Virginia Nikolaki, Bety and Panagiotis Patiniotis and Irene Kali are only some of the cooks of Astypalaia who shared their recipes with me over the years. Popie and Nikola Papanikola let me pick vegetables from their wonderful garden there.

Many thanks to Kostas Prekas and Irene and

Stefania Gianisi, from Syros; also to Margarita Marouli, Flora Stefa and Stamatis Paouris from Kea; to Morfi Diakogiorgou, from Karpathos; Christos Danassis from Folegandros; and Maria Primikiri, who gave me marvelous recipes from Folegandros, also providing clever substitutions for some hard-to-find island ingredients. I am grateful to my dear friend and accomplished cook Despina Drakaki and her mother, Pantelia Kortianou, from Paros. On Kythera, I owe many thanks to Vassilis Haros, Eleni Kalligerou, Eleni Koroneou, the bakers Giannis Koroneos and Giorgos Kasimatis and especially Elenara (Eleni Kasimati) from Drymonas, who spent a whole day with me making the cracked wheat and sour milk pasta of the island. On Santorini, I want to thank Giorgos Hatziyannakis, the owner of the wonderful Selini restaurant, and also my friend Katerina Vassiliadou. On Cyprus, I am grateful to Claire Serafim, for her knowledge and hospitality; to the veteran chef and teacher Marios Mourtzis; and also to Emilia Ekonomou, Andromachi Markidou, Panagiota Kyriakou, Maria Hartoupalou, Despoula Andreou and Christos Georgiou, as well as to my friend Niki Bahariou.

Many thanks to the fellow cooks, authors and journalists who have written books—in Greek—on the cooking of their region and unselfishly compared notes and answered my questions: Dora Parisi, author of *Tastes of the Aegean* (with recipes from Lesbos), who tirelessly cooked many dishes for me; Nikoletta Foskolou, author of *Traditional Recipes from Tinos*, who not only shared recipes but sent me her mother's homemade cheeses; Michalis Magoulas, who let me read his book *The Cooking of Ithaca* before it was published; Eleni Troullou, author of *Delicacies from Sifnos*, and her husband, Antonis. Very special thanks to Ninetta Laskari, author of a marvelous book of history, memories and recipes, *Corfu, a Glimpse in Time 1204–1864*, who, with her writings and our lengthy conversations, introduced me to the authentic old recipes of her island. To Nikos and Maria Psilakis, who have collected an unbelievable number of recipes from all parts of Crete in both their books, *Traditional Cuisine of Crete* and *Olive Oil: The Civilization of the Olive Tree*, and to my dear friend Myrsini Lambraki, author of *The Wild Greens* and *Olive Oil: 5,000 Years of Taste and Civilization*.

For helping me make some sense out of the long and complicated history of island foods, I thank Phylis Bober, author of *Art, Culture and Cuisine: Ancient and Medieval Gastronomy*, and Andrew Dalby, author of *Siren Feasts: A History of Food and Gastronomy in Greece*; also Fred Plotkin, who was immensely helpful, with his vast knowledge of Italian foods, in comparing island recipes to the modern Venetian and Genoese ones. Thanks as well to cheese expert Daphne Zepos, for suggesting substitutes for Greek cheeses.

Paula Wolfert, my dear friend, was again, as she has always been, ready to answer questions about specific dishes and techniques, using her vast knowledge of Mediterranean foods. Additionally, she also helped me compile the list of sources.

Last, but not least, I would like to thank the Livanos family—and especially John, Nick and Chryssa—who created Molyvos, a New York restaurant that treats Greek cuisine with respect, something that couldn't have been accomplished without the talent of chefs Rick Moonen and Jim Botsacos.

CONTENTS

FOREWORD

The foods you will find in this book are the ones I like to cook every day or on special occasions, traditional and contemporary dishes that I love to eat. I collected many of them on summer vacations and special trips, others were given to me by great island cooks, and quite a few were handed down to me from my family, originally from the islands of the Cyclades.

I learned to cook from my mother, my grandmother and my aunt. Even before going to school, I remember shelling peas in the large kitchen of my grandfather's old house, which had a wood-burning cooking stove with a large hood over it. I was too short to reach the sink and had to stand on a stool in order to rinse and trim the wild greens or wash the dishes. I would help my aunt roll bitter orange peels and thread them like a necklace when she made her rolled bitter-orange preserves. My mother taught me how to prepare the artichokes that overran our garden. My younger sister and I always helped shape the Christmas honey cookies. We learned how to remove the stones from cherries using a hairpin—there were no special instruments for that then—and we looked on as my mother scaled and gutted all the many kinds of fish my father brought from the port of Piraeus, where he worked.

Watching my grandfather slaughter a hen with a small ax was traumatic, and we would cover our eyes as the hen flapped, headless, around the yard. But the dark-fleshed, chewy meat we cooked in stews or soups was so much more flavorful than that of the pallid, sickly looking chicken we eat today.

Both my mother's and father's families trace their roots to the islands: My father comes from Andros, my mother from Kea. I grew up on the outskirts of Athens, beside a large garden next to my mother's family's house. Nikitas Patiniotis, my grandfather from Kea, was a handsome and remarkable man. Calm, loving and compassionate, he often went as far as to buy the worst, almost rotten vegetables from the greengrocer who passed each day with his mule. This made my grandmother furious.

"He is a poor man, Anna, and if we don't buy them, who will?" I remember him saying to her apologetically. My grandfather

NIKITAS PATINIOTIS, MY GRANDFATHER FROM KEA

taught me all about the different wild greens —how and when to collect them. He spoke to me about all the plants of the garden, relating the story of the fragrant bay, once a beautiful woman. He identified the various insects for me, explaining how they lived and what they ate, insisting that there are no bad and good creatures but that each fulfills a purpose.

When I was fourteen, we left our house in the country and went to live in a flat in the center of Athens. Ever since, I have longed to return to the country. Now that we have purchased a house on the island of Kea, I feel I have come full circle.

Traveling from island to island, reading old books and kitchen ledgers, researching history and customs and building friendships with island cooks have made me proud of my origins. This book is not an encyclopedia of Greek island cooking but a very personal selection from thousands of recipes that I have collected over the years. Besides relying on personal preference, I have chosen dishes that can be successfully cooked away from the islands and outside Greece. Some islands are better represented than others, and I have undoubtedly missed some foods worth recording. Each village on each island has many different versions of the same dish, often using diverse ingredients; and Greece has about 170 inhabited islands in all.

It would be impossible to claim that I know all there is to know about the island foods. My search continues.

—AGLAIA KREMEZI

THE FOODS OF THE
GREEK ISLANDS

INTRODUCTION

Stretching from the shores of Turkey to the Ionian Sea east of Italy, the Greek islands have always been a crossroads for the inhabitants of the Mediterranean. The word "isolated" and the Greek word for island, *nesos* (NEE-sos), probably both come from the same Latin origin, *insula*, which later became *isola* ("island" in Italian). But the islands are hardly isolated places, especially if you compare them with the mountain villages of the mainland. Although surrounded by the sea, they have seldom been cut off from the rest of the world.

Throughout their history, even the tiniest, rockiest, most remote islands have stayed in touch with their neighbors, for Greek sailors traveled all over the Mediterranean. Often, their neighbors came to them too—not always with friendship in mind. Those picturesque whitewashed buildings perched high on rocky cliffs that are so characteristic of the Greek island landscape were, in actuality, often intended to be the first defense against marauding pirates and foreign invaders. Minoans, Phoenicians, Spartans, Athenians and other inhabitants of the various ancient city-states of mainland Greece ruled the islands in antiquity. They were succeeded by the Romans and by Byzantine lords, and then by the Venetians or Genoese, who held the islands for many centuries until the Ottoman Turks took them over. Certain islands were briefly dominated by the Catalans, during the Middle Ages, and others for a short period in the eighteenth century by the Russians and French. In the more recent past, the English and Italians also laid claim to some of the islands.

The culinary traditions of all these cultures have influenced, but never dominated, Greek island cooking, which relies on flavorful local ingredients rather than on complicated techniques. Seasonal vegetables, leafy greens, assorted crops that each family gathers or cultivates, grains, olives, olive oil, beans and other legumes, local cheeses, occasionally fresh or cured fish and, sometimes, meat provide the basis of everyday cooking. The festive foods, although more elaborate, are also seasonal.

Simple but never plain, the cuisine of the islands is remarkable for its ingenuity, combining and making the most of produce and other humble ingredients. Wild fennel, for example, which grows all over the islands, is used variously as an aromatic herb, put into stuffing, mixed with onions and flour and turned into savory patties or stewed with onions and sweet wine and served as a topping for pasta. Lemons, brought to the Mediterranean by the Arabs, are by far the most common flavoring of the Greek islands, as indispensable as salt. Grown in every garden, lemons perk up all sorts of dishes, from grilled meat and fish to greens, beans, stews and sweets. Piquant capers from the bushes that thrive in the stony landscape are put in everything from the potato-garlic dip known as *skordalia* to stews, where they

are used like green beans. Tomatoes, a much later addition to the Greek repertoire, arriving on the islands from Italy at the end of the nineteenth century, complement local olive oil from the trees that grow on some of the islands. Thyme grows all over the islands, helping the bees produce exquisitely flavored honey. Oregano is gathered on most of the islands during the spring and summer months.

THOUGH UNCOMPLICATED, the food of the islands is, nevertheless, sophisticated, with inspired dishes one would not expect to find in small rocky places that seem so far away from what most people perceive as "civilization." One summer morning about fifteen years ago on Astypalaia, an island of the Dodecanese in the southeastern Aegean, I was introduced to one such specialty, a stuffed pasta called *latzania*, which is traditionally made for the February carnival that precedes Lent before Easter. On a narrow, winding street on the hill in the beautifully preserved sixteenth-century capital of the island, Mr. George Podotas, the owner of a combination grocery, garment and hardware store, described the taste of this dish, which probably originated in Venice. With admiration, he explained that the pasta is filled with the creamy fresh cheese produced from the milk of the semi-wild goats of the island, which graze on the densely flavored wild greens. Besides pepper, the filling is spiced with the fragrant local wild saffron. "Even if you don't eat the pasta and only drink the broth in which it is cooked, you will never forget its taste," Mr. Podotas told me.

I finally got a detailed recipe from Mr. Podotas' wife, Frosso, and watched her demonstrate, with a piece of paper, how I should roll the pasta and twist its ends. When, the next day, I proudly brought her my *latzania*, she looked at the bowl with disdain. She tasted one and said, "Well, I suppose you can't do better with the summer cheese. It doesn't have much flavor now that the animals are fed hay and corn. You obviously used store-bought saffron from Athens. Why didn't you ask me to get you some of the local saffron the women collect for their homes?" I must have looked very disappointed, so she hastily added: "Well, it is very good, and in any event, it is just a try, to get an idea how you will make the real *latzania* in February."

ISLAND COOKING has also been profoundly shaped by the various rules of the Greek Orthodox Church. Christmas, Easter and August 15, the Virgin Mary's Assumption—the most colorful of all island festivals—are all preceded by forty days of Lent. During those periods, as well as every Wednesday and Friday, people abstain from all foods derived from animals: meat, dairy products and eggs. These periods have inspired cooks to invent a number of exquisite vegetarian dishes that substitute for the more familiar versions made with meat: Stuffed grape leaves are often filled with rice and herbs instead of ground meat. Crisp vegetable patties are made of shredded zucchini or chopped tomatoes, flavored with onion and mint or other herbs and fried in olive oil and served in place of meatballs. On the islands, these religious rules are followed by most of the people, and the local tavernas, which usually serve grilled meat or fish, offer *ladera*, veg-

etable stews cooked with olive oil, during Lent. (Even McDonald's, Wendy's and the Greek fast-food chains advertise Lenten menus during those days of abstinence!)

The recipes of the islands are very localized. A popular dish in one village may be completely unknown to the residents of a village only a couple of miles away. This makes for a remarkably diverse repertoire. One finds some foods inspired by elaborate Venetian cuisine. Others have their roots in ancient Greek or Roman dishes, and others come from the Ottoman-Turkish tradition. Still others recall dishes of the mainland. Often, all these influences are knit together.

ASTYPALAIA

Although there are some common characteristics in the cooking of each group of islands, even in the same group, the islands show surprising individuality. The Ionian islands, to the west of the mainland, are green and fertile—especially if one compares them with the arid and rocky islands of the Cyclades to the south and east. Because they have been under Western domination for a very long time, their cuisine is more elaborate, distinctly influenced by the Venetians, particularly on Corfu, the northernmost of the Ionian islands, and to a lesser extent on Ithaca and Cephalonia. On the Sporades and Evia, off the central eastern shore of the mainland, the local cooking, while retaining some typical island traditions, especially where fish cooking is concerned, seems to be closer to that of the neighboring Thessaly, the central part of the mainland. Lesbos, Chios and the other islands of the northeastern Aegean, right off the shores of Turkey, have a rich tradition of cooking partly influenced by the nearby Turkish coast.

The Cyclades, the poorest of all the islands, arid and stony, with very little cultivable land, demonstrate how inventive Greek island cooks can create very tasty dishes with few ingredients. The large islands of the Dodecanese, Rhodes and Kos, in the southeastern part of the Aegean, are fertile but are now completely exploited by tourism. Their traditional cooking, which barely survives among the pizza parlors and the pubs, reflects their wealth, as well as their proximity to the shores of Turkey. On the other hand, although Crete and Cyprus have tourist economies, they have managed to keep their agriculture and their traditional ways of cooking alive.

THE IONIAN ISLANDS

Off the western part of the mainland, the seven islands of the Ionian Sea extend from far north, a few miles from the coast of Albania, to the southern tip of the Peloponnese. Ruled at various times by the Venetians, the French and the English, these islands were among the few parts of Greece governed by a feudal system, like the rest of Europe. This created a Greek bourgeois society many years before Athens or any other part of the mainland became urbanized. For that reason, these islands have a more refined cuisine, which also shares strong Italian as well as French influences. This cooking was later adapted by the Athenian bourgeoisie when the city became the capital of the modern Greek state.

Corfu, more than any other of the Ionian islands, has retained many words from the old Venetian dialect as well as foods, some of which seem to have been forgotten in Italy. They include *stuffato*, a stew of meat or poultry slowly cooked together with vegetables, tart with quince, or the well-balanced veal *sofrito*, flavored with plenty of garlic, parsley and vinegar. There is a sharp dichotomy, though, between this cuisine of the old nobility and that of the rural common people.

That distinction was made fully evident in the center of Corfu one sunny winter afternoon. While I was enjoying a coffee and watching a game of cricket—a remnant from the English—played on the grounds a few yards from the old Venetian fortress, I struck up a conversation with an impeccably dressed lady sitting next to me. I asked her how the women cook the wild greens I had seen at the farmer's market. "People make a dish called *tsigarelli*, sautéing various kinds of spinach-like greens in olive oil with plenty of garlic and hot red peppers," the woman replied. When I asked her to give me her favorite combination of greens, she quickly said that she herself had never cooked the dish. It was food of the peasants, she explained, who used it as a topping for polenta, one of the island's staples. Noting my interest, she told me that her maid said the dish was served in a taverna in Garitsa, a working-class neighborhood at the southern end of Corfu Town. "The dishes there are red not from tomato but from hot pepper," she said with disdain.

CORFU

About an hour later, I made my way towards Yannis's taverna in Garitsa. There, from Yannis's wife, Sofia, I learned about the wild asparagus and the other winter and spring greens of the island.

The peppers about which the aristocratic lady had spoken so disparagingly are commonly used on Corfu and on Paxi, an island a few miles to the south. The hot dishes of these islands rival those of Macedonia and the rest of the northern mainland. But while the inhabitants of northern Greece got their affinity for peppers from the Ottoman Turks, who ruled them for many centuries, the people of Corfu and Paxi were probably influenced by the cooking of nearby Albania and the rest of the Balkans. They adopted the peppers, which could be easily cultivated in their fertile soil, in their quest to find substitutes for the expensive spices used by the nobility.

On Kythera, the southernmost of the Ionian group, the peasant cooking illustrates the continuity of age-old traditions common to all the Greek islands. In the farmer's market at Potamos, a village on the island, I found *sykomyzithra*, a fresh ricotta-like cheese thickened with the sap of the fig tree instead of rennet. I also enjoyed a tasty thick soup made from coarsely ground barley. Both the cheese and the barley soup have been prepared by islanders since the Neolithic Era. Other foods, like the famous savory barley and wheat biscuits of the island, fragrant with the local sweet olive oil, are fine examples of how well the islanders use their few available ingredients.

To learn about *ksinohondros*, the local pasta made from cracked wheat, I went to Drymonas, one of the villages on the southwestern part of the island, to watch Elenara Kasimati prepare it. She had soaked the wheat grains in water

overnight, then dried them completely in the sun, and when I arrived at her house, she was ready to grind the wheat in her old-fashioned hand mill. She fired up the hearth, brought out a large old copper pot and a wooden spoon and took a bowl of milk from her goat out of the refrigerator. She mixed the wheat with the milk and sprinkled in some of the fragrant coarse sea salt that the islanders gather from the rocks around the island, then sat down on a low stool in front of the fire and started to stir. As I watched her stir the milk and wheat in the big pot which stood on a tripod in the hearth, it occurred to me that she was duplicating a procedure which generations of women had done before her, probably since the Bronze Age. Then she said, "It is a bit long, this stirring. So I open the door to the next room and watch television as I stir. That way, time passes faster."

EVIA, THE SPORADES AND THE SARONIC ISLANDS

East of the mainland, Evia is one of the largest islands of the Aegean. Farther south, in the Saronic Gulf, between Attica—the region around Athens—and the Peloponnese, are the five Saronic islands. To the northeast of Evia are scattered the four islands of the Sporades—their name means "scattered," as in the word "sporadic."

Skyros, the southernmost island and the largest of the Sporades, was the first island I ever visited as a child. Molos, the tiny fishing village where my family stayed in the 1960s, had no electricity, and life there was very different from what we were used to. We rented the whitewashed stone house of a fisherman, right on the water. The sound of the waves lulled us to sleep on calm evenings and kept us awake during the windy nights. The house consisted of a simple large room, with a fireplace in one corner. It had a stone mantelpiece and shelves carved into the walls, where blue and white pottery plates and vases were neatly displayed. Skyros has a tradition of pottery, as do many of the other islands, and its pottery, produced from local clay, was for everyday use, not decoration. Most of the pots and pans were made of clay, as they have been since antiquity. Although stovetop cooking was done in aluminum pots, people still baked in the traditional clay casseroles. We placed the unglazed clay water jars on the windowsill so that the sea breezes would cool the water, since there was no refrigeration.

Kokalenia, the wife of Thodoros, the fisherman who rented us their house, cooked the fish her husband caught each day, taking it right from the boat to the pot. I have never tasted a better fish soup than hers. Goats provided the milk to make a strongly flavored cheese, which used to be stored by burying it in the sand. Kokalenia grated it over ordinary pasta or sprinkled it on top of a soup with *trahana*, a pasta made with sour milk and cracked wheat.

North of Skyros, closer to the shores of Thessaly, Skopelos and Skiathos are strongly influenced by the cooking and customs of that part of the mainland. The coiled greens pie of Skopelos is very similar to a version made in Thessaly and Epirus, in northern Greece. During weddings and big family celebrations on Skiathos, cooks don't make sesame candy or almond cookies as they do on most other islands but, rather, baklava, much as they do in Thessaly.

Evia is hardly considered an island by Greeks, because it is so close to the mainland, linked to it with bridges. Its landscape, too, is similar to that of the central mainland, with fertile plains, olive groves and beautiful pine forests in the north. Fried cheese bread is one of the best-known specialties of the island. The local tavernas also offer excellent grilled meats, and *kokoretsi*, the famous delicacy of charcoal-grilled skewered pieces of lamb offal wrapped in lamb's intestines. Made all over the mainland, *kokoretsi* was probably brought to Greece by the Arvanites, the people of Arvanon (now Albania), who inhabited southern Evia as well as the outskirts of Athens and the islands of the Saronic Gulf— Aegina, Hydra, Poros, Spetses and Salamina. The Arvanites were excellent fighters, and Byzantine kings employed them as professional soldiers. They were invited to come and settle in various parts of Greece from the thirteenth century on to defend these regions.

Today, Albanians make up the majority of the new wave of foreign immigrants who come to Greece seeking a better life. Most of them find employment in agriculture or as builders in various parts of the country. Some of the Albanian women who work as cooks in island tavernas make excellent spicy meatballs, and our family has gotten the recipe for a delicious Albanian rice casserole with peppers, dill and feta cheese. On Kea, I have watched, fascinated, as an Albanian woman made butter from cow's milk yogurt by shaking it for about twenty minutes in a plastic water bottle.

LESBOS AND CHIOS, THE NORTHEASTERN AEGEAN ISLANDS

Just off the shores of Turkey are the northeastern Aegean islands, of which Lesbos and Chios are the largest. One of the few things these two very different islands have in common is ouzo, the anise-flavored strong alcoholic beverage that is usually served diluted with water. Ouzo is offered everywhere in Chios and Lesbos, as there is no local wine. Lesbos has managed to make its ouzo known all over Greece and exports it abroad, but the ouzo of Chios, though practically unknown outside the island, is often excellent. During my first visit to Chios, I asked for Mini, one of the most popular ouzo brands from Lesbos. The waiter looked at me and said scornfully, "Are you from Lesbos? Obviously, you know nothing about ouzo."

Unlike most of the smaller islands of the Aegean, Chios and Lesbos are self-contained, with year-round lives of their own, and don't depend on tourism. Under the Genoese for 300 years and, later, under Ottoman rule, Chios and Lesbos prospered. Both Chios and Lesbos used to be important centers of trade and industry in the eastern Mediterranean. The Greek defeat in the last war with Turkey in 1922 brought a flood of refugees into the country—the approximately two million Greeks who had been living and prospering in Izmir and other cities of Turkey. About half a million of them landed on Lesbos, and many settled on the island. As the links with the East were cut off, the economies of Chios and Lesbos declined sharply.

In many ways, however, the two neighboring islands couldn't be more different. Chians are reticent and methodical. On Lesbos, on the other hand, the people enjoy relating stories about themselves and everything around them. Lesbos is an island of artists and poets. Odysseus Elytis, the Nobel Prize–winning poet, and Stratis

MAKING SPOON SWEETS IN CHIOS

Myrivilis, one of the most famous Greek authors, came from Lesbos. It's also the birthplace of the well-known ancient lyrical poets Alcaeus and Sappho.

There are eleven million olive trees on Lesbos, an amazing number, especially when one considers the work needed to build the stone walls around most of the trees planted on the slopes of hills. After the island's industrial production declined, olive oil became its most important product. On Lesbos, more so than on any other island, there is an abundance of fish and seafood dishes, from simply boiled skate's fin, which is served drizzled with the local olive oil, to delicious rolled monkfish fillet to the exotic mahogany clams to the ubiquitous freshly salted sardines, which are served everywhere on the island.

I was fortunate to learn more about the diverse fish cookery of the island from Maria and Giorgos Koutsoumbis, who live in Molyvos, one of the loveliest places on Lesbos, as well as from Dora Parisi, Maria's sister, who wrote *Taste of the Aegean*, a book with recipes from Lesbos. The first time I visited the Koutsoumbises' house, which has a stunning view of the sea, the table was laden with all sorts of dishes. Among them were stuffed red mullet, an intensely flavored octopus stew with olives and Dora's famous pumpkin, cheese and walnut pie, as well as lacy almond cookies. Giorgos, who owns a fishing boat, told me about the various fish he catches each season, and the women shared their recipes with me, also talking about many of the island's old traditions that have unfortunately disappeared.

Mytilini, the port capital of Lesbos, is a bustling city, with a Baroque cathedral, neoclassical buildings, an abandoned mosque and Turkish baths and many shabby houses and shops that have obviously known better days. The stalls of the fishmongers are piled with fresh fish, including freshly salted sardines from the Gulf of Kalloni, and grocery stores carry the wrinkled local olives and the marvelous cheeses of Lesbos:

fresh or baked myzithra, and the famous ladotyri, the cheese that is left to mature submerged in olive oil. On the side streets, the traditional coffee shops have no signs and can be easily missed. A coffee shop in Lesbos serves not just coffee but also ouzo and *mezedes* (appetizers). Fried vegetables, bean salads, stuffed grape leaves and stuffed zucchini blossoms appear first, accompanied by a tiny bottle of ouzo followed by all kinds of seasonal seafood.

Unlike that of Lesbos, which is mainly covered by olive trees, the Chian landscape is varied. There are fertile plains where fruits, wheat and vegetables are cultivated, bare mountains with stone buildings that probably date to antiquity for goats and sheep, pine forests and hills covered with fragrant trees of the pistachio family (*Pistacia lentiscus*), which grow only in southern Chios. The fragrant sap of the trees gives the island its most famous product, mastic, which is used in Greece and in Arab countries throughout the Middle East as a licorice-like flavoring for breads and cookies, ice creams and cakes and as chewing gum.

On Chios, as on Corfu, there are really two separate cuisines: the foods cooked in the mansions of the wealthy, where Genoese and later the French influences are quite apparent, and the peasant dishes of the rural villages, which use the local seasonal produce, and are much like the foods of the Dodecanese islands. Although the upper class often turns to imported ingredients, their foods still reflect a strong local tradition, as well as that of the eastern Mediterranean. In the kitchen ledger of the Choremis, a family of cotton merchants and politicians, I found recipes for English blancmange and French sauces, right alongside instructions for chickpea-leavened bread and the local fried dough puffs.

In the Kambos region, south of the capital of Chios, citrus orchards surround the houses. A fragrant indigenous variety of tangerines was once extremely popular throughout the Mediterranean, bringing wealth to the orchard owners.

Consequently, Chios has a tradition for fruit preserves, or spoon sweets, as they are called. Whole tiny tangerines, rolled strips of lemon, bergamot or bitter orange peel, unripe pistachios or figs, even fragrant citrus blossoms and the petals of pink roses are cooked in syrup and served on tiny glass plates as a treat to guests. Unfortunately, the once-prized tangerines are now on the verge of extinction, pushed aside by less flavorful varieties that have very few or no seeds.

THE CYCLADES

Between Chios and mainland Greece, extending from the southern tip of the peninsula around Athens and dotting most of the central part of the Aegean, the Cyclades comprise about twenty inhabited islands, including Milos, Kea, Naxos, Andros and Santorini, and many more uninhabited ones.

In the Cyclades, culinary habits were shaped not by Venetian domination but by the poor land and dry climate. More than anywhere else in Greece, Cycladic cooking is amazingly ingenious, with delicious dishes created from humble ingredients. The mainstays of the cuisine—the savory barley and wheat biscuits, simple cheeses and cured pork—have remained more or less unchanged throughout the centuries. The drystone terraces on the steep hillsides were originally built in antiquity to expand the scarce cultivable land of the islands so that the people could plant barley, beans and vegetables. Cereal grains were usually planted every second year, by turns with legumes. Chickpeas, beans and favas acted as a natural fertilizer for the soil, in addition to being highly nourishing. Stone or marble paved threshing floors are scattered all over the islands. Many of these threshing floors are in use to this day, as are the ancient terraces.

Barley, which has been cultivated in the Mediterranean since the beginnings of civilization, was for centuries the basic food of the island people, up until the 1960s. "The staple food of the common people is a biscuit made of barley from which only the very outer husk has been discarded. They bake it two or three times a year," wrote François Richard, who visited Santorini in the seventeenth century. He added: "With this biscuit, which many soak in water before lunch, they eat their vegetables, their usual meal, because they only rarely taste meat, with the exception of the rich, who buy it once a year in order to secure that they will not go without it." The biscuits, which are still baked all over the islands, were convenient food for the sailors, who took them with them during their long voyages. Today, tourists love these versatile crunchy biscuits, which are crumbled and made into delicious salads with the very flavorful island tomatoes and olives, drizzled with fruity olive oil and seasoned with fragrant oregano. Or they are spread with the slightly tangy fresh local cheeses to become a tasty *meze*.

Pork plays a significant role in the diet of these islanders. Small parts of the animal are consumed fresh, on the festive Christmas table, while most is cured and stored for use throughout the year.

Louza, or *loza*—exquisite cured pork that can be compared to the best *jamón serrano* of Spain—is made from the tenderloin, which is marinated in wine, then spiced and smoked. In the old days, poor islanders often sold this cured pork to the wealthy to get badly needed cash. Today, islanders often add small pieces of cured pork to vegetable stews, bean soups and the special island omelettes, which are made with seasonal produce such as fresh fava beans, artichokes or simple wild greens gathered from the hills. Cycladic sausages, seasoned with dried orange peel and aromatic oregano or savory, are often cooked in wine before being hung from beams in the cellar.

Seafood is not plentiful in the Aegean, which may explain why it has never been one of the basic foods of the islanders. The fishermen sell most of their catch to Athens; on their own tables, it is an expensive treat.

THYME
GROWING
ON MILOS

THE DODECANESE

In the southeastern part of the Aegean, along the southern coast of Asia Minor (Turkey), is the group of islands called the Dodecanese, meaning "twelve islands." Well-known wealthy places like Rhodes and Kos, which have been exploited by tourists, belong to this group, along with smaller, less frequented islands, such as Karpathos, whose villages are almost untouched by modern civilization.

The foods of the Dodecanese are more elaborate than those of the Cyclades, and spices are one of the distinguishing characteristics of the cuisine of these islands. Rice and homemade pastas play an important role in the cuisine of the Dodecanese, which also makes ample use of tomatoes. It was probably the Italians who taught the islanders that tomatoes complement all kinds of foods. Here, more than on any of the other is-

lands, tomatoes are added not only to stews but even to ground meat, as in, for example, the fried meatballs of Rhodes.

The southernmost island of the Dodecanese, Karpathos, located between Rhodes and Crete, affords a rare opportunity to taste the traditional foods of the region, untouched by foreign influences. Although the southern part of the island booms with modern villas, holiday apartments and hotels, built with the money of emigrants who return to the island every summer, the north is isolated by high rocky mountains. It could be reached only by boat until the 1980s, when a difficult mountain road was finally built.

Olympos is one of the most impressive villages of all the islands, its old houses rising high on the cliff. It was well protected from pirates and invaders. In this remote village, which has never been inhabited by any foreign conqueror, the people still use many ancient Greek words in their local dialect. The foods of Olympos have their roots in Byzantium and are seasoned with a spice combination similar to that of North Africa.

From Morfi Diakogiorgou, the daughter of the priest of Olympos, whose mother is considered the best cook of the village, I learned more about the Olympos spice mixture. Every woman in the village has a bowl filled with an aromatic blend of coarsely crushed coriander seeds—grown and dried in the village—and ground allspice berries, cinnamon, cloves, cumin and black pepper. Each cook uses her own special proportions, Morfi said, making the mixture hotter with a generous amount of pepper or more fragrant with cinnamon and cloves. This spice combination, with the addition of some mastic or aniseeds, is also used in the breads and the sweet Easter cheese tarts.

Most savory dishes in Olympos use a base called *tsiknoma*: onions sautéed in olive oil, seasoned with the village's spice blend and often flavored with wine. Vegetables, beans and/or meat are added to make the various stews. *Tsiknoma* is also used as a sauce for the homemade shell-shaped pasta of the region.

At Easter, the women roast the heads and necks of young goats in their wood-burning ovens before boiling them to make stock for soup. They have never heard about the similar French technique of roasting bones for stock, but they discovered a long time ago that the smoky taste of roasted meat and bones deepens the flavor of their festive broth.

CRETE

The largest and southernmost of the Greek islands, Crete did not become part of Greece until 1913. The Venetians ruled it for four hundred years, until the mid–seventeenth century. Then the Ottomans took over, until the beginning of the twentieth century.

After the defeat of Greece in the war with Turkey in 1922, a political settlement called an "exchange of populations" was signed between the two countries. As a result, the Greeks who had lived in Asia Minor, in Turkey, for centuries—about two million people—had to leave their homes and relocate to Greece as refugees. At the same time, a number of Turks who had lived in Greece for centuries were obliged to go to Turkey. This affected mostly the Cretan Turks, who considered the island their home, having lived there for many years in harmony with the local population.

The long coexistence of Greeks and Turks has influenced the culinary habits of both peoples. The use of yogurt in cooking and baking as well as the Turkish names of dishes are much more prevalent on Crete than on any other Greek island.

TOMATOES ON CRETE

The wild greens of Crete, harvested from the hills and fields, have been used to prepare various dishes since antiquity. "Never eat an olive when you have a nettle," wrote the stoic philosopher Chrysippus in the third century B.C. A lemony stew of mixed greens with onions, ramp, fennel and potatoes and an omelette of wild greens are two of the most popular dishes of the island. The women who sell the greens in the farmer's markets of Herakleon display neat bunches of distinctive mixes, some for savory pies, some for stews.

A Turkish food writer told me that he used to win bets with his friends by saying he could guess the origin of people he'd never met before. Once, during an excursion in Anatolia, in Turkey, he spotted a family high up on a hill. "I'll bet you they come from Crete," the writer told his friends. Sure enough, when they climbed the hill and talked to the people, they found that their families had originally come from Crete. "Who else but the descendants of Cretans would be gathering wild greens," the writer explained to his astonished friends.

The foods of Crete are sophisticated, combining techniques from both East and West. Olive oil is one of the most important products: It has been exported ever since the sixteenth century. In the palace of Knossos, cultivated olive trees are depicted on a wall painting dating from the end of the seventeenth century B.C. In the earliest written Greek texts, the clay tablets found in the palace of Knossos (dating from the sixteenth and fifteenth centuries B.C.), olives and olive oil are mentioned. These clay tablets divide olive oil into two main categories: simple and scented. Simple oil is believed to have been used for food, while scented oil was mainly used for cosmetic purposes, especially for cleaning the body, since there was no soap.

Along with the precious fruits of the olive tree, many grains, legumes, vegetables and fruits are among the other foods local to Crete. (It should be noted that the current focus on the healthful "Mediterranean diet" started with a study of the eating habits of Crete.)

Excellent soft and hard artisanal cheeses are also made on the island. Pietro Casola, an Italian who visited the island at the end of the fifteenth century, describes a sort of mass production of them: "I saw warehouses full of them, some of which were in *salmoria* [brine] two feet deep, in which the large cheeses were floating. . . . They sell a great quantity [of cheeses] to the ships." Those large cheeses—what we would probably call kefalotyri today—seem to have been the only hard cheese available in Greece.

Crete is also famous for its paper-thin phyllo pastry, which is used here more than on any other island, almost as much as in the north of Greece. But this is a different pastry from the plain flour and water dough used for the phyllo of the north, for it contains olive oil, lemon juice and raki, the strong home-distilled alcoholic drink of the island. The phyllo is folded around all kinds of fillings, from mixed greens and fennel to sweet cheese with honey.

CYPRUS

In the far eastern part of the Mediterranean, close to the Syrian coast, Cyprus is a fascinating amalgam of East and West. The beautiful and tormented island is today a separate European country, but I decided to include it in this book not only because of its Greek heritage but also because it belongs to the same cultural corpus as the rest of the islands. Cypriot cuisine's many ties with the ancient past and its neighbors are fully apparent.

The Arabs and Venetians ruled Cyprus before the Ottomans took over, in the late sixteenth century. The English succeeded the Turks in 1878, making the island part of the British Empire. Cyprus became an independent country in 1960, when it was populated by Greeks and many Turks, living side by side. The Greek junta made an attempt to unite the island with Greece in

1974, and the Turks invaded. A large part of Cyprus is still under Turkish occupation, and the two communities have been living completely divided ever since. Turkish Cypriot attempts to have the occupied territory internationally recognized have failed. This unfortunate situation has not prevented the internationally recognized sovereign Cyprus, in the central and southern part of the island, which is populated by Greeks, from prospering and advancing.

The foods of Cyprus are a rich mixture of East and West and make wonderful use of spices, especially the aromatic local coriander seeds. Fresh coriander (cilantro), which is indigenous to the Mediterranean, was used by ancient Greeks and introduced to India by Alexander the Great, but it is almost forgotten in Greece today. On Cyprus, however, it still plays an important role in salads as well as in cooked dishes.

Cypriots have done a much better job than most Greeks in preserving their traditional foods. They have also managed to export not only haloumi, the best-known cheese of the island, but other interesting cheeses too. Their good wines, especially their famed Commandaria, a marvelous sweet wine with a long history, are available all over the world. Following the English tradition, they also make sherry-like aperitif wines, which are now becoming popular in Europe.

While in Cyprus, I met two remarkable cooks, Maria Hartoupalou and Panagiota Kyriakou, both refugees who had to flee their homes on the northern part of the island. They settled in villages around Lemesos in the south and earn a living by producing and selling traditional foods. Panagiota bakes fragrant chickpea-leavened bread every second day, and people from her village wait patiently in line to get it, fresh from the oven. In a small makeshift room in her backyard, Maria makes haloumi cheese, about which the Cypriots are very particular.

"The best haloumi is made in the spring, from April to early June, when the flocks [of sheep] feed on the delicious and fragrant wild greens that are abundant in the hills and the mountains of Cyprus," explained Claire Serafim, a member of one of the most renowned and wealthy Cypriot families. Mrs. Serafim now lives in an Athenean suburb, but every year, in May, she returns to her old house in Nicosia, the island's capital, to make haloumi as her mother taught her. For her, as for most Cypriots, this marvelous cheese is far too important to leave to commercial producers.

IT IS PROBABLY the islanders' turbulent past, with its succession of armies, overlords and pirates, and their ancestors' travels throughout the Mediterranean as well as to faraway seas that have given them a global view of life. It is a joy to hear them talk, especially the women who have never left their places of birth. They deftly convey images as they relate stories or give their view of what is going on in the world, connecting the past with the present. Speaking in local dialects, they use metaphors and colorful words that city people have almost forgotten.

For islanders, personal fulfillment and family life are much more important than money. Theodosiou, the busiest *meze* restaurant in the port of Chios, closes in August, at the peak of the tourist season, because the owner likes to go on vacation then. Even on Santorini, the most developed of all islands, the authentic old tavernas owned by locals close for three days in mid-August because people want to celebrate the Virgin Mary's Assumption. On most islands, the busy bars and restaurants are owned and run by people from Athens or Salonica (Thessaloniki), or even from other European countries. Few locals want to break their backs working day and night during the busy tourist season. They seem to have decided that earning piles of money is not a strong enough incentive to make them change their traditional way of life.

Women are the center of the life on the islands. They may not be as visible as men on the village square or in the coffee shops, but they are usually the ones who own homes and land, and if a family decides to build a house, a small hotel or a taverna, the woman is the one to deal with the contractors and builders. Since the majority of men were historically sailors or worked abroad and were away from home for extended periods of time, all the family business is traditionally handled by the women. In the village of Olympos on Karpathos, there is an unwritten law dictating that the mother's fortune go to the first-born daughter.

The ways of cooking of the islands are also an inheritance of sorts. Recipes are seldom written down and are simply passed from mother to daughter. Now that many islanders have moved to Athens and the younger women work outside the home, this oral tradition is seriously endangered. During the past few years, some island cooks or societies of women have begun to publish their local recipes. But very few of the poor islanders' foods have been recorded, and these dishes survive only as memories of a past laden with hardships that modern cooks would rather forget.

Traditional island cooking is, unfortunately, on the verge of extinction. The trend for fusion food came to the now cosmopolitan islands before the professional cooks of the tavernas and restaurants learned the authentic cooking of their region. In most places, one finds real island food only in private homes. It is that tradition which I hope to preserve in these pages.

MEZE
MORE THAN JUST
APPETIZERS

BLUE CHEESE AND TOMATO SPREAD 20
(Domata me Kopanisti)

POOR MAN'S CAVIAR 21
(To Chaviari tou Ftochou)

EGGPLANT AND PARSLEY SPREAD 22
(Melintzanosalata me Maidano)

CAPER POTATO-GARLIC DIP 23
(Skordalia me Kapari)

YELLOW SPLIT PEAS WITH GARLIC 24
(Fava Skordalia)

YOGURT, GARLIC, CUCUMBER
AND FENNEL DIP 26
(Tzatziki me Maratho)

STEWED CAPERS 27
(Kapari Magirefti)

FETA CHEESE PANCAKE 28
(Tiganopita me Feta)

OMELETTE WITH BRAISED GREENS 29
(Omeleta me Horta)

TOMATO PATTIES FROM SANTORINI 30
(Domatokeftedes)

CHICKPEA PATTIES 32
(Revithokeftedes)

ZUCCHINI-CHEESE PATTIES 34
(Kolokythokeftedes)

FRIED SUN-DRIED TOMATOES 35
(Liastes Domates Tiganites)

FRIED ZUCCHINI BLOSSOMS STUFFED
WITH FETA AND MINT 36
(Kolokithanthi Gemisti, Tiganiti)

GRILLED ARTICHOKES 37
(Aginares sta Karvouna)

LENTEN GRAPE LEAVES
STUFFED WITH RICE 38
(Dolmades Nistisimi)

EGGPLANT STUFFED WITH TARAMA 40
(Chiotikes Melitzanes)

OCTOPUS WITH GARLIC SAUCE 41
(Ktapodi me Skordalia)

OCTOPUS SALAD WITH GRILLED PEPPER,
FRISÉE AND ARUGULA 42
(Ktapodi Salata)

CRAB CAKES WITH GARLIC SAUCE,
DILL AND FENNEL 44
(Kavourokeftedes)

TERRINE OF FISH WITH LEEKS,
ORANGE AND LEMON 46
(Psari Pikti)

"The cook sets before you a large tray on which are five small plates. One of these plates holds garlic, another a pair of sea urchins, another a sweet wine sop, another ten cockles, the last a small piece of sturgeon. While I'm eating this one, another is eating that one; and while he is eating that one, I have made away with this. What I want, good sir, is both the one and the other, but my wish is impossible. For I have neither five mouths nor five hands . . ."

Lynceus, Centaur, 4th to 3rd century B.C.

The sharing of food whenever a whole family or a bunch of friends gather around the table is typical of the traditional Greek way of life. The meal begins with alcoholic drinks and a communal course of *meze* (plural, *mezedes*), little plates containing various kinds of cold and hot foods: green and black olives; feta or other local cheeses drizzled with olive oil and sprinkled with oregano; raw, cured or simply cooked seafood and fish; pickled vegetables and spreads; garlicky dips; intensely flavored rice-and-herb-filled grape leaves; and vegetable or meat stews. Offered in small portions together with pieces of fresh country bread, the *mezedes* arrive at the table together with the drinks. Each *meze* is something like what the French call an *amuse-gueule* (a taste-teaser), but together, several of them can become a substantial meal.

Each diner, fork in hand, dives into the small treats that keep coming at a steady pace. Whoever manages "the quickest fork," as the saying goes, succeeds in tasting all the dishes. The temptations posed by the procession of dishes can be formidable, leaving the diners wishing they had "five mouths and five hands" to enjoy them all, as the above passage from Lynceus's comedy *Centaur* attests.

Ouzo, the aniseed-flavored strong alcoholic drink, and raki (equally strong, but unscented) are the drinks most often served with *mezedes*, but wine is another option. Traditionally, Greeks never drink alcohol on an empty stomach, and they always urge foreigners to take a bite together with drinks. There is even a special word for drinking that is not accompanied by some sort of food, *kserofiri*, and it is always pronounced with contempt: "You can't drink this *kserofiri!*"—which, on the other hand, doesn't mean that you can't, or shouldn't, drink so long as you keep eating as the little plates with the various *mezedes* keep coming.

The ancient dishes described by Lynceus are particularly characteristic of the *mezedes* served on the islands, where seafood plays a very important role. During the summer, at seaside tavernas all over the islands of the Aegean, you can inhale the tantalizing smells of charcoal-grilled octopus; freshly cut vine-ripened tomatoes and cucumber seasoned with oregano; and fried zucchini, eggplants and tiny crunchy fish mingled with garlic and fennel. Meat—never plentiful in Greece, a country that has no large plains for cattle—is traditionally reserved for special occasions. Instead of small fried meatballs, you are more likely to be served fragrant chickpea patties. Cured pork is too precious to be served as a *meze* by itself, but it is used to flavor the omelettes of the islands, which are filled with seasonal vegetables or greens.

Other *mezedes* typical of the islands include a tangy caper, onion and tomato stew; seafood, such as mahogany clams, boiled skate wing fin or raw sea urchins; flavorful seasonal vegetables, such as fresh chickpeas, fava beans and wild artichokes; and pickled delicacies, such as grape hyacinth bulbs and rock samphire.

When islanders invite you into their homes for *mezedes*, the food is more casual. The cook will serve you some items from the pantry—olives, cheese, sun-dried fish or freshly salted sardines, pickled vegetables and greens—and some dishes made at the last minute, like batter-fried fresh vegetables, vegetable patties, omelettes stuffed with almost anything available in the kitchen or harvested from the kitchen garden. Most cooks try to have on hand rice-and-herb-stuffed grape leaves—usually prepared once a week in large quantities and refrigerated, since their taste improves over time. They also may have some *fava* (mashed fava beans or yellow split peas) mixed with herbs and scallions and drizzled with lemon and olive oil.

An elaborate *meze* course can take longer to prepare than a regular meal, but many of the dishes can be cooked more than one day in advance and served at room temperature. A main course may or may not follow. If you plan to serve a *meze* course as a prelude to a lunch or dinner, choose two or three light vegetable and fish dishes, which can be set on a side table when your guests arrive so that they can help themselves. On the other hand, if you plan to make a *meze* meal, follow the traditional Greek custom by starting with cold vegetable dishes, continuing with the cold fish and seafood and finishing with the warm ones—the fried vegetables, then the hot fish or meat dishes.

Some Greek *mezedes* tend to have strong flavors, which may overpower delicate wines like the popular Chardonnay. Ouzo diluted with two parts water goes well with most *mezedes*, as do the new light and fruity resinated Greek wines.

"Only soup cannot be made into *meze*," my grandmother used to say. This chapter contains only some of the dishes that are suitable as *meze*.

The following dishes from other chapters, served in small portions, would be equally suitable as part of a *meze* table:

DOMATA ME KOPANISTI
Blue Cheese and Tomato Spread

2 pounds ripe tomatoes, cored, halved and seeded

1 cup crumbled blue cheese, preferably aged Gorgonzola, at room temperature

½ cup crumbled feta cheese

1–3 tablespoons vodka or white rum (optional)

⅓ cup extra-virgin olive oil, or more to taste

2 tablespoons chopped fresh mint

Preheat the oven to 375°F.

Arrange the tomatoes cut side up in a single layer on a baking sheet. Bake for 1 hour, or until they shrink to half their original size. Let cool completely, then puree them using a food mill. (The tomatoes can be baked a day in advance and refrigerated.)

Just before serving, mash the cheeses in a bowl with a fork, then mix in the tomatoes. Don't try to make a homogenous paste; it should be somewhat coarse. Add the vodka or rum, if using. Drizzle with the oil and stir to mix, but don't try to completely incorporate it into the spread. Transfer the spread to a shallow serving bowl, drizzle with more oil, if desired, sprinkle with the mint and serve.

MAKING KOPANISTI

THIS DELICIOUS spread from Olympi and other villages of southern Chios is made with the local tiny and intensely flavored tomatoes and the sharp *kopanisti*—a blue-type spreadable cheese, very similar to the *ricotta forte* of Italy's Puglia. Neither of these two key ingredients is available outside the island, but I was determined to find substitutes, because I love this spread. In the summer, use ripe red tomatoes and bake them to concentrate their flavor—in other seasons, good-quality canned tomatoes are fine. Because the more common blue cheeses lack the pungency of *kopanisti*, add a few tablespoons of rum or vodka. Good fruity olive oil binds all the flavors together.

Serve with plenty of fresh crusty bread or Savory Barley and Wheat Biscuits (page 228) and/or some cut-up raw vegetables.

TO CHAVIARI TOU FTOCHOU

Poor Man's Caviar

MAKES 8 TO 10 SERVINGS (ABOUT 2½ CUPS)

½ pound juicy black olives, such as Pelion or Kalamata, pitted

½ pound green olives, such as Nafplion, pitted

1 cup capers, preferably salt-packed

3–6 tablespoons freshly squeezed lemon juice

5 garlic cloves

½ cup coarsely chopped fresh flat-leaf parsley

3–4 tablespoons extra-virgin olive oil

1 teaspoon dried savory or oregano, crumbled

½–1 teaspoon freshly ground white pepper

2–3 teaspoons dried whole wheat bread crumbs (optional)

Thin slices whole wheat bread, toasted

A KIND OF Greek *tapenade*, this spread of olives, garlic and capers from the island of Syros was traditionally made by patiently pounding the ingredients in a mortar with a pestle, and there are purists who insist that the flavor is inferior if you use a food processor. I think the difference, if any, is that you end up with a somewhat moister spread.

Rinse the olives and capers thoroughly under cold running water and drain well on paper towels.

In a food processor, combine the olives, capers, 3 tablespoons lemon juice and the garlic and process into a smooth paste. Add the parsley and process until incorporated. Add 3 tablespoons oil, savory or oregano and ½ teaspoon white pep- per and process until blended. Taste and adjust the seasonings, adding more lemon juice and white pepper, if needed. If the mixture is too dry, add more oil. If the mixture is too moist, stir in the bread crumbs.

Transfer to a serving bowl, cover and refrigerate for at least 2 to 3 hours, or overnight. Serve small portions on the bread.

MELINTZANOSALATA ME MAIDANO

Eggplant and Parsley Spread

MAKES 6 TO 8 SERVINGS (ABOUT 3 CUPS)

2–3 large eggplants (about 2 pounds total)

⅓ cup extra-virgin olive oil

2 cups packed fresh flat-leaf parsley leaves, plus a few leaves for garnish

3 scallions (white and most of the green parts), chopped

2–3 tablespoons red wine vinegar

2 garlic cloves, quartered

2 tablespoons capers, preferably salt-packed, rinsed and drained (optional)

Salt and freshly ground black pepper

2 ripe tomatoes, cored, peeled, seeded, diced and drained (optional)

Slices of country bread, toasted if desired

Preheat the broiler.

Rub the eggplants with a little of the oil, place on a baking sheet and broil, turning often, for 25 to 30 minutes, or until the skin chars and turns black all over. Let the eggplants cool, then peel them and chop the flesh; drain in a colander.

In a blender or a food processor, combine 1 cup of the parsley leaves, the scallions, 2 tablespoons vinegar, half of the remaining oil and the garlic and process into a smooth paste.

Finely chop the remaining parsley leaves. Place the eggplant flesh in a medium bowl and stir in the parsley-scallion mixture, then add the 1 cup finely chopped parsley, capers (if using) and the remaining oil. Taste and season with vinegar, salt and pepper. Cover and refrigerate for at least 3 hours, or overnight.

Just before serving, fold the tomatoes, if using, into the eggplant mixture. Transfer to a serving bowl, garnish with parsley leaves and serve with the bread.

THIS fresh-tasting spread comes from the island of Tinos. Each year, thousands of Greeks visit the island on August 15, the Virgin Mary's Assumption, to see a legendary miracle-performing icon in its cathedral. But, although the island has beautiful old villages and excellent beaches, these visitors seldom go beyond the main square of the port. The countryside is scattered with stone dovecotes that resemble modern sculptures emerging from the reddish brown hills. Unlike most islands of the Cyclades, Tinos produces very interesting fresh cow's milk cheeses, which are left to drain in wonderful presses carved from white marble.

The recipe is adapted from one by Nikoletta Foskolou, a remarkable lady from the village of Xinara, who collected recipes from her mother, her grandmother and other good island cooks and published them in a nice little book called *Traditional Recipes from Tinos*.

SKORDALIA ME KAPARI
Caper Potato-Garlic Dip

MAKES 6 TO 8 SERVINGS (ABOUT 2 CUPS)

2	cups cubed day-old whole wheat bread, soaked in water until softened
3–5	garlic cloves, quartered
1/3	cup extra-virgin olive oil
1/4	cup capers, preferably salt-packed, rinsed and drained
3–4	tablespoons freshly squeezed lemon juice
1/2	cup blanched whole almonds, soaked overnight in water and drained
1	medium potato, boiled, peeled and mashed
	Freshly ground white pepper
	Salt (optional)

Squeeze the soaked bread to extract the excess water and place it in a food processor. Add the garlic and process into a smooth paste.

With the motor running, add the oil, a little at a time. Add 3 tablespoons of the capers and 3 tablespoons lemon juice. Add the almonds and pulse a few times, until they are coarsely ground.

Scrape the mixture into a medium bowl and fold in the potato. (Do not be tempted to use the food processor for this; the potato would become gluey.) Season with white pepper. Taste and add salt, if needed—the capers are usually salty enough—and more pepper and/or lemon juice. Cover and refrigerate for at least 2 hours.

Sprinkle the remaining 1 tablespoon capers over the *skordalia* before serving.

ONE OF THE most popular *meze* in Greece is *skordalia*, a light-textured dip of garlic pounded with soaked bread, potatoes and almonds, flavored with extra-virgin olive oil and plenty of fresh lemon juice. *Skordalia* can be made more or less pungent by varying the amount of garlic used. Similar sauces are found in Spain, southern France, Italy and the Middle East.

This particular version, from the island of Tinos, is flavored with capers. Hanging from cliffs and rocks over the sea, caper bushes grow in abundance all over the Cycladic islands. Their fragrant buds, collected in early summer and cured or dried in the sun, give a unique taste and aroma to all kinds of island dishes.

Although *skordalia* traditionally accompanies salt cod fritters, it can also be served with crudités. With the addition of a few tablespoons of water or broth, it becomes a sauce for fried, poached or steamed fish or for grilled or steamed vegetables, such as broccoli or potatoes. It is also excellent as a dressing for cooked beans and is often served with fried eggplant, fried zucchini, or Chickpea Patties (page 32).

CAPER BUSH

FAVA SKORDALIA
Yellow Split Peas with Garlic

MAKES 8 SERVINGS

THIS VERSATILE variation on the traditional garlicky dip, which comes from Cyprus, uses yellow split peas instead of the usual potatoes. It can be served as a dip, spread on crudités or Savory Barley and Wheat Biscuits (page 228) or used as a sauce for fried or grilled fish, poultry or meat, steamed or grilled vegetables or even pasta.

Instead of yellow split peas, you can also make this with dried peeled fava beans or with the same amount of cooked mashed chickpeas or white beans, such as cannellini.

2 cups yellow split peas, picked over and rinsed

2 bay leaves

2 teaspoons salt

4–6 garlic cloves

1/2 cup extra-virgin olive oil

3–4 tablespoons red wine vinegar

3–4 tablespoons dry white wine

2 tablespoons dried oregano, crumbled, plus more for garnish

Freshly ground black pepper

ALL OR A FEW
OF THE FOLLOWING TOPPINGS

1 cup chopped fresh cilantro

2–3 tablespoons pitted and chopped Kalamata olives

4–5 oil-packed sun-dried tomatoes, drained and coarsely chopped

1 medium tomato, cored, peeled, seeded, diced and drained

2–3 green garlic bulbs or ramps (white plus most of the green parts), thinly sliced

A few sprigs of arugula, coarsely chopped

A few sprigs of purslane or fresh flat-leaf parsley, coarsely chopped

Extra-virgin olive oil

Place the split peas in a large pot, add water to cover by 4 inches and bring to a boil. Reduce the heat to low and simmer, skimming often, for 5 minutes. Add the bay leaves and simmer for 40 minutes more, stirring occasionally and adding a little warm water as needed to keep the peas covered as they cook. Add 1 teaspoon of the salt and simmer for 15 to 20 minutes more, or until the peas are soft and almost dry.

Puree the peas with a stick (immersion) blender, or transfer to a food processor and puree. Let the puree cool completely; it will thicken considerably.

In a large mortar, grind the garlic with the remaining 1 teaspoon salt into a smooth paste. Add 2 cups or so of the puree and continue grinding to incorporate the garlic. Or use a blender or a small food processor.

In a large bowl, combine the garlic mixture, the remaining pea puree, the oil, 3 tablespoons each vinegar and wine, the oregano and pepper to taste, stirring vigorously to incorporate. Taste and adjust the seasonings as necessary. Cover and refrigerate for at least 3 hours, or overnight.

If the *skordalia* seems too thick, add a little vinegar, wine or water to thin. Spread on a large plate, sprinkle with oregano, garnish with toppings of your choice and serve.

TZATZIKI ME MARATHO

Yogurt, Garlic, Cucumber and Fennel Dip

1 small cucumber, peeled, grated and drained

2/3 cup finely shredded fennel (1 small or 1/2 large bulb; fronds and tender stalks reserved, if desired; see below)

2–3 garlic cloves, minced

1/2–1 fresh chile pepper, seeded and minced, or plenty of freshly ground black pepper

2 cups thick sheep's milk yogurt or Drained Yogurt (page 266)

1/2 cup finely chopped fennel fronds plus tender stalks, or fresh dill

1–2 tablespoons freshly squeezed lemon juice

Salt

2–3 tablespoons extra-virgin olive oil

Squeeze the grated cucumber, pressing it hard between your hands to extract most of its juices. In a medium bowl, mix the cucumber with the shredded fennel, garlic, chile or pepper and yogurt. Add the chopped fennel or dill (reserve 1 teaspoon for garnish), 1 tablespoon lemon juice and salt to taste and stir well to mix. Taste and add more lemon juice, salt and/or pepper, if needed. Cover and refrigerate for at least 30 minutes but no more than 3 hours before serving. (If the cucumber sits longer, it will release more liquid.) Transfer to a serving bowl, drizzle with some oil and sprinkle with the reserved fennel or dill.

IN THIS fresh-tasting dip, the cooling taste of yogurt complements the bite of the garlic. Enjoy it with carrot sticks and other raw vegetables or with chips or crackers, or serve it with fried vegetables, like Fried Sun-Dried Tomatoes (page 35). Brought to Greece by the Turks, *tzatziki* seems to have its roots in Persian cuisine. In its more common form, it is made with only cucumber, but this version includes shredded fennel.

KAPARI MAGIREFTI
Stewed Capers

MAKES 4 TO 6 SERVINGS

    1 cup good-quality large capers, preferably
        salt-packed
 $^1/_2$ cup olive oil, or more to taste
    2 cups halved and thinly sliced onions
    1 cup sweet red wine, such as
        Mavrodaphne or sweet Marsala
 $^1/_2$ cup water
  2–3 tablespoons good-quality red wine
        vinegar (optional if using brine-
        packed capers)
      Freshly ground black pepper

If you are using salted capers, place them in a
colander and rinse under lukewarm running water for about 4 minutes, or until they lose most of
their saltiness. If using brine-packed capers, rinse
them well, until most of their tartness is gone.

In a medium saucepan, heat $^1/_4$ cup of the oil
and sauté the onions over medium heat until
soft, about 6 minutes. Add the capers and the remaining $^1/_4$ cup oil and cook for 2 minutes, or until the capers start to sizzle. Pour in the wine and
simmer for 1 minute. Add the water, reduce the
heat to low and cook for 10 minutes, or until the
onions and capers are tender and most of the water has evaporated. Add vinegar and pepper to
taste; you may not need to add vinegar if using
capers packed in brine. Let cool completely before serving. The capers can be made up to 3
days in advance, covered and refrigerated; bring
to room temperature before serving.

"CLOSE YOUR EYES and add olive
oil," the old cooks from Sifnos used to say, writes Eleni
Troullou in her book *Delicacies from Sifnos*. What she
means is that this caper stew needs lots of olive oil.

Try to get good-quality large capers packed in salt
for this recipe. Serve the stew on toasted country bread
or in a bowl for people to dip their bread into. Or serve
it as a sauce for any kind of pasta. On Santorini, a similar caper stew is used as topping for pureed yellow
split peas.

VARIATION

Instead of the water, add $^2/_3$ cup grated ripe or
diced canned tomatoes.

NOTE: To grate tomatoes, cut in half, remove
the stem and grate on a large-holed grater, cut
side facing the holes. Discard the skin.

TIGANOPITA ME FETA
Feta Cheese Pancake

MAKES 4 SERVINGS AS AN APPETIZER, 2 SERVINGS AS A MAIN COURSE

$1/2$ cup all-purpose flour

2 large eggs, lightly beaten

1 cup water

1 tablespoon olive oil

$1^1/2$ cups crumbled feta cheese

Freshly ground black pepper

In a medium bowl, beat the flour and eggs with a whisk or an electric mixer until blended, then gradually beat in the water. Cover and let stand for at least 30 minutes, or up to 2 hours.

Preheat the oven to 400°F. Coat an 11-x-7-inch or other $1^1/2$-quart baking dish with the oil.

Stir 1 cup of the cheese and pepper to taste into the batter. Pour the batter into the baking dish and sprinkle the remaining $1/2$ cup cheese and more pepper over the top. Bake for 30 minutes, or until the top is golden brown and the sides are pulling away from the dish. Cut into squares and serve warm or at room temperature.

TIGANOPITA is the name used for various quick Greek flatbreads that are fried on top of the stove or cooked on the hearth. They are usually made with bread dough and topped with cheese and dried herbs. This particularly easy *tiganopita* from Chios is made from a simple egg batter. It can be eaten warm or at room temperature, served in the pan in which it was baked. Cut it into squares and offer it as an appetizer or as the main course of a light lunch, accompanied by a green salad.

OMELETA ME HORTA
Omelette with Braised Greens

MAKES 6 TO 8 SERVINGS AS AN APPETIZER, 4 SERVINGS AS A MAIN COURSE

- $1/3$ cup olive oil
- 3 scallions (white and most of the green parts), chopped
- $1/2$ pound spinach, coarsely chopped
- $1^1/2$ cups coarsely chopped arugula
- $1^1/2$ cups coarsely chopped sorrel (or increase the arugula to 3 cups)
- $1/2$ cup coarsely chopped fennel fronds plus tender stalks, or fresh dill
- 6 large eggs, lightly beaten
  Salt and freshly ground black pepper
- 1 cup crumbled feta cheese (optional)
  Thick sheep's milk yogurt or Drained Yogurt (page 266; optional)

Preheat the oven to 350°F.

In a large ovenproof skillet, heat the oil and sauté the scallions over medium heat until translucent, 3 to 4 minutes. Add the spinach, arugula and sorrel and sauté, stirring, for 5 minutes, or until wilted. Stir in the fennel or dill, then pour the eggs over the greens. Season with salt and plenty of pepper to taste and sprinkle with the cheese, if using. Cook for 2 minutes, then transfer the skillet to the oven and bake the omelette for 5 minutes, or until set and bubbly.

Cut into wedges and serve warm or at room temperature, with the yogurt if desired.

THERE ARE AS many combinations of different wild greens in Crete as there are cooks. Sweet, sour and peppery greens are mixed together to make many different dishes, including this light omelette, which is really more like an Italian frittata.

In the tavernas of Herakleon, Crete's capital, it's brought to the table in the baking dish, then cut into squares or wedges and served warm or at room temperature, with a dollop of the local sheep's milk yogurt on the side.

VARIATION
FROUTALIA ME KOUKIA KE PASPALA
Fresh Fava Bean and Pancetta Omelette

Sauté $1/4$ pound diced pancetta and $1/2$ cup diced spicy sausage with the scallions. Substitute $1^1/2$ cups shelled fresh fava beans (peeled, if desired) for the greens and fennel, and cook the omelette as directed.

DOMATOKEFTEDES
Tomato Patties from Santorini

MAKES 6 TO 8 SERVINGS

2 pounds ripe tomatoes

6 dry-packed sun-dried tomatoes

3 tablespoons olive oil, plus more for frying

1/2 cup chopped onion

3 garlic cloves, minced

1–2 teaspoons Aleppo pepper or 1/2–1 teaspoon crushed red pepper flakes

1 cup chopped fresh flat-leaf parsley

1 cup finely chopped scallions (white and most of the green parts)

2 tablespoons all-purpose flour

1 teaspoon baking powder

1 large potato, boiled, peeled and mashed, or 2 tablespoons instant mashed-potato flakes

Salt

1–2 teaspoons sugar (optional)

1 bunch fresh mint, stemmed

TINY Santorini tomatoes, ripened under the blazing island sun, with little rain and almost no irrigation, are intensely flavorful, with hardly any juice. When making this simple *meze* with Santorini tomatoes, one doesn't need to drain them or to add much else.

Trying to duplicate the taste with ordinary tomatoes, I came up with this recipe. Following the same principle, you can make other patties using seasonal vegetables (see the variations).

Blanch the fresh tomatoes in a large saucepan of boiling water for 20 seconds, then remove and plunge into a bowl of cold water. Core, peel, halve, seed and dice the tomatoes. Drain in a colander set in the sink for 30 minutes.

Meanwhile, place the sun-dried tomatoes in a bowl of warm water and let stand for 30 minutes.

Drain the sun-dried tomatoes and squeeze out as much liquid as possible. Finely chop them.

In a small skillet, heat the 3 tablespoons oil and sauté the onion until translucent, about 4 minutes. Stir in the garlic and pepper or pepper flakes and remove from the heat.

In a medium bowl, combine the diced tomatoes, sun-dried tomatoes, parsley, scallions and onion mixture. In a small bowl, combine the flour and baking powder. Add to the tomato mixture, along with the potato or potato flakes and season with salt to taste. Taste the mixture; if it is too acidic, add the sugar.

In a large skillet, heat about 1 inch of oil to 350°F. In batches, place tablespoonfuls of the tomato mixture in the skillet; do not crowd. Place 1 or 2 mint leaves on top of each patty and fry, turning once, until golden, about 3 minutes. Drain on paper towels and serve warm.

CHIAN MALATHROPITES
Fennel Patties

Substitute 4 fennel bulbs, trimmed (reserve half of the fronds and tender stalks), for the fresh and sun-dried tomatoes and mince them in a food processor or with a sharp knife. Sauté the fennel with the onion until softened. Chop the reserved fennel tops and add to the sautéed-onion mixture; omit the sugar and mint. Fry the patties as directed.

PRASSOKEFTEDES
Leek Patties

Substitute 4 leeks, white part only, trimmed and chopped, for the fresh and sun-dried tomatoes. Blanch the leeks in a saucepan of boiling water for 4 minutes; drain well. Sauté the leeks with the onion. Omit the garlic and use plenty of Aleppo pepper or crushed red pepper flakes. Omit the sugar and mint.

DRYING TOMATOES

REVITHOKEFTEDES
Chickpea Patties

MAKES 4 TO 6 SERVINGS

CHIOS

2 cups chickpeas, soaked overnight in water and drained

Salt

1/3 cup olive oil, plus more for frying

1 1/2 cups chopped onions

6 scallions (white and most of the green parts), chopped

1 cup cornstarch

1 cup chopped fresh mint

1 tablespoon dried oregano, crumbled

Freshly ground black pepper

Olive oil and safflower oil for frying

About 1 cup all-purpose flour

CHICKPEA patties, made from mashed cooked chickpeas seasoned with onions and herbs, are traditional on the island of Chios and in many other places throughout Greece, served as appetizers, especially on days of religious abstinence.

These patties are always served at Kastro, an excellent taverna in the village of Avgonima, on Chios. Kalliopi Delios prepares the mixture every day or so and shapes and fries the patties on demand.

Because I love chickpea patties but don't like frying—especially when I have guests—I invented this baked version. Serve them on their own or accompanied by Caper Potato-Garlic Dip (page 23) or Yogurt, Garlic, Cucumber and Fennel Dip (page 26).

Place the chickpeas and 2 tablespoons salt in a medium saucepan and add water to cover by 2 inches. Bring to a boil and skim off the foam that rises to the surface. Reduce the heat to low and simmer for 1 to 1½ hours, or until the chickpeas are tender. Add a little warm water if needed during the cooking to cover the chickpeas by 1 to 2 inches. Drain the chickpeas, reserving about ¾ cup of the cooking liquid.

In a medium skillet, heat the ⅓ cup oil and sauté the onions over medium heat for 4 minutes. Add the scallions and sauté for 3 to 4 minutes more, or until tender. Remove from the heat.

Set aside 1 cup of the chickpeas and place the rest in a food processor. Add the cornstarch, onion mixture and about ½ cup of the reserved cooking liquid. Pulse to puree. If the mixture seems too thick, add a little more cooking liquid. Transfer to a medium bowl.

In a small bowl, mash the reserved 1 cup chickpeas with a fork. Add to the chickpea puree, along with the mint, oregano and plenty of pepper. Taste and adjust the seasonings. The puree can be used immediately but is easier to shape if it is refrigerated for at least 1 hour and up to 2 days.

In a large deep skillet, heat 1½ to 2 inches of a combination of half olive and half safflower oil to 350°F.

Meanwhile, for each patty, roll about 2 tablespoons of the chickpea mixture into an oblong about the size of your index finger. Dredge in the flour, shaking off the excess. Fry the patties a few at a time, turning once, until golden brown, 2 to 3 minutes. Drain on paper towels. Serve warm.

VARIATION

Instead of frying the chickpea mixture, you can bake it. Spread the mixture about ¼ inch thick on a well-oiled nonstick baking sheet. Drizzle the top with 2 to 3 tablespoons olive oil and bake in a preheated 450°F oven for 15 to 20 minutes, or until the top starts to brown. Let stand for 5 minutes, then cut into small wedges with a spatula. Serve warm or at room temperature.

KOLOKYTHOKEFTEDES
Zucchini-Cheese Patties

MAKES 6 TO 8 SERVINGS

4 cups grated zucchini (3–4 zucchini), drained in a colander for at least 1 hour

1 cup chopped scallions (white and most of the green parts)

1 cup chopped fresh flat-leaf parsley

1 cup grated hard myzithra, kefalotyri, pecorino Romano or Parmesan cheese (optional)

1 cup cornstarch

1/2 cup chopped fresh mint

1 tablespoon dried oregano, crumbled
   Salt and freshly ground black pepper
   Olive oil and safflower oil for frying

In a large bowl, combine the zucchini, scallions, parsley, cheese (if using), cornstarch, mint, oregano and salt and pepper to taste. Let stand at room temperature for 15 minutes.

In a large, deep skillet, heat 1¹/2 inches of a combination of olive and safflower oil over medium-high heat to 350°F. To make a test patty, stir the zucchini mixture and, using the spoon, scoop up an amount about the size of a golf ball. With the help of a second spoon, shape it into a patty and place it in the hot oil. Fry, turning once, until browned, about 3 minutes. Taste the patty and adjust the seasonings in the remaining zucchini mixture, if necessary. Shape and fry the remaining patties, in batches, and transfer to paper towels to drain. Serve hot, warm or at room temperature.

ZUCCHINI patties are a very common *meze* and are often served during Lent, when those who observe the Greek Orthodox religious traditions abstain from any foods derived from animals. You will find many variations of these patties throughout Greece: Some cooks, for example, prefer to boil the zucchini, then mash it and drain it in a cheesecloth bag before mixing it with sautéed onions and other ingredients. This recipe uses grated raw zucchini, scallions and plenty of fresh herbs. The cheese, which would be omitted during Lent, is optional.

These patties are adapted from a recipe that Kalliopi Delios makes at her taverna, Kastro, in Avgonima. To bind the patties, she uses cornstarch instead of flour, with the result that the patties are particularly light-textured.

Serve with Yogurt, Garlic, Cucumber and Fennel Dip (page 26) or plain Drained Yogurt (page 266), or Caper Potato-Garlic Dip (page 23).

LIASTES DOMATES TIGANITES
Fried Sun-Dried Tomatoes

MAKES 4 SERVINGS

2/3 cup beer

1 cup all-purpose flour

1/3 cup finely chopped onion

3 tablespoons chopped fresh flat-leaf
  parsley

2 tablespoons chopped fennel fronds
  plus tender stalks, or fresh dill

1/4 cup grated hard myzithra, kefalotyri or
  pecorino Romano cheese (optional)

  Salt and freshly ground black pepper

  Olive oil and safflower oil for frying

12 oil-packed sun-dried tomatoes, drained
  on paper towels

In a medium bowl, whisk the beer into the flour
to make a thick batter. Stir in the onion, parsley,
fennel or dill and cheese, if using. Season with
salt (if the tomatoes are not salty) and a few
grindings of pepper.

In a medium skillet, heat about 1 1/2 inches of oil
over medium-high heat to 350°F. Dip each sun-
dried tomato into the batter, turning to coat on
all sides. In batches, fry, turning once, until
golden, about 3 minutes. Drain on paper towels
and serve hot.

BATTER-FRIED vegetables are a standard
part of any *meze* spread. Sliced zucchini and eggplant
as well as zucchini blossoms are the most popular.
These fried sun-dried tomatoes from Tinos are really
spectacular. All sorts of vegetables were sun-dried for
winter use in the old days, when fresh ones were not
available year-round. Fried cauliflower florets, dipped
in the same batter, are a specialty of the island of Syros (see the variation).

Traditionally, fried vegetables are served with Caper Potato-Garlic Dip (page 23) or Yogurt, Garlic, Cucumber and Fennel Dip (page 26).

VARIATION
KOUNOUPIDI TIGANITO
Fried Cauliflower

Cut 1/2 head cauliflower into florets. Blanch in a
medium saucepan of boiling salted water for a
few minutes, until just tender. Drain well on paper towels. Dip in the batter and fry as directed.

KOLOKITHANTHI GEMISTI, TIGANITI

Fried Zucchini Blossoms Stuffed with Feta and Mint

MAKES 3 OR 4 SERVINGS

12 zucchini blossoms

 2 ounces feta cheese, cut into 12 pieces

12 large fresh mint leaves, plus 1–2 sprigs
      for garnish

 1 cup all-purpose flour

2/3 cup warm water

 1 large egg

 3 tablespoons ouzo

 1 tablespoon olive oil

 1 teaspoon Aleppo pepper or pinch
      crushed red pepper flakes

 1 teaspoon salt

    Olive oil and safflower oil for frying

One at a time, carefully open each zucchini blossom (see Note) and insert 1 piece of cheese and 1 mint leaf. Place on a plate, cover and refrigerate for up to 4 hours (the blossoms can be stuffed ahead).

In a medium bowl, whisk together the flour, water, egg, ouzo, oil, pepper or pepper flakes and salt.

In a large, deep skillet, heat about 1½ inches of a combination of olive and safflower oil over medium-high heat to 350°F.

In batches, carefully dip each stuffed blossom into the batter, turning to coat on all sides, and fry, turning, until golden brown on all sides, about 3 minutes. Drain on paper towels and serve at once, garnished with the mint sprigs.

THROUGHOUT the Greek islands, zucchini blossoms are stuffed with bulgur, rice, nuts, ground meat and a variety of other ingredients. I prefer this absolutely simple filling of feta and mint, which takes on a complex flavor when the blossoms are dipped in an ouzo-scented batter and fried. I first tasted the dish in Mytilini, the capital of Lesbos, at Hermes, one of the historic coffee and ouzo bars in the old market. As with all vegetable *meze*, batter-fried zucchini blossoms are brought to the table first in Greece. More substantial fish and seafood *mezedes* follow.

It's best to pick the blossoms in the daytime, since they close at night. (If they are closed, make sure there are no bees hidden inside.)

NOTE: The blossoms have a tendency to close up. To keep them open, place them upside down on the work surface as you proceed, as my friend Katerina Vassiliadou taught me. She learned the trick from her mother, an excellent Santorini cook.

AGINARES STA KARVOUNA

Grilled Artichokes

MAKES 4 SERVINGS

2 lemons, quartered

12 baby artichokes, preferably with stems

$^1/_2$ cup extra-virgin olive oil

Coarse salt and freshly ground black pepper

Place about 1$^1/_2$ quarts cold water in a bowl and squeeze the juice from the lemons into it; set the lemon quarters aside. One at a time, cut off the stem of each artichoke, leaving only about 1 inch. Snap off the bottom three rows of leaves, rubbing the cut surfaces frequently with the lemon quarters, and cut off the tip of the artichoke. Halve the artichoke lengthwise and rub generously with the lemon quarters. Using a grapefruit spoon, remove the hairy chokes from the center of the artichoke. As you work, place the prepared artichokes in the lemon water.

Prepare a charcoal or gas grill.

Drain the artichokes and dry with paper towels. Place them cut side down on a work surface and flatten with your hands. Brush generously on both sides with the oil. Thread 3 artichoke halves each onto 8 soaked bamboo or metal skewers. Grill 3 to 4 inches from the fire, turning once, for 4 minutes per side, or until thoroughly softened. Sprinkle with salt and pepper to taste and serve warm or at room temperature.

ITWAS summertime when I first visited Kythera, and everybody I met told me that I had missed the island's famous grilled artichokes, a dish made only in early spring, when the artichokes are very tender. When I finally had the chance to try them, I couldn't believe how exquisite they were. Frequently served as an appetizer at an outdoor Easter lunch, these are easy to make and can be eaten warm or at room temperature.

DOLMADES NISTISIMI
Lenten Grape Leaves Stuffed with Rice

MAKES 8 TO 10 SERVINGS

1 8-ounce jar brine-packed grape leaves, or half a 16-ounce jar, drained

3 cups chopped onions

1 fennel bulb, trimmed and finely chopped

5 scallions (white and most of the green parts), finely chopped

1 teaspoon coarse sea salt or kosher salt

1 cup medium-grain rice, such as Arborio

1 cup chopped fresh dill

1 cup chopped fresh mint

1 cup olive oil

Freshly ground black pepper

About 1 cup water

$^1/_3$–$^1/_2$ cup freshly squeezed lemon juice to taste

2 lemons, cut into wedges

Thick sheep's milk yogurt or Drained Yogurt (page 266; optional)

Bring a large pot of water to a boil. Carefully separate the grape leaves and blanch them, in batches, for about 1 minute, in the boiling water. Rinse with cold water and drain.

In a large bowl, combine the onions, fennel, scallions and salt and work the mixture between your hands to wilt the vegetables. Stir in the rice, dill, mint, $^1/_2$ cup of the oil and plenty of pepper.

Line the bottom of a large pot with the smaller and/or torn grape leaves. Place a large leaf, vein side up, on a work surface, with the stem toward you. Cut off the stem with scissors. Place about 1 tablespoon of the filling near the stem. Fold the two sides of the leaf over the filling. Fold over the bottom and roll up the leaf tightly like a cigar (see illustrations). Place seam side down in the pot. Continue with the remaining leaves, placing the *dolmades* tightly next to each other. When the bottom of the pot is filled, make a second layer.

TANGY rice-stuffed grape leaves are served throughout Greece and the Middle East. While those of northern and mainland Greece tend to be more complex, with pine nuts and various spices, the simple fennel-and-mint-scented grape leaves of the islands have a clear flavor that brings to mind the aromas of summer. The recipe is my adaptation of a dish that Kalliopi Delios, from Avgonima, Chios, serves as a *meze*.

Her grape leaves are never served warm, as being prepared a day ahead allows their taste to develop. "I always make them on a Friday afternoon, let them cool in the pot and store in the refrigerator overnight. Then they are ready to be served as a *meze* during the weekend," Kalliopi told me. Like most Greek women, she uses fresh or home-frozen grape leaves, and that makes all the difference. If you can get even a few fresh leaves, use them as flavoring, layering them between the *dolmades*. Fresh leaves need to be blanched in boiling water for about 3 minutes, while frozen ones can be used directly after thawing.

In Rhodes, Lenten stuffed grape leaves are still made with bulgur (see the variation), as in the old days, before rice became readily available.

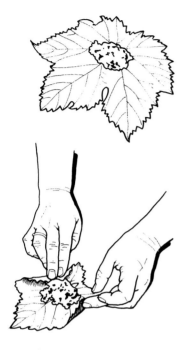

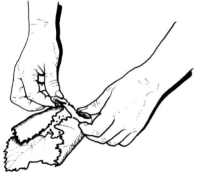

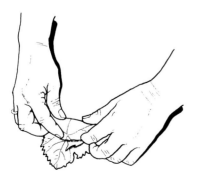

Pour the water, the remaining ½ cup oil and the lemon juice over the *dolmades*. The liquid should almost cover them; if it does not, add a little more water. Place an inverted heatproof plate over the *dolmades* to keep them from unrolling as they cook. Bring the liquid to a boil, cover, reduce the heat to low and simmer for 30 minutes, or until the rice is cooked. Remove from the heat. Let the *dolmades* cool completely. Refrigerate overnight. To serve the *dolmades*, bring to room temperature. Arrange on a plate and serve, accompanied by lemon wedges or thick yogurt, if using.

VARIATION
DOLMADES ME HONDRO
Bulgur-Stuffed Grape Leaves

Omit the fennel and add ½ cup grated fresh or diced canned tomatoes to the stuffing. Substitute 1 cup coarse bulgur (see Sources, page 285) for the rice. If you like, add ½ to 1 teaspoon cumin, preferably freshly ground.

CHIOTIKES MELITZANES

Eggplant Stuffed with Tarama

MAKES 4 SERVINGS

12 small slender eggplants (about
   2 pounds total)

   Coarse sea salt or kosher salt

   FILLING

4 ounces day-old whole wheat bread,
   cut into pieces (about 2 thick slices)

2/3 cup milk

5 scallions (white and most of the green
   parts), coarsely chopped

3 tablespoons good-quality white tarama
   (about 2 ounces)

6 tablespoons extra-virgin olive oil,
   plus more for brushing

1 1/2–2 tablespoons good-quality red wine
   vinegar

1/2 cup chopped fresh flat-leaf parsley

2 tomatoes, cored, peeled and diced
   (optional)

THIS IS an excellent but simple appetizer that you can prepare in advance and serve at room temperature. Stefanos Kovas, a talented chef from Chios, often cooks this traditional recipe from the northern villages of the island. He serves it with pickled vegetables, like the crunchy Jerusalem artichokes that are a common *meze* in Nenita, in the southern part of Chios. The eggplants are stuffed with a rustic version of *taramosalata*—a delicate dip made with cod roe (tarama)—and stale whole wheat bread. You can double the ingredients and serve this filling as a dip, with raw vegetables and crackers, or use it as a sauce for steamed or baked potatoes.

Cut a deep lengthwise slit in each eggplant and generously salt the interiors. Place the eggplants in a colander and drain for at least 1 hour and up to 3 hours.

MEANWHILE, MAKE THE FILLING: Place the bread in a medium bowl, add the milk and let stand for 10 minutes.

Mash the bread with a fork. Place the bread with its liquid, the scallions and tarama in a blender or food processor and process into a paste. Add the oil and vinegar and pulse to combine. Transfer the mixture to a medium bowl and stir in the parsley.

Preheat the broiler.

Wipe the eggplants with a paper towel and place them on a baking sheet cut side up and brush with oil. Broil, turning once, for 10 minutes, or until soft. Let cool slightly.

Preheat the oven to 400°F. Oil a baking dish large enough to hold the eggplants.

Stuff the eggplants with the tarama mixture. Place them in the oiled baking dish and sprinkle a few pieces of tomato, if using, on top of the filling in each one. Bake for 15 minutes, then brush the stuffed eggplants with oil and bake for 5 minutes more, or until the stuffing starts to brown. Let cool to room temperature before serving.

KTAPODI ME SKORDALIA

Octopus with Garlic Sauce

MAKES 6 TO 8 SERVINGS

2 pounds cleaned fresh or frozen octopus (not thawed)

1 Caper Potato-Garlic Dip (page 23)

If using fresh octopus, rinse it well and place it in a heavy nonreactive pot. Cook over medium heat for about 10 minutes (it will release liquid). Reduce the heat to low and simmer for 20 minutes, or until the octopus is fork-tender, adding a few tablespoons of water as needed.

If you are using frozen octopus, place it in the pot, still frozen, and cook over medium-low heat, turning frequently, until thawed. Simmer until fork-tender. Remove from the heat.

Drain the octopus, reserving the cooking liquid. Cut the octopus into bite-sized pieces. Place the octopus in a serving bowl.

Add a few tablespoons of the reserved cooking broth to the garlic dip to give it a slightly more liquid consistency. Pour the dip over the octopus and let it cool to room temperature.

Sprinkle the octopus with the reserved capers from the dip recipe and serve.

THIS PUNGENT and garlicky octopus *meze* comes from the island of Cephalonia. Serve it with Mixed Green Salad from Lesbos (page 179) and steamed potatoes together with plenty of crusty bread to soak up the wonderful sauce.

KTAPODI SALATA

Octopus Salad with Grilled Pepper, Frisée and Arugula

FROM MOLYVOS RESTAURANT

MAKES 4 SERVINGS

2 gallons water

2 cups white wine vinegar

Juice of 4 lemons

1/2 cup kosher salt

6 bay leaves

2 pounds octopus (cleaned by your fishmonger), fresh or frozen

MARINADE

1 cup extra-virgin olive oil

1/4 cup white wine vinegar

Juice of 2 lemons

2 garlic cloves, finely chopped

1 teaspoon dried oregano, crumbled

VINAIGRETTE

6 tablespoons extra-virgin olive oil

Juice of 2 lemons

1 teaspoon dried oregano, crumbled

Salt and freshly ground black pepper

SALAD

1 red bell pepper

1 yellow bell pepper

3 cups chopped frisée (white part only)

1 cup sliced arugula

12 caper berries

PRECOOKING the octopus and marinating it with garlic and oregano before grilling it will ensure tenderness. Chef Jim Botsacos complements his version of this popular island *meze* with a salad of slightly bitter greens and sweet grilled peppers.

Combine the water, vinegar, lemon juice, salt and bay leaves in a large pot, bring to a simmer and cook for 10 minutes.

Add the octopus and cook for 20 minutes, or until tender. Drain and let cool.

MARINATE THE OCTOPUS: Combine all the marinade ingredients in a large bowl or baking dish. Cut the blanched octopus lengthwise in half, place in the marinade and turn to coat. Cover and refrigerate overnight.

MAKE THE VINAIGRETTE: In a small bowl, whisk together the oil, lemon juice, oregano and salt and pepper to taste. Set aside.

MAKE THE SALAD: Prepare a charcoal grill or preheat a gas grill (or preheat the broiler). Grill or broil the peppers, turning occasionally, until uniformly blackened on all sides. Place in a paper bag, seal the bag and let cool.

Peel off the blackened skins from the peppers and remove the cores and seeds. Dice the peppers. Set aside.

Drain the octopuses and pat dry. Grill (or broil) for 4 to 5 minutes per side. Cut the octopuses into bite-sized pieces.

TO SERVE: Place the frisée and arugula in a large bowl and toss with the peppers. Add the octopus and the vinaigrette and toss. Mound the salad in the center of four serving plates and garnish with the caper berries.

VARIATION

You can substitute small squid for the octopus, omitting the blanching and marinating steps. Brush the squid with the marinade during and after grilling.

FROM MOLYVOS RESTAURANT

KAVOUROKEFTEDES
Crab Cakes with Garlic Sauce, Dill and Fennel

MAKES 6 SERVINGS

CRAB CAKES

- 1 pound jumbo lump crab meat, picked over for shells and cartilage
- 1 tablespoon chopped fresh lovage or celery leaves
- 1 tablespoon chopped fresh dill
- 1½ tablespoons chopped fennel fronds plus tender stalks, or fresh dill
- ½ cup Garlic Sauce (page 188)
  Salt and freshly ground black pepper

LEMON-CAPER MAYONNAISE

- 3 large egg yolks
- 1 tablespoon Dijon mustard
- 3 tablespoons freshly squeezed lemon juice
  Pinch of salt
- 1½ cups olive oil
- ¼ cup capers, drained and chopped
  Freshly ground black pepper

- ½ cup cornstarch
- 1 cup all-purpose flour
- 1 tablespoon salt
- ½ teaspoon freshly ground black pepper
- 4 large eggs
- 2 cups toasted whole wheat bread crumbs or panko (Japanese bread crumbs)
- 1 teaspoon Aleppo pepper or pinch crushed red pepper flakes
- ¼ cup chopped fresh flat-leaf parsley

About ½ cup olive oil for frying

Bean Salad with Lemon-Caper Mayonnaise (page 183)
A few sprigs of fresh flat-leaf parsley

INSPIRED by the salt cod fritters that are beloved all over the islands, Chef Jim Botsacos created these fresh crab cakes with a Greek accent. He serves them with a lemon-caper mayonnaise over a white bean salad.

MAKE THE CRAB CAKES: In a medium bowl, combine the crab, lovage or celery leaves, 1 tablespoon dill, fennel or more dill, garlic sauce and salt and pepper to taste. Line a small baking sheet with parchment paper or waxed paper and scoop 6 equal-sized portions of the crab mixture (about $^{1}/_{4}$ cup each) onto the paper. Cover loosely with plastic wrap and refrigerate for 1 hour.

MAKE THE LEMON-CAPER MAYONNAISE: With an electric mixer on low speed, beat the egg yolks, mustard, lemon juice and salt in a medium bowl. With the mixer on medium speed, slowly add the oil in a slow, steady stream, beating until incorporated. The mayonnaise will be thin in consistency, like an easy-to-pour creamy vinaigrette, not thick like regular mayonnaise. Stir in the capers with a wooden spoon and beat for 1 minute. Season to taste with pepper and additional salt if necessary. Set aside.

Preheat the oven to 325°F.

In a shallow bowl, combine the cornstarch, flour, 1 tablespoon salt and $^{1}/_{2}$ teaspoon pepper. Put the eggs in a second shallow bowl and beat well. Combine the bread crumbs, pepper or pepper flakes and parsley in a third shallow bowl.

Remove the crab cakes from the refrigerator. Working with one portion at a time, roll it into a ball, then drop into the flour mixture and shake off any excess. Dip it in the egg, then roll it in the bread-crumb mixture, patting lightly so it adheres. Place on a work surface and press lightly to flatten.

Place a medium skillet over medium heat and add $^{1}/_{4}$ cup of the oil. When it is hot, place 3 crab cakes in the skillet and cook, turning once, until golden brown on both sides, about 2 minutes per side. Place on paper towels to drain. Repeat with the remaining crab cakes, adding more oil as necessary.

Transfer the crab cakes to a baking sheet and bake until heated through, 3 to 4 minutes.

To serve, divide the white bean salad among six serving plates. Place the crab cakes on top. Drizzle with the mayonnaise. Garnish with parsley, if desired.

PSARI PIKTI

Terrine of Fish with Leeks, Orange and Lemon

MAKES 4 TO 6 SERVINGS

FISH TERRINES are found on many Greek islands. For this one from the island of Chios, the fish is simmered in a fragrant broth of orange and lemon juices, seasoned with cinnamon, cloves, saffron and bay leaves. In my version, I have substituted a combination of orange juice and zest for the Chian bitter oranges.

This recipe is a wonderful illustration of many influences, both Eastern and Western, that come into play in this part of the Aegean. The original that inspired my version, attributed to Marianthi Kalouta, was published by Vasso Kritaki, a passionate Chian researcher, in a booklet she wrote tracing the influences of Chian cooking in Turkey.

Only seven miles of sea stand between the Turkish coastal city of Çesme and Chios Town. Chian upper-class families like the Kaloutas often had close ties with Greeks living "on the other side" in Turkey, while women from the poorer villages of Chios found work in the homes of the wealthy residents of Izmir (formerly known as Smyrna), a once-flourishing cosmopolitan city a few miles north of Çesme. Greeks and Turks lived and prospered side by side in this beautiful city until 1922, when war broke out. After the Greeks were defeated in the last Greek-Turkish war, the armies of Kemal Atatürk almost completely destroyed Smyrna. Its Greek inhabitants, together with the Greeks living in the other towns of Turkey, returned to Greece as refugees.

Serve the chilled terrine as an appetizer, accompanied by steamed potatoes, beets and Swiss chard or other greens dressed in a simple lemon vinaigrette. You can also omit the gelatin that sets the terrine and serve the fish and broth warm in bowls as a fish course (see the variation).

1/4 cup olive oil

3 leeks (white parts plus 2 inches of the green parts), halved lengthwise and cut into 1-inch-wide slices

1 medium onion, halved lengthwise and cut crosswise into 1/2-inch-thick slices

2 cups dry white wine

1 1/2 cups fish stock or bottled clam juice

1 tablespoon black peppercorns, crushed in a mortar, or coarsely ground black pepper

1 cinnamon stick

2 bay leaves

5 cloves

Pinch of saffron threads

1 tablespoon grated orange zest

1 cup freshly squeezed orange juice

1/4 cup freshly squeezed lemon juice

Salt

2 pounds firm-fleshed fish fillets, such as cod, mackerel, halibut, haddock or monkfish

1 envelope unflavored gelatin

A few sprigs of fresh flat-leaf parsley

3–4 thin orange slices, quartered

In a large, deep skillet, heat the oil and sauté the leeks and onion over medium heat, stirring often, until just soft, about 4 minutes. Add 1 cup of the wine, the stock, pepper, cinnamon stick, bay leaves, cloves and saffron, reduce the heat to low, cover and simmer for 15 minutes, or until the leeks are very tender.

Add the remaining 1 cup wine, the orange zest and juice, lemon juice and salt to taste. Bring to a boil, add the fish and cook for 6 to 8 minutes, or until the fish is just cooked through. With a slotted spoon, carefully transfer the fish to a plate and set aside. Boil the broth for a few minutes longer to reduce it until you have about 3 cups broth. Remove from the heat.

Remove and discard the cinnamon stick and bay leaves and puree the broth mixture in a food mill or food processor. Pass it through a sieve into a bowl, pressing on the solids to extract all the juice. Discard the solids. Taste the broth and adjust the seasonings.

Place 1/2 cup of the broth in a small bowl and sprinkle the gelatin over it. In a small saucepan, heat 1/2 cup of the broth. Remove from the heat and add the gelatin-broth mixture and stir to dissolve. Stir into the remaining leek broth.

Pour about 1/2 cup of the broth mixture into a rectangular, oval or round mold. Arrange the parsley and orange slices in an attractive pattern in the broth mixture. Place the mold in the freezer for 10 minutes, or until the liquid is set.

Meanwhile, add the fish to the remaining broth mixture and let cool completely.

Remove the mold from the freezer and pour in the fish mixture. Cover and refrigerate overnight, or until set.

To unmold, dip the mold briefly in hot water and invert onto a plate.

VARIATION

Omit the gelatin and serve the fish and broth as a soup, adding some steamed potatoes, carrots and spinach or Swiss chard leaves.

SAVORY PITAS
AND PIES

FINGER-SIZED FRIED GREENS PIES 51
(Nistisimes Hortopites)

ONION, TOMATO AND FETA TURNOVERS 52
(Kremydokalitsouna)

CRETAN PHYLLO 53
(Kritiko Phylo)

CHEESE AND ONION PIE 54
(Kalasouna)

ZUCCHINI AND EGGPLANT COUNTRY PIES
FROM KYTHERA 56
(Hortopites ton Kythiron)

COILED SPINACH, LEEK AND FENNEL PIE 58
(Hortopita Rollo)

SAVORY PUMPKIN AND FENNEL PIES 60
(Bourekia me Kolokytha)

MEAT PIE FROM CEPHALONIA 62
(Kreatopita Kefalonitiki)

FESTIVE PORK, CURRANT AND PISTACHIO PIE
FROM CRETE 64
(Tzulamas)

MEAT AND MACARONI PIE FROM SYROS 66
(Pasticcio)

LAMB AND FENNEL TORTA 68
(Chaniotiki Tourta)

OCTOPUS OR SALT COD PIE 70
(Ktapodopita or Bakaliaropita)

The *pites* (plural of *pita*, meaning "closed pie") of the islands are diverse and wonderful, the kind of convenient seasonal food that only resourceful cooks with limited ingredients could invent. Wheat flour, water and olive oil are the main ingredients of the basic crusts. Enclosed between the two thin layers of pastry, you'll find homemade cheese, greens and herbs gathered from the hills, zucchini, eggplant or other vegetables from the garden or perhaps some meat that wouldn't be enough to feed the family on its own, mixed with some rice, or even octopus or other seafood.

The pies of today probably evolved from ancient flatbreads (also called *pites*), which were topped with cheese, herbs and olive oil or other ingredients. Or they may have evolved from the Renaissance torte, the festive pie that contained many diverse ingredients, sweet ones as well as savory. Later, in the hands of skilled cooks, probably in the kitchens of the Ottoman sultans, the crusts gradually became thinner and thinner, finally as thin as the commercial phyllo we now use. Today, the flavorings of *pites* may be arranged on top of the bread, like an Italian *focaccia*, or enclosed within a thin crust.

The crust used for many of the diverse island pies, however, is not paper-thin, like the phyllo of northern Greece. Often, in fact, it is a thin casing of bread dough. Phyllo is used in the pies of Crete, which frequently take the form of small fried turnovers, and most respectable Cretan tavernas have sheeters in the kitchen— electric machines that roll out phyllo the way pasta machines do. Although it looks like commercial phyllo, the Cretan pastry is not simply made from flour and water, as phyllo usually is, but also contains olive oil, lemon juice and raki—the strong distilled alcoholic drink of the island. Consequently, it has a delightful crunchy texture, even when the *pites* are served cold.

Because it's not easy for a novice to roll perfectly thin phyllo, I've provided alternatives in those recipes when commercial frozen phyllo is not appropriate. The dough does not have to be rolled paper-thin, and you can use a pasta machine if you have one. If there is a Middle Eastern shop in your area, you may be able to get fresh handmade phyllo. For some of the pies in this chapter, you can use good-quality commercial puff pastry, as do many cooks on the Ionian islands. Readily available wonton or spring-roll wrappers are another acceptable alternative in many cases, especially for fried pies or turnovers.

Having our electric or gas ovens makes us forget that not so long ago, the difficulty for Greek island cooks was not making the crust for a pie but baking it. A village cook could not bake whenever she chose, for on the nearly treeless islands, wood for the oven was probably the most valuable of the components needed to make a pie. Firing an oven was a lengthy process, done once a week, and the cook always planned to bake a series of dishes, besides the family's bread, in order to use every bit of the precious oven heat. The *pites* were usually baked after the bread, as the oven started to cool. Lower temperatures were essential to allow the crust and filling to cook evenly.

A shortage of wood is the reason that many island pies are not large, like the pies of northern Greece. The scarcity of wood also led islanders to invent a bell-shaped clay cover that enabled them to bake small amounts of food in an open fireplace. Called *tserepa* in Cephalonia and Ithaca, the thick terra-cotta cover was made from local clay, mixed with either hay (in Cephalonia) or goat's hair (in Ithaca). The pan containing the pie was placed on a cleaned area in the center of the hearth and covered with the *tserepa*, which had been well heated in the fireplace. The fading heat from the tiles at the bottom of the pan and from the bell-shaped cover on top slowly cooked the pie to perfection.

Because these island dishes can be somewhat time-consuming to make, I've adapted the recipes for our modern ovens to produce pies that are quite large, since a bigger pie takes no more effort than a small one. The *pites* can be served as an appetizer or a main course, and they are ideal party and picnic foods, because they can be eaten warm or at room temperature. Whole or cut into wedges, they can be refrigerated for up to 4 days or frozen for up to 3 months. To reheat, warm refrigerated pies in a preheated 375°F oven for 10 to 15 minutes or frozen pies directly from the freezer for about 25 minutes.

NISTISIMES HORTOPITES
Finger-Sized Fried Greens Pies

MAKES ABOUT FIFTY 3½-INCH-LONG PIES

¹/₃ cup olive oil

1 small fennel bulb, trimmed and finely chopped

1 leek (white part plus 3 inches of the green part), finely chopped

¹/₂ cup chopped onion

5 scallions (white and most of the green parts), thinly sliced

1 pound mixed greens (such as spinach, Swiss chard, dandelion greens, arugula and/or mesclun), coarsely chopped

1 cup coarsely chopped fresh flat-leaf parsley

¹/₂ cup coarsely chopped fresh dill

Salt and freshly ground black pepper

1 recipe Cretan Phyllo (page 53)

Olive oil and safflower oil for frying

In a large skillet, heat the oil and sauté the fennel, leek and onion for 4 minutes, or until soft. Add the scallions and sauté for 1 minute more. Add the greens and sauté, stirring frequently, until they start to wilt. Stir in the parsley and dill and cook just until wilted. Remove from the heat and add salt and pepper to taste. Let cool.

Working with 1 portion at a time, cut the phyllo into 4-inch squares. Place 1 tablespoon of the filling near the bottom of each phyllo square, fold over about ¹/₄ inch of each side, fold the bottom edge over the filling and then roll up like a cigar. Set aside on a plate. (If you are not going to fry the *hortopites* immediately, arrange them on baking sheets lined with paper towels, cover and refrigerate for up to 1 day.)

In a large skillet, heat 2 inches of a combination of olive and safflower oil over medium-high heat to 350°F. In batches, fry the *hortopites*, turning once, until golden brown, about 3 minutes. With tongs, transfer to paper towels to drain. Serve warm or at room temperature.

~~~~~~~~~~~~~~~~~~~~~~~~~~~~~~~~~~

THESE PIES are traditionally made on Clean Monday, the first day of Lent in the Greek Orthodox tradition, so they have no cheese, unlike most greens pies. A great finger food for a buffet lunch or dinner, a *meze* spread or a picnic, *hortopites* can be fried in advance and served at room temperature.

KREMYDOKALITSOUNA

Onion, Tomato and Feta Turnovers

MAKES ABOUT 50 TURNOVERS; 6 TO 8 SERVINGS AS A LIGHT MEAL

⅓ cup olive oil

2½ cups thinly sliced onions

⅔ cup grated ripe tomatoes (see page 27)

½–1 teaspoon Aleppo pepper or ¼–½ teaspoon crushed red pepper flakes

2–3 tablespoons dried whole wheat bread crumbs

1 cup crumbled feta cheese

Salt

1 recipe Cretan Phyllo (opposite page)

Olive oil and safflower oil for frying

In a large skillet, heat ⅓ cup oil and sauté the onions over medium heat until soft, about 5 minutes. Add the tomatoes and pepper or pepper flakes and cook until most of the juices have evaporated, 4 to 5 minutes. Remove from the heat and add the bread crumbs as needed to thicken the filling. Let cool completely, then add the cheese and salt to taste.

Working with 1 portion at a time, cut the phyllo into 3½-inch rounds, using a cookie cutter, biscuit cutter or glass. Place 1 tablespoon of the filling in the middle of each round, fold over the dough to make a half circle and press the edges with the tines of a fork to seal. Set aside on paper towels. (If you are not going to fry the turnovers immediately, arrange them on baking sheets, cover and refrigerate for up to 1 day.)

THESE SMALL pastries are just one example of the hundreds of different kinds of turnovers that are served as a *meze* in Crete, but they make a fine meal in themselves as well. They disappear quickly, so you'll be glad that this recipe makes plenty. The fried turnovers will keep for several days, but they taste best fresh. You can make similar turnovers using grated zucchini instead of the tomatoes, or substitute pancetta or spicy sausage for the feta (see the variation).

In a large skillet, heat 2 inches of a combination of olive and safflower oil over medium-high heat to 350°F. In batches, fry the *kalitsouna*, turning once, until golden brown, 3 to 4 minutes. With tongs, transfer to paper towels to drain. Serve warm or at room temperature.

VARIATION

Omit the cheese and sauté 3 ounces of pancetta or crumbled spicy sausage, chopped, with the onions.

KRITIKO PHYLO
Cretan Phyllo

MAKES ENOUGH FOR 1 PIE OR 50 SMALL TURNOVERS

$3^1/_2$–4 cups all-purpose flour

1 teaspoon coarse sea salt or kosher salt

$^1/_2$ cup vodka

$^1/_2$ cup freshly squeezed lemon juice

$^1/_4$ cup olive oil

About $^2/_3$ cup water

Place $3^1/_2$ cups flour and the salt in a food processor. Pulse a few times to mix. With the motor running, add the vodka, lemon juice and oil, then add just enough water to make a soft dough.

Let the dough rest in the processor for 15 minutes.

Process the dough for 1 to 2 minutes longer, or until it is slightly elastic. Let rest in the food processor for 20 to 30 minutes.

On a lightly floured surface, knead the dough briefly, until it is smooth and elastic, adding a little more flour if it is sticky. Divide the dough into 4 pieces. Cover 3 of them with plastic wrap and, with a rolling pin, roll out the dough as thin as possible, dusting often with a little flour. Or, if you have a pasta machine, roll out strips of phyllo as described in the manufacturer's instructions. Repeat with the remaining dough. Use immediately, and proceed as instructed in the individual recipes.

THIS CRUNCHY phyllo has a pleasing texture similar to that of a thin biscuit, which it retains as it cools. When fried, tiny bubbles form in the pastry, making it crispy, almost like a rustic puff pastry. The soft and pliable dough can be easily rolled out with a rolling pin. Cretan Phyllo is particularly good for making small fried pies, like Finger-Sized Fried Greens Pies (page 51) and Onion, Tomato and Feta Turnovers (opposite page).

In the Cretan town of Chania, the same dough is rolled out and cut into long 2-inch-wide ribbons with a pastry wheel, then submerged in hot oil to make festive fried dough sweets that are drizzled with honey and sprinkled with almonds and walnuts.

KALASOUNA

Cheese and Onion Pie

MAKES 8 TO 10 SERVINGS

CRUST

4 cups all-purpose flour

1 tablespoon baking powder

Pinch of salt

2/3 cup olive oil or a combination of olive oil and safflower oil

2/3–1 cup water

FILLING

2 cups finely chopped red onions

3 scallions (white and most of the green parts), thinly sliced

Salt

10 1/2 ounces feta cheese, crumbled

1 1/2 cups thick sheep's milk yogurt or Drained Yogurt (page 266)

1/4 cup toasted bread crumbs

Freshly ground black pepper

2 large eggs, lightly beaten

3–4 tablespoons milk

1/4 cup sesame seeds

MAKE THE CRUST: In a large bowl, mix together the flour, baking powder and salt. Add the oil and rub the ingredients between your hands until the texture is like bread crumbs. Gradually add enough water to make a soft, elastic dough. Cover with plastic wrap and let rest for 2 to 3 minutes. Alternatively, you can make the dough in a food processor. Combine the dry ingredients and pulse to mix, then, with the motor running, add the liquids. (Let the dough rest in the food processor for 2 to 3 minutes.)

MAKE THE FILLING: Place the onions and scallions in a colander and sprinkle generously with salt. Knead with your hands for a few minutes to wilt the onions and scallions, then rinse under very warm running water. Drain well and squeeze with your hands to extract as much liquid as possible.

In a large bowl, combine the onions and scallions, cheese, yogurt, bread crumbs and pepper to taste. Taste and add salt if necessary—feta is usually quite salty. Stir in the eggs.

ON THE island of Folegandros, the filling for this cheese pie is flavored with plenty of onions and enclosed in a thick bread crust. The name for the rustic pastry is also a scornful term used on the island to describe a woman with a bad figure. The pie was traditionally made on Saturdays, the day bread was baked, since the crust was made from a piece of the leavened dough, with some olive oil added. Maria Primikiri developed this simpler version.

Preheat the oven to 400°F. Oil the bottom and sides of a 13-x-9-inch baking dish and sprinkle with 2 tablespoons of the sesame seeds.

Divide the dough into 3 pieces. Take 2 of the pieces and cover the other. Briefly knead together the pieces and roll the dough out on a lightly floured surface into a sheet large enough to cover the bottom and sides of the baking dish, with a ½-inch overhang. Fit the dough into the dish and add the filling.

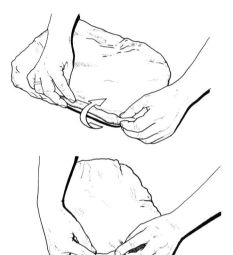

Roll out the remaining piece of dough into a rectangle just a little larger than the dish and place it over the filling.

Fold the overhanging bottom crust inward. Pinch the two edges together, turn them inward and press to seal, making a neat cord around the edge of the pan (see illustrations).

Flatten the cord with the tines of a fork, to prevent it from sticking out, because it will burn during baking.

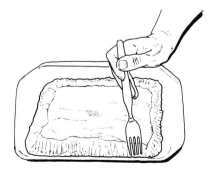

If you like, with a pastry wheel, score parallel lines on the top of the crust, crossing them to make diamond-shaped patterns on the pie, being careful not to cut through the crust. Brush with the milk and sprinkle with the remaining 2 tablespoons sesame seeds.

Bake for 1 hour, or until the crust pulls away from the sides of the pan and is golden brown on top. Let cool before cutting. Serve warm or at room temperature.

HORTOPITES TON KYTHIRON

Zucchini and Eggplant Country Pies from Kythera

MAKES 16 SMALL PIES

THE MIXED-VEGETABLE pies of Kythera, which are closely related to dishes like Spanish *empanadas* and Italian *tortas* that are found in many versions all around the Mediterranean, offer the ideal balance of crust and filling. Eleni Georgiou-Kalligerou, who gave me her recipe for this bread-like crust, said that she always prepares more dough than she needs for the pies, so she can make the remainder into a flatbread, which she drizzles with olive oil and sprinkles with coarse sea salt while still warm.

Country pies can be eaten warm or cold, making them ideal for picnics. They can be made ahead and stored in the refrigerator for up to 4 days or in the freezer for up to 3 months. If you want to serve them hot, just reheat them in a 350°F oven for 15 to 20 minutes or for about 30 minutes for frozen pies.

CRUST

2 cups all-purpose flour

2 cups bread flour

1 teaspoon active dry yeast

1/3 cup olive oil

1²/3–2 cups warm water

1 teaspoon coarse sea salt or kosher salt

FILLING

1 pound zucchini (4–5 medium), grated

1 large eggplant, peeled and cut into 1/2-inch cubes

Coarse sea salt or kosher salt

1/2 cup olive oil

3 cups chopped onions

3 ripe tomatoes, cored, peeled and diced, or 1¹/2 cups canned diced tomatoes, drained

1–2 teaspoons Aleppo pepper or 1/2–1 teaspoon (or to taste) crushed red pepper flakes

2/3 cup coarse or fine bulgur (see Sources, page 285)

2¹/2 cups grated hard myzithra, kefalotyri or pecorino Romano cheese

3 large eggs

Cornmeal
About 3 tablespoons milk

MAKE THE CRUST: Place the flours and yeast in a food processor. Mix for a few seconds to combine, then add the oil and 1 cup of the water and mix for 1 to 2 minutes. Add the salt and more water as needed to make a soft dough.

Turn the dough out onto a lightly floured surface and knead for 6 to 8 minutes with lightly oiled hands, until smooth and elastic. Shape the dough into a ball. Oil a large bowl and place the dough in it, turning to coat on all sides. Cover with plastic wrap and let rise in a warm spot for 1½ to 2 hours, or until doubled in volume. (You can also refrigerate the dough overnight, but allow it to rise at room temperature for 2 hours before proceeding.)

MAKE THE FILLING: Place the zucchini and eggplant in separate colanders, salt them generously and let drain in the sink (or on two plates) for at least 30 minutes or up to 2 hours.

In a large, deep skillet, heat the oil and sauté the onions over medium heat until translucent, about 10 minutes. Squeeze out the excess liquid from the zucchini and eggplant with your hands and add them to the skillet. Increase the heat to high and sauté until most of the liquid has evaporated, 10 to 15 minutes. Add the tomatoes and 1 teaspoon of the pepper or ½ teaspoon of the pepper flakes, and cook for about 2 minutes more; the mixture should still be wet. Add the bulgur, reduce the heat to low and simmer for 5 minutes, or until most of the liquid has evaporated. Remove from the heat and let cool slightly. (You can prepare the filling to this point up to 2 days in advance; cover and refrigerate.)

Add the cheese to the filling, taste and adjust the seasonings. Break the eggs into a small bowl, reserving a tablespoon or so of egg white in a small cup. Add the eggs to the filling and stir to combine.

Preheat the oven to 400°F. Oil large baking sheets and sprinkle them lightly with cornmeal.

Place the dough on a lightly floured work surface and divide it into 16 pieces. Cover all but 1 piece with plastic wrap. Sprinkle the piece of dough with flour and flatten it with your hands. With a floured rolling pin, roll out the dough into a 7-inch round. (It doesn't matter if it's not a perfect circle.)

Spread about 3 tablespoons of the filling on one side of the dough round, leaving a 1-inch border. Fold the dough over to cover the filling and press the edges together with a fork to seal. Place on the prepared baking sheet and repeat with the remaining dough and filling.

Mix the reserved egg white with the milk and brush on the pies. Bake for 30 to 35 minutes, or until golden brown. Let cool on a rack, then serve warm or at room temperature.

VARIATION
PITES ME KOLOKYTHI KE DOMATA

To make Zucchini and Tomato Pies, omit the eggplant and double the amount of zucchini.

HORTOPITA ROLLO
Coiled Spinach, Leek and Fennel Pie

MAKES 8 TO 10 SERVINGS

~~~~~~~~~~~~~~~~~~~~~~~~~~~~~~~~~~~~

THIS PIE is also called *skopelitiki*—from Skopelos, the island in the northern Aegean where it originated. Its thick and tasty crust is very easy to make, but if you don't have the time, you can use strudel leaves. Thick commercial phyllo pastry (#7) will do too, but not the very thin, brittle kind. You can also make about 10 small individual *hortopites* using spring-roll wrappers (see page 60).

CRUST

4–4½ cups all-purpose flour
  2 teaspoons baking powder
  ⅔ cup olive oil
  1 cup dry white wine or beer

FILLING

  2 pounds mixed greens (such as spinach, Swiss chard, dandelion greens, arugula and/or mesclun)
  1 cup olive oil
  3 leeks (white parts plus 3 inches of the green parts), thinly sliced
  6 scallions (white and most of the green parts), thinly sliced
  1 cup coarsely chopped fresh flat-leaf parsley
  2 cups crumbled feta cheese
  1 cup coarsely chopped fennel fronds plus tender stalks, or fresh dill
  1 cup Zante currants
    Freshly ground black pepper
    Salt (optional)

MAKE THE CRUST: In a large bowl, mix 4 cups flour with the baking powder. Add the oil and wine or beer and mix briefly with a food processor until a soft dough forms. If necessary, add a bit more flour. Shape the dough into a ball and let rest in the food processor for 15 minutes.

MAKE THE FILLING: Rinse the greens, drain briefly and place in a large pot while still wet. Cook over high heat, stirring, until wilted. Let cool.

Squeeze the excess liquid from the wilted greens with your hands, then coarsely chop them.

In a large skillet, heat ¼ cup of the oil and sauté the leeks over medium heat for 6 to 8 minutes, or until tender. Add the scallions and sauté for 3 minutes more. Add the wilted greens, the parsley and 3 tablespoons of the oil and sauté for 4 minutes, or until most of the liquid has evaporated. Remove from the heat and add the cheese, fennel or dill, currants and pepper to taste. Taste and add salt if necessary—feta is usually quite salty. Set aside to cool.

Preheat the oven to 375°F. Pour the remaining oil into a small bowl and use some of it to oil a 12-inch pie pan.

Divide the dough into 4 pieces. Cover 3 of the pieces with plastic wrap. On a floured surface, roll 1 piece into a 15-x-10-inch rectangle. Brush both sides of the phyllo sheet with oil and place one-quarter of the filling on it, leaving a 1-inch border all around. Roll it up from a long side like a cigar and then coil it into a spiral shape and place seam side down in the center of the pan (see illustrations). Continue with the remaining phyllo and filling, coiling the rolled pieces, starting the next one where the last one leaves off. Brush the dough generously with oil and prick with a fork in several places.

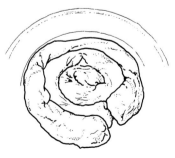

Bake for 45 minutes, or until golden brown. Let cool for 15 minutes before cutting. Serve warm or at room temperature.

BOUREKIA ME KOLOKYTHA
Savory Pumpkin and Fennel Pies

MAKES 20 TO 25 SMALL PIES

PUMPKIN and fennel pies—with or without cheese—are made all over Chios. I prefer the cheese version, which is more common in the southern villages of the island, because it is the most flavorful. In the village of Olympi, I also found little ring-shaped pies called *vrachiolia* (bracelets), which are similar but are made with a strong cheese and contain sugar and cinnamon. This recipe is based on Katina Kritouli's *bourekia*, from the village of Pitios in northern Chios, but I put in some cheese for extra flavor, as they do in Olympi—and left out the sugar and cinnamon.

Traditionally, *bourekia* are wrapped in homemade phyllo pastry. But making thin phyllo is not an easy task, and I have found that spring-roll wrappers are an excellent substitute.

FILLING

- 1/3 cup olive oil
- 1 cup diced onions
- 2 1/2 cups diced pumpkin or winter squash, such as butternut or Hubbard (about 3/4 pound)
- 1 fennel bulb, trimmed (fronds and tender stalks reserved) and coarsely grated
- 1/3 cup coarse or fine bulgur (see Sources, page 285)
- 1/2 teaspoon Aleppo pepper or pinch of crushed red pepper flakes
- 1/2 cup chopped fennel fronds plus tender stalks, or fresh dill
- 1 1/2 cups crumbled feta cheese
- 2/3 cup grated hard myzithra or pecorino Romano cheese

  Salt (optional)

- 1 recipe Cretan Phyllo (page 53) or 25 (8-inch square) spring-roll wrappers, thawed, if frozen

  Olive oil for brushing
- 1 large egg white, lightly beaten

  Olive oil and safflower oil for frying

MAKE THE FILLING: In a large skillet, heat the oil and sauté the onions over medium heat for 4 to 5 minutes, or until soft. Add the pumpkin or squash and grated fennel, increase the heat to high and sauté for 10 to 12 minutes, or until the vegetables are soft. Add the bulgur and pepper or pepper flakes and cook for 2 minutes more; remove from the heat. Stir in the fennel fronds or dill, cover and let stand for 15 minutes.

Stir the cheeses into the filling mixture. Taste and add salt if necessary—the cheeses are quite salty.

If using phyllo, cut it into 8-x-6-inch rectangles. Cover all but 1 piece of phyllo or 1 spring-roll wrapper with plastic wrap. Place the piece of phyllo or the wrapper on a work surface, with a longer side facing you, if using phyllo, and brush with oil. Place about 2^1/$_2$ tablespoons of the filling about 1 inch from the edge closer to you, leaving a ^{1}/$_2$-inch border on either side. Form the filling into a log. Fold the bottom of the sheet up over the filling, and then fold in the sides. Roll loosely, away from you, to form a cylinder. Brush the top edge of the dough or wrapper with egg white and press to seal, then bend the cylinder into a horseshoe shape. Transfer to a baking sheet and set aside. Continue with the remaining phyllo or wrappers and filling.

In a large skillet, heat about 1^1/$_2$ inches of a combination of olive and safflower oil to 350°F. Add no more than 2 or 3 *bourekia* and fry, turning once, until golden brown, about 4 minutes. Repeat with the remaining *bourekia*. Transfer to paper towels to drain.

Serve warm or at room temperature.

NOTE: *Bourekia* keep well, covered, in the refrigerator for up to 5 days. Reheat them in a preheated 400°F oven for about 15 minutes.

KREATOPITA KEFALONITIKI

Meat Pie from Cephalonia

MAKES 10 TO 12 SERVINGS

FILLING

1 pound boneless lamb, finely chopped or coarsely ground

½ cup olive oil

4 large garlic cloves, coarsely chopped

1 teaspoon dried rosemary, crumbled

1 teaspoon dried thyme, crumbled

1 teaspoon ground allspice

1 teaspoon Aleppo pepper or ½ teaspoon crushed red pepper flakes

1 pound lean pork, finely chopped or coarsely ground

2 cups coarsely chopped onions

1 cup dry red wine

1 tablespoon tomato paste

1 pound ripe tomatoes, diced or grated, or 1½ cups canned diced tomatoes with their juice

⅓ cup medium-grain rice, such as Arborio

1½ cups grated hard myzithra or pecorino Romano cheese

1 cup beef or Chicken Stock (page 267)

1 cup packed coarsely chopped fresh flat-leaf parsley

½ cup chopped fresh dill

1 tablespoon orange zest

1 teaspoon ground cinnamon
   Salt

2 large eggs, lightly beaten

1½ 17¼-ounce packages (3 sheets) frozen puff pastry, thawed according to the package instructions
   About 3 tablespoons milk

THIS FAMOUS pie, whose spices bring to mind the meat pies of Arab and Sephardic traditions, is unique to Cephalonia and very different from the pies baked in other parts of Greece. Marinated finely chopped lamb and pork, tomato, rice and cheese are mixed together, seasoned with cinnamon, allspice, orange zest and all sorts of fresh and dried herbs and cooked slowly in the oven between two layers of rich phyllo pastry. My version is loosely based on a recipe I got from Gerasimos Konstantatos, a friend from Cephalonia. It was passed down from his mother, and he assures me it is the best he has ever tasted on the island or in the homes of his relatives in Athens.

This is an ideal party dish, since it can be made ahead and it serves a large group. It can easily be halved, but since the preparation involves quite a bit of time, I suggest you bake a large pie anyway, then freeze half of it as soon as it cools.

MAKE THE FILLING: In a medium bowl, combine the lamb, 2 tablespoons of the oil, half the garlic, ½ teaspoon each of the rosemary, thyme and allspice and ½ teaspoon of the pepper or ¼ teaspoon of the pepper flakes. Cover and refrigerate for at least 2 to 3 hours, or overnight. In a separate bowl, combine the pork, the remaining garlic, the remaining ½ teaspoon each rosemary, thyme and allspice and the remaining ½ teaspoon pepper or ¼ teaspoon pepper flakes. Cover and refrigerate for at least 2 to 3 hours, or overnight.

Preheat the oven to 450°F.

In a large, deep skillet with a lid, heat the remaining 6 tablespoons oil and sauté the onions over high heat until soft, 4 to 5 minutes. With a slotted spoon, transfer to a large bowl. Add the lamb to the pan and sauté, stirring often, until no longer pink, 4 to 5 minutes. With the slotted spoon, transfer to the bowl. Add the pork to the pan and sauté for about 4 minutes until it is no longer pink. Add the wine and tomato paste and cook for 1 minute more. Reduce the heat to low, cover and simmer for 15 minutes. Stir in the tomatoes and rice and add to the onions and lamb.

Add the cheese, stock, parsley, dill, orange zest, cinnamon and salt to taste to the lamb mixture. Add the eggs and mix well.

Briefly knead 2 sheets of the puff pastry together, then roll out on a lightly floured surface. Line a 12-x-18-inch baking dish with the pastry, trimming it to a 1-inch overhang. Add the filling and smooth with a spatula. Stretch the remaining sheet of puff pastry to cover the filling.

Fold the overhanging bottom pastry up over the top crust and pinch the edges together to seal, crimping them to make a neat cord around the edge of the pan (see illustrations, page 55). Flatten the cord with the tines of a fork to prevent it from sticking up, or it will burn during baking. Brush the top generously with the milk.

Bake for 15 minutes, sprinkling the top of the pie with water 8 to 10 times. Bake for 10 minutes more, then reduce the oven temperature to 350°F and bake for 1 hour more, or until golden brown. Check often, and if the pastry puffs up, prick it in several places with a knife. If the top browns too soon, cover it loosely with aluminum foil. Bake for 20 minutes more. Turn off the oven, but leave the pie in the oven for 15 minutes. Let cool at room temperature for at least 30 minutes before cutting and serving.

NOTE: The baked pie can be covered and refrigerated for up to 5 days and reheated in a preheated 350°F oven for about 20 minutes before serving.

TZULAMAS

Festive Pork, Currant and Pistachio Pie from Crete

MAKES 6 TO 8 SERVINGS

IN MESARA, on the fertile plain of Crete, the three weeks before the 40-day period of Lent are days of mad parties, fancy dressing and meals rich in dairy products and meat, with public dances and carnival parades marking the end of winter. Hovering between sweet and savory, this festive pie, which is traditional during Carnival, is reminiscent of *bisteya*, the famous Moroccan pastry stuffed with pigeon (or chicken) and almonds. Though the name comes from the Turkish word *çullama*, meaning "pastry-covered food," this pie is not Turkish, for it is made with pork, a meat that Muslim Turks are prohibited from eating. But Middle Eastern and Arab influences are present nonetheless, and the combination of ingredients—ground meat, nuts, currants and cinnamon—is certainly very old. In my version, I substitute a mixture of ground pork and chicken livers for the traditional pork liver. You can make your own pastry, but commercial puff pastry works equally well.

Serve as a main course, accompanied by a salad of wilted greens or a simple mixed green salad.

FILLING

3 tablespoons olive oil or unsalted butter

1/2 pound chicken livers, finely chopped

1 pound lean ground pork

1 cup sweet red wine, such as Mavrodaphne or sweet Marsala

1 cup Zante currants

2 cinnamon sticks

1 teaspoon Aleppo pepper or pinch of crushed red pepper flakes

1 cup medium-grain rice, such as Arborio

2 cups Chicken Stock (page 267)

1/2 cup coarsely chopped almonds

1/2 cup coarsely chopped pistachios

1–2 tablespoons sugar

1/2 teaspoon ground cinnamon

Salt and freshly ground black pepper

1 1/2 17 1/4-ounce packages (3 sheets) frozen puff pastry, thawed according to the package instructions, or 1 recipe Cretan Phyllo (page 53)

Olive oil or melted unsalted butter for brushing, if using phyllo dough

2–3 tablespoons milk

Confectioners' sugar and ground cinnamon

MAKE THE FILLING: In a large, deep skillet, heat the oil or butter and sauté the livers over medium heat until firm, about 4 minutes. Add the pork and sauté for 4 minutes more. Add the wine, currants, cinnamon sticks and Aleppo pepper or pepper flakes, reduce the heat to low and simmer for 15 minutes, or until the pork is no longer pink. Remove from the heat and stir in the rice, 1 cup of the stock, the almonds, pistachios, sugar, cinnamon and salt and pepper to taste. Let cool. Remove the cinnamon sticks.

Preheat the oven to 400°F. Oil or butter a 13-x-9-inch baking dish.

If using phyllo, divide the dough into 4 pieces and fit 2 sheets into the bottom and up the sides of the dish, brushing each sheet with oil or butter, and trim to a 1-inch overhang. Add the filling, smoothing it with a spatula, and pour the remaining 1 cup stock over it. Cover with the remaining 2 sheets phyllo, brushing each with oil or butter. Fold the overhanging bottom crust up over the top crust and pinch the top edges together to seal, crimping them to make a neat cord around the edge of the pie (see illustrations, page 55). Flatten the cord with the tines of a fork to prevent it from sticking up, or it will burn during baking. Brush the top generously with the milk.

If using puff pastry, divide into 3 portions. Cover 1 piece with plastic wrap. Briefly knead the other 2 pieces together, then roll out on a lightly floured surface. Fit 1 sheet of pastry into the dish, and trim to a 1-inch overhang. Add the filling, smoothing the top with a spatula, and pour the remaining 1 cup stock over it. Cover with the other sheet. Pinch the two edges together, turn them inward and press to seal. Brush the top generously with milk.

Bake for 15 minutes, sprinkling the top of the pie 8 to 10 times with water. Bake for 10 minutes more, then reduce the oven temperature to 350°F and bake for 30 to 40 minutes more, or until golden brown. Check often, and if the pastry puffs up, prick it in several places with a knife. If the top browns too quickly, cover it loosely with aluminum foil. Turn off the oven, but leave the pie in the oven for 10 minutes more.

Let the pie cool on a rack for 15 minutes (see Note), then sprinkle with confectioners' sugar and cinnamon and serve.

NOTE: If you let the pie cool completely and then reheat it in a 400°F oven for about 15 minutes, you will be able to cut it into neater slices.

PASTICCIO
Meat and Macaroni Pie from Syros

MAKES 8 SERVINGS

GREEKS love *pasticcio*, a dish of ground meat cooked with onions and tomatoes and mixed with macaroni, cheese and cream, topped with a thick layer of béchamel sauce and baked. Although its name is Italian (it means, literally, "a mess"), *pasticcio* as such does not exist in Italy, but its roots are in the elaborate old *timbales*—pastry-enrobed pasta, meat, vegetable and egg pies prepared there for special occasions.

I found this recipe in a marvelous book published in 1828 in Ermoupolis, the capital of Syros. Written by an unknown author, believed to be a doctor who had come to Syros from Asia Minor, the book was the first Greek-language cookbook, and it appeared just after the modern Greek state was established, at a time when Syros was one of the most important ports of the eastern Mediterranean. The book is full of translated Italian, English and French recipes, with some local additions, and it is obvious that the author either cooked himself or spent much time as an observer in the kitchen. The original recipe calls for chopped tender veal, some cured pork and bone marrow, which are simmered in meat stock spiced with pepper, nutmeg and cinnamon, then mixed with cooked "Neapolitan macaroni" and prunes and cooked for a while longer. Lots of "cheese from Crete or from Parma" is added, together with butter, and the rich mixture is poured into a deep pan lined with a sheet of pastry dough, covered with a second sheet and baked until golden brown.

The "cheese from Parma" obviously means Parmigiano-Reggiano. The name may have been translated from the Italian recipe, or the cheese may have been readily available on the island. There is no tomato in this dish, since the book came out just when tomatoes were first becoming available in Greece.

"Be careful to send it to the table while still warm," the author advises.

FILLING

1 tablespoon olive oil or unsalted butter

¼ pound bacon, diced

1½ cups coarsely chopped onions

1½ pounds ground lean veal or beef

2–3 tablespoons bone marrow (optional; see Note)

1 teaspoon Aleppo pepper or pinch of crushed red pepper flakes

Salt

½ cup sweet red wine, such as Mavrodaphne or sweet Marsala

1 cup beef stock or Chicken Stock (page 267), or more if needed

2 cinnamon sticks

15 pitted prunes, coarsely chopped

2 tablespoons unsalted butter

1 pound ziti

1½ cups grated Parmigiano-Reggiano or grana cheese

1 cup grated pecorino Romano cheese

1 cup whole milk, or more if needed

1 teaspoon freshly grated nutmeg

Freshly ground black pepper

1½ 17¼-ounce packages (3 sheets) frozen puff pastry, thawed according to the package instructions

About 3 tablespoons milk

MAKE THE FILLING: In a large, deep lidded skillet, heat the oil or butter and sauté the bacon over medium-high heat until crisp, 3 to 4 minutes. With a slotted spoon, transfer to paper towels to drain. Add the onions to the skillet and sauté until soft, about 4 minutes. Add the veal or beef and sauté, stirring, until no longer pink, about 4 minutes. Add the bone marrow (if using), pepper or pepper flakes and salt to taste and sauté for 1 minute. Add the wine and simmer for 30 seconds. Reduce the heat to low, add the stock and cinnamon sticks, cover and simmer for 10 minutes. The mixture should still be moist. Remove from the heat, discard the cinnamon sticks and stir in the prunes and the butter.

Meanwhile, cook the ziti in a large pot of boiling salted water until just slightly undercooked (2 minutes less than directed on the package). Drain.

Transfer the ziti to a large bowl and stir in the meat mixture, cheeses, milk, nutmeg and pepper to taste. Taste and adjust the seasonings. The mixture should be moist; if it is too dry, add a little more milk or stock.

Preheat the oven to 400°F. Oil or butter a 13-x-9-inch baking dish.

Divide the puff pastry into 3 portions. Cover 1 piece with plastic wrap. Briefly knead the other 2 pieces together, then roll out on a lightly floured surface. Line the dish with the puff pastry, trimming it to a 1-inch overhang; reserve the trimmings. Add the filling and smooth it with a spat-

ula. Roll the remaining puff pastry and stretch it to cover the *pasticcio*. Cut off some of the overhanging bottom pastry; reserve the scraps. Fold the overhanging bottom pastry over the top crust and pinch the edges together to seal, crimping them to make a neat cord around the edge of the pie. Flatten the cord with the tines of a fork to prevent it from sticking up, or it will burn during baking (see illustrations, page 55). Roll the remaining puff-pastry trimmings and cut ribbons. Brush the pie generously with the milk, decorate with the pastry ribbons and brush again with the milk.

Bake for 15 minutes, sprinkling the top of the pie 8 to 10 times with water. Bake for 10 minutes more, then reduce the oven temperature to 350°F and bake for 30 minutes more, or until golden brown. Check often, and if the pastry puffs up, prick it in several places with a knife. If the top browns too quickly, cover loosely with aluminum foil. Turn off the oven, but leave the pie in the oven for 10 minutes more.

Let the pie cool for 15 minutes on a rack, then serve.

NOTE: For the bone marrow, buy a 4-to-5-inch-long marrow bone, place it in a medium saucepan, cover with cold water, and bring to a boil. Reduce the heat to low and simmer for 10 to 15 minutes, or until the marrow is firm. Drain, then scoop the marrow out of the bone with an iced-tea spoon.

CHANIOTIKI TOURTA
Lamb and Fennel Torta

MAKES 12 SERVINGS

CRUST

1/3 cup warm water

2 teaspoons active dry yeast

5 cups all-purpose flour

2–3 teaspoons aniseeds or fennel seeds

2 teaspoons coarse sea salt or kosher salt

2 large eggs, lightly beaten

1/4 cup olive oil

About 3/4 cup milk

FILLING

1/3 cup olive oil

1/2 cup chopped onion

1 fennel bulb, trimmed (fronds and tender stalks reserved) and finely chopped

1 pound boneless lamb, trimmed of most fat and cut into tiny cubes

1 cup water

1/2 teaspoon freshly ground black pepper

1 1/2 cups coarsely chopped fresh flat-leaf parsley

1 cup fennel fronds plus tender stalks

5–6 scallions (white and most of the green parts), thinly sliced

1 teaspoon fennel seeds, preferably freshly ground or crushed in a mortar

1/2 teaspoon salt

1/3 cup chopped fresh mint

3 ounces manouri cheese (about 2/3 cup), mashed with a fork

1/2 cup thick sheep's milk yogurt or Drained Yogurt (page 266)

A few drops of milk or water

2–3 teaspoons sesame and/or nigella seeds

THE DOUGH for this rich Easter bread from Chania, on Crete, is very similar to that for Jewish challah, which is found all over Greece as *tsoureki*, a sweet festive bread shaped like a braid. The filling comes in many variations, but lamb or young goat and fresh cheese are its main ingredients. In some recipes, the meat is not cooked separately before it is added to the other filling ingredients; in others, including this version, the meat is partially cooked with herbs and spices before it is mixed with the cheese.

When I first tasted it, I thought that it was a variation of an old Venetian recipe. But it seems that although the word *tourta* clearly derives from the Re-

naissance and Italian *tortas*, this meat-stuffed loaf has nothing to do with any modern Venetian *torta*. As far as I know, it is unique to Greece.

After trying many versions, I came up with this recipe. To duplicate the marvelous fresh, rich and slightly tangy Cretan cheese, which is not available outside the island, I have substituted manouri, the creamy rich cheese from the north of Greece, mixed with some yogurt.

This is not a stuffed bread but, rather, a *pita* with a thick bread-like crust, so you need to remove it carefully from the pan and let it cool to just warm before serving it, or the filling will be too soft and runny and its flavor not yet fully developed.

MAKE THE CRUST: In a small bowl, combine the water and yeast and let stand for 2 minutes.

In a food processor, place the flour, aniseeds or fennel seeds and salt and pulse to blend. With the motor running, add the yeast mixture, all but 1 tablespoon of the beaten eggs, the oil and enough milk to form a soft dough. Process the dough for 2 to 3 minutes, or until it forms a ball.

Turn the dough out onto a lightly floured surface and knead it for 2 to 3 minutes, or until soft and elastic. Shape the dough into a ball. Oil a large bowl and place the dough in it, turning to coat. Brush a piece of plastic wrap with oil and cover the dough. Let rise in a warm spot for 45 minutes to 1 hour, or until doubled in volume.

MAKE THE FILLING: In a large skillet, heat the oil and sauté the onion over medium heat until soft, 4 to 5 minutes. Add the fennel bulb and sauté for 3 to 4 minutes, or until soft. Add the lamb and sauté, stirring, until no longer pink, about 10 minutes. Add the water and pepper and cook for 20 minutes more. Add the parsley and cook for about 10 minutes more, or until the meat is almost done. Stir in the wild fennel or fennel fronds, scallions, fennel seeds and salt and remove from the heat. Stir in the mint and let cool. (You can prepare the filling up to this point 1 day in advance, cover and refrigerate. Remove from the refrigerator at least 1 hour before using.) Stir the cheese and yogurt into the filling, taste and adjust the seasonings.

Preheat the oven to 425°F.

Turn the dough out onto a lightly floured surface. Cut off a piece of dough the size of a tennis ball and set aside. Cut the remaining dough into 2 pieces, 1 slightly larger than the other. Lightly

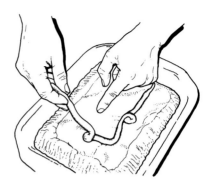

oil a 12-x-18-inch baking pan and place the larger piece of dough in it, flattening it with your hands and pressing it up the sides of the pan, making a slight overhang. Add the filling, distributing it evenly.

On a lightly floured surface, flatten the second piece of dough with your hands into a rectangle the size of the pan. Place it over the filling. Fold the overhanging bottom pastry over the top crust and pinch the edges together to seal, crimping them to make a neat cord around the edge of the pie. Flatten the cord with the tines of a fork to securely seal to prevent it from sticking up, or it will burn during baking (see illustration, page 55).

Roll the reserved piece of dough with your palm into a rope as thick as your little finger. Cut into several pieces, and decorate the surface of the pie with them (see above). Whisk the reserved 1 tablespoon egg with a few drops of milk or water and brush over the dough. Sprinkle the top with the seeds.

Bake for 15 minutes, then reduce the oven temperature to 350°F and bake for 45 minutes more, or until golden brown.

Let cool before cutting. Serve at room temperature, or refrigerate and serve cold.

KTAPODOPITA OR BAKALIAROPITA
Octopus or Salt Cod Pie

~~~~~~

THE FILLING of this delicious pie from Cephalonia is unusual. The salty taste of seafood is complemented by the fresh flavor of zucchini, tomatoes, onions and garlic. The pie needs long, slow baking so that the rice can absorb the moisture in the filling and cook. The result is unbelievable. Octopus pies, a typical Lenten dish, are also prepared on Lesbos and other islands of the Aegean, but I love this particular version because of the special fragrance the cinnamon gives it.

This is a large pie, but any leftovers keep well for about 3 days in the refrigerator or can be frozen for up to 3 months, wrapped in aluminum foil and sealed in a zipperlock bag.

2 pounds fresh or frozen octopus (1 large or several small) or 1 pound salt cod soaked overnight in several changes of water

½ cup dry red or rosé wine

2 tablespoons olive oil, plus ¼ cup if using salt cod

4 cups coarsely chopped onions

4 garlic cloves, coarsely chopped

1 teaspoon Aleppo pepper or pinch crushed red pepper flakes

1½ pounds zucchini, coarsely grated

1 pound ripe tomatoes, cored and diced or grated (see page 27)

1 cup packed coarsely chopped fresh flat-leaf parsley

⅔ cup medium-grain rice, such as Arborio, soaked in warm water for 10 minutes and drained

½ teaspoon ground cinnamon

1 teaspoon salt

1½ 17¼-ounce packages (3 sheets) frozen puff pastry, thawed according to the package instructions

If using fresh octopus, wash it well and place in a large nonreactive pot. (The octopus releases water as it cooks, so there is no need to add any.) Cook over medium heat for 10 minutes, or until the octopus changes color and curls up. If using frozen octopus, place it in the pot directly from the freezer and cook over low heat, turning frequently, until it curls up. Increase the heat to high and cook to evaporate the excess liquid. Add the wine, reduce the heat to low and simmer for 10 to 15 minutes, or until the octopus is tender when tested with a fork. Remove from the heat. Remove the octopus from the cooking liquid (set the pot aside) and let stand until cool enough to handle. Finely chop the octopus and set it aside in its liquid.

If using salt cod, drain on paper towels, then remove any bones and skin and cut into thin strips. Sauté in the 1/4 cup oil in a large skillet for about 5 minutes, or until firm. Pour in the wine and let cook for 1 minute. Remove from the heat and set aside.

Preheat the oven to 450°F.

In a large skillet, heat the 2 tablespoons oil and sauté the onions over medium heat until translucent, 3 to 5 minutes. Stir in the garlic and pepper or pepper flakes and remove from the heat.

In a large bowl, combine the octopus or salt cod with the cooking liquid, the onion mixture, zucchini, tomatoes, parsley, rice, cinnamon and salt.

Barely knead 2 sheets of the puff pastry together, then roll out on a lightly floured surface. Line a 12-x-18-inch baking dish with the pastry, trimming it to a 1-inch overhang. Add the octopus or salt cod mixture, smooth the top with a spatula. Stretch the remaining sheet of puff pastry to cover the filling. Fold the overhanging bottom pastry over the top crust and pinch the edges together to seal, crimping them to make a neat cord around the edge of the pan (see illustrations, page 55). Flatten the cord with the tines of a fork to prevent it from sticking up, or it will burn during baking. With a sharp knife, cut two slashes in the top, making a cross.

Bake for 15 minutes, sprinkling the top of the pie with water 8 to 10 times. Bake for 10 minutes more, then reduce the oven temperature to 350°F. Bake for 1 hour more, or until golden brown. Cover loosely with aluminum foil and bake for 15 minutes more. Turn off the oven, but leave the pie in the oven for 15 minutes.

Remove from the oven and let cool for at least 30 minutes, before cutting and serving.

NOTE: The pie can be cooled completely and refrigerated. Reheat in a preheated 350°F oven for about 20 minutes before serving.

FISH AND SEAFOOD
SCARCE
BUT EXCELLENT

SHRIMP BAKED IN TOMATO SAUCE
WITH FETA 76
(Garides Saganaki)

CRISP-FRIED SMELT OR WHITEBAIT
AND ONIONS 77
(Begoto)

COD WITH ARTICHOKES 78
(Psari Filleto me Aginares)

COD WITH LEAFY GREENS
IN EGG-LEMON SAUCE 80
(Bakaliaros me Horta Avgolemono)

STUFFED RED MULLET 82
(Barbounia Gemista)

MARINATED WHITE FISH WITH CURRANTS
AND ROSEMARY 83
(Savoro me Stafides)

GRILLED BONITO STEAKS
WITH GARLIC AND LEMON 84
(Palamida Psiti me Skordo ke Lemoni)

GRILLED WHOLE FISH
WITH LEMON, OLIVE OIL AND OREGANO 85
(Psari Psito)

FISH WITH SPLIT PEA AND TOMATO
GARLIC SAUCE FROM SANTORINI 86
(Brandada Santorinis me Fava)

SQUID WITH GREEN BEANS 87
(Kalamarakia me Fassolakia)

SPAGHETTI WITH LOBSTER
IN LIGHT TOMATO SAUCE 88
(Astakomakaronada)

CALAMARI OR OCTOPUS STEW
WITH MACARONI 90
(Ktapodi me Kofto Makaroni)

"The best fish is the freshest," every fisherman will tell you, and by "fresh," they mean it has been out of the water for no more than a day, often less. A large number of the inhabitants of the islands are professional or amateur fishermen: There are more boats in Greece than there are cars. And just as the fruits and vegetables in this land of blazing sun and scarce rains are small but intensely flavorful, so the fish of the Aegean are neither large nor plentiful but exceptionally delicious. Freshness definitely plays an important role in the incredible taste of even the most simply prepared fish, as anyone who has tasted the grilled fish of the island tavernas can testify.

Because seafood is not plentiful in Greek waters, fish has never been the staple food of the islanders. The fishermen sell most of their catch to merchants in Athens or to the large hotels and tavernas of the popular resorts. On most of the islands, except the larger ones, there are no

fishmongers. People catch their own fish, or they wait at the port for the boats to return and pick from what is available. Because fish is expensive, fishermen keep just the smallest of their catch or the kinds they can't sell. Only on special occasions like the Day of Annunciation, the 25th of March, or Clean Monday, the first day of Lent, do islanders cook the choicer fish and seafoods. Winter, not summer—when most tourists visit the islands—is the best time to sample seafood, not only because there is more fish available in the winter but also because it tastes better then.

Islanders usually prepare fish very simply so as to highlight its flavor. Twenty-four centuries ago, Archestratus, who was born in Sicily and is considered by many to be the father of modern gastronomy, counseled that the best fish should be prepared with a minimum of ingredients. "Bake them gently," he advised, "and serve without any greasy sauce. And let no Syracusan or Italian Greek come near you when you and fried in olive oil, always accompanied by garlic sauce.

Octopus, calamari and cuttlefish are very popular, usually served in fish restaurants as *meze*. In island homes, the three are cooked in many ways, particularly during Lent preceding Easter, at Christmas and on August 15, the Virgin Mary's Assumption, the biggest of all island feasts. Octopus, calamari and cuttlefish are made into stews with greens or onions and wine. Often, they are cooked with rice or pasta to make a hearty one-pot meal. Although octopus and calamari were once relatively inexpensive and easy to get, today most of the catch goes to the tavernas and restaurants, so fresh octopus and calamari are less common in the market. During the summer, though, most Greeks vacationing on the islands catch their own small octopuses, diving in the shallow waters and grabbing one with a bare hand. They beat it on the rocks to soften its flesh before cooking it right there on the shore on a makeshift grill fired with driftwood. The succulent freshly grilled octopus is complemented with a glass of ouzo, enjoyed while admiring the sunset.

The spiny lobster of the Aegean is considered one of the best of its kind, while the smaller langoustine is less common but much appreciated. Both are expensive, and very few Greeks buy and cook them at home, but instead enjoy them occasionally in seaside tavernas and restaurants.

The most common inexpensive fish of the islands and the mainland alike, often called "the mountain fish" of the poor, is salt cod (*bakalarios pastos*). Imported from Portugal or the Scandinavian countries, salt cod is sold in all grocery stores. After soaking for about 24 hours in several changes of water, the cod is skinned, boned and cooked in many different ways. Pieces are dipped in batter, fried and served with garlic sauce (*skordalia*), or stewed with tomatoes, onions and potatoes or wild greens or with artichokes

are preparing this dish. For they don't know how to treat delicate fish, but they ruin them by pouring cheese all over them and adding vinegar and silphium." (Silphium, which is known as asafetida today, was a strong-tasting and much esteemed condiment that only the rich could afford.) Archestratus's words are echoed by Yannis Foskolos, the cook at an excellent fish taverna in Syros, who asserts, "Masters of fish cookery take care to prepare it as simply as possible so that the exceptional taste of each different kind is not lost."

That said, there are some ground rules about the specific ways of cooking each of the most common fish of the Aegean that even the younger generation of Greeks—people who may never have prepared fish at home—know.

Red mullet and small bogue are always fried in olive oil after being dredged in flour; so are tiny fresh anchovies and whitebait. All are eaten whole as they come crunchy out of the frying pan, head and bones included, and are served as a *meze*. Daurade (sea bream) and red snapper are grilled whole, drizzled with olive oil, lemon and oregano, while grouper, fresh cod and hake are poached with some white wine, celery, fennel and carrots, and the broth is served separately as soup. Smooth houndfish and many other dogfish are much loved by Greek islanders, and you will often find them serving portions dipped in batter in a lemony sauce. *Brandada* — a dish common to other Mediterranean countries — is made in Santorini; grilled or fried salt cod is topped with a very tasty mixture of mashed yellow split peas, garlic and tomatoes and baked again. Salt cod is also cooked with chickpeas or beans as a hearty one-pot meal.

The islanders tend to keep the more unusual species of fish for themselves. *Moungri* (conger eel) is one of the fishermen's favorites, adding deep flavor to fish soups and making the best fish terrine.

Other more exotic sea delicacies include sea anemones, which are dipped in batter and fried. The much-loved bright orange eggs of sea urchins, dressed with lemon juice, are served in seaside tavernas in Crete. On Syros, you may find sea urchin roe served in tiny shot glasses. Of the Greek clams, *kydonia*, a kind of cockle, are the most popular, eaten raw, drizzled with lemon juice. *Fouskes*, which look like gray rocks, are another rare delicacy. They have an irregular, leathery outer skin, which, when cut open with a knife, reveals bright yellow flesh. Delightfully briny and chewy, they also are eaten raw.

Whenever they visit a fish taverna, Greeks follow a routine: The most knowledgeable person at the table (usually a man) goes to the restaurant kitchen to choose the fish. The restaurant owner or the head waiter opens one refrigerator drawer after another, digging into crushed ice and taking out smaller or larger fish to show to the customer. "Be suspicious when you find a taverna's fridge full of all kinds of fish," my father, a self-proclaimed expert, used to say. "This means that most of it is imported." By "imported," Greeks mean the fish from the coast of North Africa, which is cheaper but has less flavor than locally caught fish.

Although fish from the Aegean and fish from the Atlantic may belong to the same species, they are very different in size and taste. It is therefore difficult to find equivalents for all the simple but wonderful fish dishes cooked on the islands. *Kakavia*, the fish soup of the islands, which is prepared with a mixture of various local fish and flavored with lemon and perhaps a couple of fresh tomatoes, is one example of a dish that cannot be duplicated outside Greece. When you want to make a Mediterranean soup using fish from the Atlantic, you are better off making bouillabaisse, which has more herbs and flavorings to compensate for the fact that the fish are less flavorful.

The recipes you will find in this chapter were chosen because they lend themselves to adaptation without losing their original character. They will be equally tasty if cooked with fish from the Aegean, the Atlantic or the Pacific Ocean.

GARIDES SAGANAKI
Shrimp Baked in Tomato Sauce with Feta

MAKES 4 SERVINGS

₁/4 cup olive oil

₁/2 cup finely chopped onion

₁/2–1 teaspoon Aleppo pepper or ¹/4–¹/2 teaspoon crushed red pepper flakes

3 garlic cloves, minced

1¹/2 pounds medium shrimp, peeled and deveined, tails left on

¹/2 cup finely diced tomato, drained in a colander for 5 minutes

Salt

²/3 cup coarsely grated hard feta cheese (see Note)

¹/4 cup chopped fresh flat-leaf parsley

Preheat the oven to 400°F.

In a large skillet, heat the oil and sauté the onion over medium heat for 5 minutes, or until soft. Add the pepper or pepper flakes and the garlic and sauté for 30 seconds. Add the shrimp and sauté for 2 minutes, or until they start to become firm. Add the tomato and salt to taste and cook for 2 minutes more, or until the sauce begins to thicken. Transfer to a baking dish or four individual gratin dishes.

Bake for 10 minutes, or until the sauce is bubbly. Sprinkle with the cheese and bake for 2 to 3 minutes more. Sprinkle with the parsley and serve.

NOTE: If you leave feta cheese uncovered in the refrigerator overnight, it will dry a bit and can then be easily grated.

GARIDES (shrimp) *saganaki* (from the Turkish *sahan*, meaning "a large copper dish") is not a traditional recipe. It was probably created in the early 1960s, as tourists began to flood the Greek islands. Soon, though, the dish became a favorite starter for both Greeks and foreigners, served in upscale seaside tavernas all over the country. Each portion usually comes to the table in its own two-handled pan, right out of the oven.

The sauce is scrumptious, so make sure you provide plenty of fresh crusty bread for dipping.

BEGOTO
Crisp-Fried Smelt or Whitebait and Onions

MAKES 4 SERVINGS

1 pound smelt or whitebait, rinsed

1 medium onion, halved lengthwise and thinly sliced into half-moons

½ cup all-purpose flour

Salt

Hot Pepper and Herb Mix (page 270) or freshly ground black pepper

Olive oil or a combination of olive oil and safflower oil for frying

2 tablespoons chopped fresh flat-leaf parsley

In a large bowl, combine the fish, onion, flour, salt and hot pepper and herb mix or pepper to taste. Toss well.

In a large skillet, heat ½ inch of oil over medium-high heat to 350°F. Fry the fish mixture, in batches, until golden brown on the first side, 2 to 3 minutes. Turn with a large spatula and fry on the other side. Transfer to paper towels to drain. Place on a warmed platter and serve hot, sprinkled with the parsley and more herb mix or pepper, if you like.

THIS SIMPLE dish is one of the traditional foods served in Chian tavernas and is usually eaten as a *meze*, accompanied by the local ouzo. To make it, tiny Aegean fish—a kind of tasty smelt or whitebait—are mixed with onions and fried in olive oil, a delicious combination.

Of the various *begoto* that I have tasted, I prefer the one served at Theodosiou, a tiny old taverna at the harbor of Chios Town. The place is always packed when it's open, but as the owner prefers to enjoy life rather than get rich, he closes his taverna in August—right at the peak of the tourist season!

PSARI FILLETO ME AGINARES
Cod with Artichokes

MAKES 4 SERVINGS

1½ quarts cold water

2 lemons, quartered

12 baby artichokes with stems

½ cup fruity extra-virgin olive oil

1 fennel bulb, trimmed (fronds and tender stalks reserved), halved and very thinly sliced

½ cup chopped onion

4 scallions (white and most of the green parts), thinly sliced

1 cup dry white wine

¼ cup freshly squeezed lemon juice, or more to taste

About 1 cup fish stock, bottled clam juice or water

Salt and freshly ground black pepper

4 cod fillets or thick steaks, halibut steaks or haddock, scrod or sea trout fillets (1½–2 pounds total), rinsed and patted dry

½ cup chopped fresh fennel fronds plus tender stalks, or fresh dill

1 teaspoon cornstarch, dissolved in 2 tablespoons cold water (optional)

ARTICHOKE
FLOWER

IN HER BOOK on wild greens, Myrsini Lambraki gives a recipe for fish fillets cooked with wild artichokes. She writes that the dish was traditionally prepared with salt cod in the high plains of Ziros on Crete, where there is an abundance of thorny wild artichokes in the spring. Substituting baby artichokes for the wild ones produces an equally memorable dish.

Serve warm or at room temperature, with plenty of crusty bread to dip in the marvelous lemony sauce.

Fill a large bowl with water and squeeze the juice of the 2 lemons into it (reserve the lemon quarters). Trim the stem of each artichoke to about 1 inch, then snap off the bottom three rows of leaves, rubbing the cut surfaces of the artichokes frequently with the squeezed lemon quarters as you work. Cut off the tips of the artichokes. Halve the artichokes and rub generously with the lemons. Using a knife or a grapefruit spoon, remove the choke from the center of each artichoke. Place the prepared artichokes in the lemon water.

In a large, deep skillet with a lid, heat $1/4$ cup of the oil and sauté the fennel bulb and onion over medium heat until just tender, about 5 minutes. Add the scallions and sauté for 2 minutes more. Add the artichokes and the remaining $1/4$ cup oil and toss to coat. Add the wine, increase the heat to high and cook for 1 minute. Add the lemon juice, enough stock, clam juice or water to cover and salt and pepper to taste. Bring to a boil, reduce the heat to low, cover and simmer for 10 minutes, or until the artichokes are tender. With a slotted spoon, transfer the artichokes to a plate, cover and set aside.

You should have about $1^1/2$ cups liquid in the skillet: if not, add a little more stock or water. Bring to a boil, add the fish and cook for 10 minutes, or until just cooked through. Taste and adjust the seasonings, adding more salt, pepper and/or lemon juice if needed. Add the artichokes to the skillet. Reserve 2 tablespoons of the fennel fronds or dill for garnish and sprinkle the artichokes and fish with the remainder. Cook for about 1 minute more, until the artichokes are heated through.

Add the cornstarch mixture, if using, to the skillet, stir, bring to a boil and cook for about 30 seconds to thicken the sauce.

Sprinkle with the reserved fennel fronds or dill and serve.

BAKALIAROS ME HORTA AVGOLEMONO

Cod with Leafy Greens in Egg-Lemon Sauce

MAKES 4 SERVINGS

~~~~~~~~~~~~~~~~~~~~~~~~~~~~~~~~~~~~

THIS DELICATE winter dish is prepared on almost every island, using the wild greens gathered from the hills and mountains. It is often made with "mountain fish," as salt cod is called, since that is the cheapest and most readily available. Its robust taste complements the tart and somewhat bitter greens.

Instead of mixed greens, you can use tender Swiss chard leaves, as is customary on Syros, or add a couple of thinly chopped ramps (wild leeks) or a small leek along with the fennel, as cooks on Crete do. You can even omit the egg-lemon sauce if you prefer, adding just the lemon juice at the end of the cooking when you turn the fish fillets. If you like, accompany the dish with small steamed or boiled potatoes.

4 cod fillets (about 1½ pounds total), rinsed and patted dry

Salt

⅓ cup freshly squeezed lemon juice, or more to taste

⅓ cup olive oil

1 teaspoon crushed fennel seeds

Freshly ground black pepper

1 large fennel bulb, trimmed (fronds and tender stalks reserved), halved and thinly sliced

3–4 scallions (white and most of the green parts), thinly sliced

1 pound mixed tender greens (such as baby spinach, small Swiss chard leaves, miner's lettuce, pea shoots, orache, fresh amaranth, outer leaves of escarole or romaine lettuce and/or beet greens), washed but not dried

½ cup plus 3 tablespoons water

1 cup dry white wine

½ cup fish stock or bottled clam juice

½ cup chopped fresh fennel fronds plus tender stalks, or fresh dill

4 small carrots, peeled

2 large egg yolks

1 teaspoon cornstarch, dissolved in 3 tablespoons cold water

Season the cod with salt to taste and place in a baking dish or shallow bowl. In a small bowl, whisk 3 tablespoons of the lemon juice, 2 tablespoons of the oil, the fennel seeds and pepper to taste. Pour the lemon-juice mixture over the cod, turn to coat, cover and refrigerate for at least 30 minutes and up to 3 hours.

In a large, deep skillet with a lid, heat the remaining oil and sauté the fennel bulb over medium heat until tender, about 4 minutes. Add the scallions and sauté for 1 minute more. Add the greens and ½ cup of the water, cover and steam for 3 minutes. With tongs, turn the greens, then cover and steam for 2 to 3 minutes more, or until all the greens have wilted. Transfer to a medium bowl and set aside.

Add the wine to the skillet and simmer for 2 minutes. Add the stock or clam juice and bring to a boil. Add the cod and any remaining liquid and cook for 3 to 4 minutes, then turn the fish. Reserve 2 tablespoons of the fennel fronds or dill for garnish and sprinkle the fish with the remainder. Cover the fish with the greens and cook for 3 to 4 minutes more, or until the fish is just cooked through. Remove from the heat and let stand for 10 minutes. Meanwhile, steam the carrots until crisp-tender, about 10 minutes.

With tongs or a slotted spoon, transfer the greens to four plates, letting them drain into the skillet for a few seconds. Place the fish over the greens. Arrange the carrots next to the greens. Keep warm.

Transfer the cooking liquid to a medium saucepan over medium heat. In a small bowl, whisk the egg yolks with the remaining lemon juice and 3 tablespoons water. Slowly add most of the cooking liquid to the egg mixture, whisking constantly. Pour the egg mixture into the saucepan, add the cornstarch mixture and reduce the heat to low. Simmer, whisking constantly, for 2 minutes, or until the sauce thickens. Taste and adjust the seasonings; the sauce should be quite lemony.

Pour some of the sauce over the fish, greens and carrots, sprinkle with the reserved fennel or dill and serve warm, with the remaining sauce on the side.

BARBOUNIA GEMISTA
Stuffed Red Mullet

MAKES 4 SERVINGS

1 small tomato, cored, peeled and diced

²/₃ cup chopped fresh flat-leaf parsley, plus 4–5 sprigs for garnish

1 cup extra-virgin olive oil

Salt and freshly ground black pepper

4 large red mullet, snapper or sea bass (about ¹/₂ pound each), cleaned, rinsed and patted dry

¹/₄ cup freshly squeezed lemon juice

2 tablespoons water

1 lemon, sliced

In a small bowl, combine the tomato, ¹/₃ cup of the parsley, 2 tablespoons of the oil and salt and pepper to taste.

Stuff each fish with one-quarter of the tomato mixture. Tie a length of kitchen twine around each fish to keep the stuffing intact. Cover and refrigerate for at least 30 minutes and up to 1 hour.

Prepare a charcoal or gas grill or preheat the broiler. Brush the fish on both sides with some of the oil and grill or broil for 8 to 10 minutes per side, or until cooked through.

Meanwhile, in a shallow bowl, whisk the remaining oil, the remaining ¹/₃ cup parsley, the lemon juice, water and salt and pepper to taste. Place the fish on a platter, pour over the lemon mixture and turn to coat. Decorate with the lemon slices and parsley sprigs and serve warm or at room temperature, with the remaining sauce on the side.

DORA PARISI and her sister Maria Koutsoumbis, from Molyvos, Lesbos, serve this dish to guests. The stuffing of chopped fresh tomato and parsley, placed in the cavity of the fish a few minutes before grilling, doubles as a kind of marinade. As the fish cooks, the flavor of the stuffing permeates the flesh, making the mullet equally wonderful warm or at room temperature.

The fish that Dora and Maria use comes straight from the fishing boat of Giorgos Koutsoumbis, Maria's husband and the cousin of John Livanos, the owner of Molyvos restaurant.

SAVORO ME STAFIDES
Marinated White Fish with Currants and Rosemary

MAKES 4 SERVINGS

1/2 cup all-purpose flour

Olive oil and safflower oil for frying

4 firm-fleshed white fish fillets, such as snapper, grouper or monkfish (about 2 pounds total), rinsed and patted dry

Salt

1/2 cup olive oil

1 medium onion, halved lengthwise and thinly sliced into half-moons

1–2 teaspoons Aleppo pepper or 1/2–1 teaspoon crushed red pepper flakes

2/3 cup Zante currants

4–5 garlic cloves, thinly sliced

1 tablespoon dried rosemary, crumbled

2/3 cup red wine vinegar

1/3 cup balsamic vinegar

Freshly ground black pepper

3–4 sprigs fresh rosemary (optional)

THE SWEET-AND-SOUR combination of vinegar and currants and the aroma of rosemary make this dish irresistible for a summer buffet dinner or lunch. This recipe, similar to the Spanish *escabeche*, comes from the islands of the Ionian Sea, where a vinegar marinade was the usual way to preserve cooked fish before refrigeration was available. Today, the reason to make this dish is its exquisite taste. Small whole fish are usually cooked this way, but fillets also work well.

This dish tastes best if the fish is left to marinate for 1 to 2 days. Serve with steamed potatoes and/or grilled or steamed vegetables drizzled with olive oil.

Place the flour in a shallow bowl. In a large skillet, heat 2 inches of a combination of olive and safflower oil over medium-high heat to 350°F. Dredge the fish in the flour, shaking off the excess. Fry the fish in batches, turning once, for 5 to 6 minutes, or until just cooked through. Sprinkle the fish with salt to taste and transfer to paper towels to drain.

Discard the oil and wipe out the skillet with paper towels. Heat the 1/2 cup oil and sauté the onion and Aleppo pepper or pepper flakes for 2 to 3 minutes, or until the onion is soft. Stir in the currants, garlic and dried rosemary. When the currants start to swell, add the vinegars and bring to a boil. Add the fish and cook, turning once, for 2 minutes. Remove from the heat. Taste and adjust the seasoning, adding black pepper to taste.

Transfer to a shallow dish and let stand, covered, for 1 to 2 days in the refrigerator. Bring to room temperature before serving, and garnish with the rosemary sprigs, if desired.

PALAMIDA PSITI ME SKORDO KE LEMONI

Grilled Bonito Steaks with Garlic and Lemon

MAKES 4 SERVINGS

4 1-inch-thick bonito, tuna, mahi-mahi or swordfish steaks (about 1½ pounds), rinsed and patted dry

Salt

2 teaspoons dried oregano, crumbled

4 garlic cloves, quartered lengthwise

Extra-virgin olive oil

½ cup freshly squeezed lemon juice

Freshly ground black pepper

4 sprigs fresh oregano (optional)

Sprinkle the fish on both sides with salt and 1 teaspoon of the dried oregano. Place the fish in a colander set over a bowl and refrigerate for at least 1 hour and up to 3 hours to season it.

Prepare a charcoal or gas grill or preheat the broiler.

Cut 2 small slits in the side of each fish steak, insert 2 garlic quarters and brush on both sides with oil. Grill or broil until cooked through, 4 to 5 minutes per side.

Meanwhile, combine the lemon juice and the remaining 1 teaspoon oregano in a shallow bowl. Dip each fish steak in the lemon mixture, turning to coat, and arrange on a serving platter. Whisk a few tablespoons of oil into the remaining lemon mixture (use about twice as much oil as lemon mixture) and drizzle over the fish steaks. Sprinkle with salt and pepper to taste and serve, garnished with the oregano sprigs, if desired.

THIS recipe comes from a magnificent little book, *The Cooking of Ithaca*, by Michalis Magoulas, an ophthalmologist who also happens to be a dedicated cook. He perfected and recorded his mother's and grandmother's recipes from the island of Ithaca. The cuisine there has been influenced by the Venetians, the French and the English, who ruled the island until 1864. "As a result of this long European domination over Ithaca (and the rest of the islands of the Ionian Sea), a middle class, a bourgeois society, was created much sooner than in the rest of Greece," writes Magoulas.

Bonito (*palamida*) is a relatively cheap fish. It is one of the very few fish of the Mediterranean that is sturdy enough to be grilled over a charcoal fire.

Serve with steamed potatoes and a mixed green salad or boiled wild greens.

PSARI PSITO

Grilled Whole Fish with Lemon, Olive Oil and Oregano

MAKES 6 SERVINGS

LEMON VINAIGRETTE

½ cup freshly squeezed lemon juice
 Pinch of salt

1 cup extra-virgin olive oil

½ teaspoon dried Greek oregano,
 crumbled

6 snapper or sea bass (1¼–1½ pounds
 each), cleaned, rinsed and patted dry
 Olive oil for brushing
 Salt and freshly ground black pepper

½ teaspoon dried Greek oregano,
 crumbled

3 lemons, cut into wedges

Soak 1 cup wood chips (preferably cherry or pecan) in cold water for 30 minutes. Prepare a charcoal or gas grill. Just before you are ready to grill, brush or rub the grill with oil to prevent the fish from sticking.

MEANWHILE, MAKE THE VINAIGRETTE: Place the lemon juice and salt in a blender. With the motor running, add the oil in a slow, steady stream, then add the oregano. Set aside.

WITH THIS recipe, Chef Jim Botsacos is able to serve fish that really tastes like fish on the islands. It's important to use Greek oregano.

When the fire is ready, place the soaked wood chips on top of the coals. Brush the fish on both sides with oil, and season inside and out with salt and pepper. Place the fish on the grill, cover and cook for 8 to 10 minutes, or until there are pronounced grill marks on the first side of the fish and it is lightly charred. Turn and cook for 8 to 10 minutes more.

Place the fish on a heated serving platter. Top each fish with 3 to 4 tablespoons of the lemon vinaigrette, sprinkle the oregano over it and serve with the lemon wedges.

BRANDADA SANTORINIS ME FAVA
Fish with Split Pea and Tomato Garlic Sauce from Santorini

MAKES 4 SERVINGS

4 firm white-fleshed fish fillets or steaks,
    such as snapper, grouper or monkfish
    (about 2 pounds total), rinsed and
    patted dry

    About 5 tablespoons olive oil

1 tablespoon dried oregano, crumbled
    Salt and freshly ground black pepper

2 tablespoons tomato paste

2½ cups Yellow Split Peas with Garlic (page
    24), without the toppings (or see
    Note)

½ cup oil-packed sun-dried tomatoes,
    coarsely chopped

1 teaspoon Aleppo pepper or pinch of
    crushed red pepper flakes (optional)

2–3 tablespoons water or dry white wine

1 medium tomato, cored and thinly sliced

3 tablespoons chopped fresh flat-leaf
    parsley

Preheat the broiler.

Brush the fish on both sides with oil and sprinkle with the oregano and salt and pepper to taste. Broil, turning once, for about 10 minutes, until just cooked through. Set aside.

Preheat the oven to 400°F.

In a large skillet, heat 2 tablespoons of the oil and cook the tomato paste over medium heat, stirring, for 1 to 2 minutes, or until shiny. Stir in the split peas, sun-dried tomatoes and Aleppo pepper or pepper flakes. The mixture should have the consistency of cake batter; if it is too thick, dilute it with a few tablespoons of water or wine.

Brush four individual gratin dishes with oil. Place 1 fish fillet or steak in each, pour a little more than ½ cup of the split-pea mixture over each and arrange the tomato slices on top. Drizzle with a little oil and bake for 15 to 20 minutes, or until bubbly. Turn the heat to broil, and broil for 2 minutes, or until golden.

Let stand for 5 minutes at room temperature, sprinkle with the parsley and serve.

VARIATION

If you wish to use salt cod, soak 2 pounds salt cod for 24 hours in cold water, changing the water several times. Rinse well under cold running water and pat dry with paper towels. Dredge in flour. Heat about 1 inch olive oil over medium-high heat to 350°F and fry, turning once, until golden, about 3 minutes per side. (Salt cod is not suitable for broiling.)

NOTE: Instead of the Yellow Split Peas with Garlic, you can use Caper Potato-Garlic Dip (page 23), with or without the capers.

THIS IS the Cypriot version of *brandada*, or *brandade*, the salt cod dish that is also native to Spain and the south of France. Salt cod is cheap and readily available all over Greece, and it can be easily found in the United States, but I have adapted the recipe so it can be prepared with either fresh or salted fish (see the variation). The fish is briefly baked, covered with a garlicky sauce and topped with sliced tomatoes. The result is a tasty, hearty dish.

Serve with a green salad or with steamed vegetables and greens and plenty of fresh crusty bread.

KALAMARAKIA ME FASSOLAKIA
Squid with Green Beans

MAKES 4 SERVINGS

1½ pounds small squid, cleaned, rinsed
    and patted dry

    Juice of 1 lemon

5 tablespoons olive oil

½ cup chopped onion

2 garlic cloves, thinly sliced

    Pinch of Aleppo pepper or crushed red
    pepper flakes

1 cup grated ripe tomatoes (see page 27)
    or canned diced tomatoes with their
    juice

½ cup dry white wine

1–2 tablespoons squid ink (optional)

½ cup fish stock or bottled clam juice

1 pound green beans, trimmed

    Salt

⅔ cup chopped fresh flat-leaf parsley, plus
    a few sprigs for garnish

In a large bowl, toss the squid with the lemon juice. Cover and refrigerate for 30 minutes.

In a large skillet, heat the oil and sauté the onion over medium heat until soft, 3 to 4 minutes. Add half of the garlic and sauté for 1 minute; do not let it color. Add the squid and pepper or pepper flakes and cook over high heat for 10 minutes, or until most of the liquid has evaporated. Add the remaining garlic and cook for 1 minute more. Add the tomatoes, wine and squid ink, if using. Reduce the heat to low, cover and simmer for 10 minutes, or until the squid is almost cooked.

Add the stock or clam juice and bring to a boil. Add the green beans and salt to taste and toss gently. Cover and cook for 10 minutes, or until

the green beans are tender. Add the chopped parsley and cook for 2 minutes more. If the sauce is watery, boil briefly over high heat to reduce.

Remove from the heat and let cool to give the flavors time to develop. Reheat very gently and serve warm, garnished with the parsley sprigs.

NOTE: To clean squid, cut the tentacles off the head and remove the cartilage in the center. Wash and peel off the purplish outer skin. Squeeze out the insides and wash and remove the center bone.

VARIATION
KALAMARAKIA ME BIZELIA
Calamari with Snow Peas

Substitute snow peas for the green beans; cook them for 3 to 5 minutes.

THIS COMBINATION might have escaped me if I hadn't tried the particularly inspiring version Lefteris Lazarou cooks at Varoulko, his Piraeus restaurant, one of the best places in Greece to try creative fish and seafood dishes. Originally, this dish was eaten during Lent, since squid and cuttlefish have no red blood and can be eaten on the days when all animals, even fish, are banned from the tables of good Greek Orthodox Christians. Unlike most Greek home cooks, Lefteris uses some squid ink in the sauce, and if you can get it, I suggest you do the same, since it intensifies the flavor.

Serve warm, with good crusty bread to dip in the sauce.

ASTAKOMAKARONADA
Spaghetti with Lobster in Light Tomato Sauce

MAKES 6 TO 8 SERVINGS

2 2-pound live lobsters

2/3 cup olive oil

1 1/2 cups coarsely chopped onions

5–6 garlic cloves, thinly sliced

1 1/2 cups chopped ripe tomatoes or canned diced tomatoes with their juice

1 cup dry white wine

1 teaspoon Aleppo pepper or pinch of crushed red pepper flakes

Salt

About 3 cups fish stock or Chicken Stock (page 267)

4 cups water

1 pound spaghetti

3 tablespoons chopped fresh flat-leaf parsley

Freshly ground black pepper

I TRIED this dish for the first time in a taverna, in a remote seaside village on Kythera about six years ago. The cook would set aside a little of the tasty fish stock he used in the many fish soups served at lunch. At dinner, if he had taken a liking to you, he would offer you his signature dish, made with pasta which he cooked in the reserved stock. He stewed the lobster separately with onions and tomatoes and mixed it with the pasta at the last moment. It was delicious, but difficult to duplicate in a home kitchen.

In the past few years, spaghetti with lobster has become a standard dish at almost every respectable island taverna. I have tasted many inferior versions and finally decided that the best is this simple version from Irene Kali, who lives in Maltezana, a seaside village on Astypalaia.

Place the live lobsters in the freezer for 2 to 3 hours (or see Note).

Split the lobsters lengthwise with a large, heavy knife. Cut off the claws and crack them with the back of the knife; do not shell them.

In a large, deep skillet or Dutch oven, heat the oil and sauté the onions over medium heat until soft, about 4 minutes. Add the garlic and sauté for 30 seconds; do not let it color.

Place the lobster in the skillet and sauté for 2 minutes. Add the onion mixture, tomatoes, wine, Aleppo pepper or pepper flakes and salt to taste and sauté over high heat for 10 minutes, or until the lobster meat is firm and the shells are red. With a slotted spoon, transfer the lobster to a large plate; set the skillet aside. Let the lobster cool slightly; then remove the meat, reserving the lobster shells. Cover and keep warm.

Place the lobster shells on a large square of cheesecloth and crack them with the back of a large knife. Tie the cloth into a bundle and place it in the skillet. Add the stock or clam juice and water, bring to a boil and add the spaghetti. Boil, stirring occasionally and adding a little more stock if needed, for about 15 minutes, or until al dente. The pasta will absorb the liquid as it cooks. Taste and adjust the seasonings. Squeeze the liquid out of the cheesecloth bundle, then discard the bundle.

Transfer the spaghetti to a large heated serving platter. Arrange the lobster on top, sprinkle with the parsley and black pepper to taste and serve immediately.

NOTE: If you don't want to freeze a live lobster, cook it for 2 minutes in a pot of boiling water to kill it, then cut it up.

KTAPODI ME KOFTO MAKARONI
Calamari or Octopus Stew with Macaroni

MAKES 4 SERVINGS

SIFNOS

½ cup olive oil

2 onions, halved lengthwise and thinly sliced into half-moons

3 garlic cloves, sliced

1½ pounds squid or fresh or frozen octopus (about 2 octopuses), cleaned and cut into bite-sized pieces (see Note)

1 cup dry rosé or red wine

2 cups grated ripe tomatoes (see page 27) or canned diced tomatoes with their juice

Pinch of Aleppo pepper or crushed red pepper flakes

1½ quarts fish stock or bottled clam juice, heated

1 pound elbow macaroni

Salt

Hot Pepper and Herb Mix (page 270) or 1 teaspoon dried oregano, crumbled

Freshly ground black pepper

3 tablespoons chopped fresh oregano, plus 1–2 sprigs for optional garnish

DURING my childhood, octopus and macaroni was a favorite picnic food on our Easter holiday excursions. We always began our trip on Holy Thursday, near the end of Lent. I had almost forgotten this classic dish until I tasted it again on the island of Chios. Although we used to eat octopus and macaroni cold, it tastes infinitely better served piping hot. We would never add cheese—forbidden during Lent—but you can certainly add some grated feta.

In a large, deep skillet with a lid or a Dutch oven, heat the oil and sauté the onions over high heat until translucent, about 5 minutes. Add the garlic and sauté for 1 minute more. Add the squid or octopus and bring to a boil, then reduce the heat to medium and cook for 15 minutes, or until most of the liquid has evaporated. Add the wine and simmer for 1 minute. Add the tomatoes and Aleppo pepper or pepper flakes and bring to a boil. Reduce the heat to low, cover and simmer for 20 minutes, or until the squid or octopus is soft when tested with a fork.

Add the stock or clam juice and bring to a boil. Add the macaroni and cook for 10 to 15 minutes, stirring often, until al dente. Add the salt, herb mix or oregano and black pepper to taste. Taste and adjust the seasonings. Transfer the stew to a serving bowl, sprinkle with the chopped oregano, garnish with the oregano sprigs, if desired, and serve at once.

NOTE: Cutting up slippery uncooked octopus is somewhat tedious, but Spanish chefs have convinced me that octopus tastes better if it is cut before stewing. However, you can cook the octopuses whole for the first 15 minutes, or until firm, turning them often with tongs or a large fork, then remove from the pan and cut them before continuing.

SUCCULENT MEAT
LAMB, PORK, VEAL AND CHICKEN

LEG OF LAMB STUFFED
WITH GREENS AND FETA 96
(Arni Gemisto me Horta ke Feta)

ROAST LEG OF LAMB WITH POTATOES 98
(Arnaki me Patates)

BAKED LAMB WITH PASTA
IN TOMATO SAUCE 100
(Youvetsi)

BRAISED LAMB CHOPS IN OLIVE OIL,
GARLIC AND LEMON SAUCE 102
(Arni Riganato)

OVEN-BAKED PORK LOIN WITH OLIVE OIL,
GARLIC, THYME AND OREGANO 103
(To Chirino tis Annas)

BAKED CHICKPEA AND LAMB STEW 104
(Revithia me Arni sto Fourno)

BRAISED LAMB (OR PORK) CHOPS
WITH ARTICHOKES 106
(Aginares me Kreas)

PORK WITH CABBAGE 108
(Hirino me Lahano)

CABBAGE LEAVES STUFFED
WITH MEAT AND RICE FROM CORFU 110
(Yaprakia tis Kerkyras)

MEATBALLS WITH RICE AND HERBS
IN LEMON BROTH 113
(Soutzoukakia Lemonata)

MEATBALLS FROM RHODES 114
(Keftedes Roditiki)

MEATBALLS WITH BULGUR IN ONION
AND TOMATO SAUCE 116
(Voli me Plyguri)

BAKED MEATBALLS FROM SYROS
WITH WALNUTS, ALMONDS AND PRUNES 118
(Koubeba Syriani)

MEAT-FILLED GRAPE LEAVES
WITH CANNELLINI BEANS 120
(Dolmades me Kreas ke Fassolia)

ONIONS STUFFED WITH GROUND MEAT
AND PINE NUTS 122
(Kremydodolmades)

VEAL STEW WITH GARLIC, PARSLEY
AND VINEGAR 124
(Moschari Sofrito)

BRAISED VEAL WITH ZUCCHINI 126
(Moschari me Kolokythakia)

VEAL AND VEGETABLE STEW
FROM CORFU 128
(Stoufado tis Kerkyras)

VEAL STEW WITH QUINCES 130
(Moschari Kydonato)

VEAL STEW WITH CORIANDER SEEDS 132
(Kreas Afelia)

BRAISED TURKEY (OR CHICKEN)
WITH SCALLIONS, LEMON AND DILL 133
(Galopoula me Freska Kremydakia)

CHICKEN SOUP WITH EGG-LEMON SAUCE 134
(Kotopoulo Soupa, Avgolemono)

CHICKEN AND FENNEL STEW
WITH QUINCE 136
(Kota me Krasi, Maratho ke Kydoni)

CHICKEN STUFFED WITH TOMATOES
AND FETA 138
(Kotopoulo Gemisto me Domata ke Feta)

STUFFED POACHED CHICKEN 140
(Kota Gemisti stin Katsarola)

BAKED CHICKEN WITH ORZO 142
(Kotopoulo Youvetsi)

RABBIT BAKED IN GARLIC,
FETA AND LEMON SAUCE 143
(Kouneli me Skordo ke Feta)

RABBIT STEW WITH PEARL ONIONS
IN TWO-WINE SAUCE 144
(Kouneli Stifado)

If you ask any Greek what his or her favorite dish is, the reply will probably be "roasted lamb." If you inquire further, people will start to describe the heavenly taste of the sweet crackling skin of a spring lamb, brushed with olive oil and seasoned with oregano or savory. Roasted either on the spit or on a grill over a charcoal fire, the lamb has an incomparable flavor. I often wonder whether the Greek obsession with roasted baby lamb is due to the fact that for ages, it has been *the* festive dish enjoyed on important religious and family occasions or whether it is the fabulous taste of the succulent meat alone that makes people dream.

There are no large lambs or mutton in Greece; lambs weigh no more than 20 pounds. Some supermarkets used to import large legs of lamb from Australia and New Zealand, but they stopped because of lack of demand. And no wonder: Baby lamb is far more flavorful.

There is general consensus that the baby lamb from the islands is the best. Butchers advertise their meats as coming from Tinos or Naxos or other islands where the lambs are fed on wild greens and herbs. Their flesh is tender and somewhat gamy at the same time. At Easter, families order a whole lamb from a distant relation or the relation of a friend, who will bring it from Folegandros or Astypalaia, where lamb is raised only for local consumption. During the days before Easter, the ferries coming from the islands are packed with slaughtered lambs, and people wait impatiently in taxis or private cars to get their precious cargo. Most Americans, used to neat packages of meat, would be appalled at the sight of the sloppily wrapped whole lambs, heads still attached, but the meat is utterly fresh and wholesome.

Greeks also love kid (young goat), which is leaner than lamb, with slightly darker meat. It tends to dry out when roasted on a spit, and it is therefore more suitable for stewing. Meat from mature goats is also favored and is occasionally available in some butcher shops during the winter. People simmer the tough but tasty dark meat for hours and serve it with its delicious broth, to which they add home-made pastas like trahana or *fide*.

In addition to lamb and kid, pork is raised on the islands. Pigs were traditionally reared in all households and usually slaughtered in December, before Christmas. Small amounts of pork were consumed fresh, and the rest was cured in many ways and stored for use throughout the year. Pigs were fed vegetable peelings, leftovers from the family's table and the nourishing whey from the daily production of cheeses. On some islands, particularly on Kea, pigs are fed acorns from the age-old oaks that grow there. In the mid-nineteenth century, there were more than a million oaks in Kea, producing four to eight tons of acorns a year, the main product of the island, most of which were exported to Italy, where they are used in tanneries to treat leather. Today, only about 200,000 trees remain. The oaks of Kea are now a protected forest, but with the recent development of the island, their future does not look promising. Pork from that island is especially succulent, though it is becoming harder to get, now that most Keans have abandoned farming and become rich from selling land to people who build weekend houses.

Island veal is rare and much sought after. Calves are brought to Tinos, Syros, Naxos, Evia and Kea at an early age to fatten naturally by munching grass, barley and vegetables. Although the island veal is chewier than American veal, it has a memorable flavor, very different from the soft and tasteless meat one gets in supermarkets. On Kea, butchers stay open even on Sunday afternoons, as weekend visitors wait patiently in line to stock their cars with this pricey but excellent meat before boarding the ferry for Athens.

Hens are raised by many islanders primarily for their eggs, an important source of protein. Hens used to be slaughtered only on special occasions or to feed small children and the sick. The meat from these older birds was tough and stringy, good for stews or soups but not for roasting. Only during the last 30 years or so has chicken become readily available and inexpensive.

Most Greek islands harbor plenty of game birds in late fall, and hunters from all over Greece come to shoot them during the short game-bird season. There are also hares, which Greeks love. *Stifado* is the classic way of cooking hare, and since the dish is so much loved, it is often prepared with the more available rabbit, which many farmers raise.

Traditionally, meat was never an everyday dish on the islands. Large pieces of grilled meat were served only at Easter or at important family feasts. When meat was cooked at home, it was made into a stew or baked with vegetables, potatoes or pasta so that a small piece would go a long way. Everything except the bones was eaten. The tripe, spleen, heart, liver and kidneys of the lamb are considered to be among the best parts of the animal. They are fried in olive oil, drizzled with lemon, sprinkled with oregano and eaten as a *meze*. Even the lamb's intestines are prized—cooked in *magiritsa*, the Easter soup, or wrapped around skewered diced innards and grilled.

Now that most islanders can afford as much meat as they like, families often gather on weekends at a *hasapotaverna*, or butcher's taverna. These large restaurants serve charcoal-grilled meat—usually lamb or, less often, pork chops—priced by weight. With such affluence and with more women working, there is less time for making the traditional slow-cooking and more frugal dishes like stews and stuffed vegetables.

With meat becoming more plentiful, I

wonder if the next generation will continue to dream about baby lamb. Perhaps they will instead begin to long for the almost forgotten foods of the poorer past, like *trahana* (sour milk and cracked wheat pasta) or a *hortopita* (wild greens pie) in homemade phyllo.

ARNI GEMISTO ME HORTA KE FETA

Leg of Lamb Stuffed with Greens and Feta

MAKES 4 TO 6 SERVINGS

⅓ cup olive oil, plus more for brushing

1 fennel bulb, trimmed (fronds and tender stalks reserved), halved and thinly sliced

1½ cups thinly sliced scallions (white and most of the green parts)

1 tablespoon coarsely chopped garlic, plus 2 garlic cloves, quartered

1½ cups coarsely chopped mixed greens (such as baby spinach, tender Swiss chard leaves, miner's lettuce, pea shoots, orache, green amaranth, outer leaves of escarole or romaine lettuce, and/or beet greens)

1 teaspoon fennel seeds, preferably freshly ground or crushed in a mortar

Freshly ground black pepper

¼ cup chopped fresh mint

1 3½-to-4-pound half leg of lamb (shank half), some fat left on, shank bone left in, hip end of bone removed (have the butcher do this, or see Note)

½ cup crumbled feta cheese

Salt

1 teaspoon dried oregano, crumbled

½ cup dry white wine, plus more if needed

½ cup chopped fennel fronds plus tender stalks, or fresh dill

THIS RECIPE comes from Andros, and it is one of the most delicious ways to cook a whole Easter spring lamb or kid. The various spring wild greens on the island, seasoned with fennel, mint and other aromatic herbs, together with the local slightly sour fresh cheese, are used to make the stuffing. In my version, instead of a whole tiny lamb, I use a shortened leg of lamb (shank half) partly boned, to make room for the stuffing. The result is quite different but equally enticing.

Serve with Roasted Potatoes with Garlic, Lemon and Oregano (page 202).

In a large skillet, heat the oil and sauté the fennel bulb over medium heat until just tender, about 3 minutes. Add the scallions and chopped garlic and sauté for 2 minutes more. Add the greens and sauté, stirring, until wilted. Remove from the heat and stir in the fennel seeds and pepper to taste. Let cool, then add the mint.

Make 8 small slits randomly in the lamb and insert the garlic quarters.

Transfer half of the greens mixture to a small bowl. Add the cheese to the greens remaining in the skillet. Taste and adjust the seasonings, adding salt if necessary (feta is usually quite salty). Stuff the lamb with the cheese mixture, squeezing it to extract the excess juices; add some of the remaining greens if needed; the lamb should be well stuffed. Close the opening with toothpicks. Rub the lamb all over with the remaining greens. Cover and refrigerate for at least 3 hours, or overnight.

Preheat the oven to 450°F.

Scrape the greens off the surface of the lamb and reserve. Brush the lamb with oil and sprinkle with the oregano and salt and pepper to taste. Place the lamb in a roasting pan that just holds it comfortably, preferably a clay or Pyrex one. Roast for 20 minutes.

Meanwhile, in a medium saucepan, bring the wine to a boil and simmer for 1 minute. Add the reserved greens.

Pour the greens mixture over the lamb and roast for 5 minutes more. Reduce the oven temperature to 350°F and roast the lamb, basting frequently with the pan juices, adding a little more wine to the pan if necessary, for about 30 minutes longer, or until an instant-read meat thermometer inserted into the thickest part of the meat registers 135°F for medium. Remove the lamb from the oven, sprinkle with the chopped fennel or dill, cover with aluminum foil and let rest for 15 minutes.

Carve the lamb and serve, passing the pan juices in a bowl or sauceboat at the table.

NOTE: Alternatively, you can use a butterflied leg of lamb. Spread the stuffing over the lamb, roll it up and tie it. Marinate and roast as directed.

ARNAKI ME PATATES

Roast Leg of Lamb with Potatoes

MAKES 6 SERVINGS

THIS IS the food Greeks associate with religious and family feasts—Easter, weddings and other joyous occasions—although now special occasions are not required to enjoy the dish. Fragrant with garlic and herbs, the lamb is basted with fresh lemon juice and white wine, both of which complement the flavor of the meat. The potatoes, cooked in the same pan, absorb all the flavors and become tender, with crispy tops.

American and New Zealand lamb is larger and leaner than Greek baby lamb, with darker meat that has a gamier flavor. In contrast, Greek spring lamb, which weighs only about 20 pounds, has very little meat and dries out easily. For larger legs, marinating the meat and inserting a mixture of garlic and herbs into the flesh is essential, as these cuts won't otherwise absorb the flavors.

I like to bring the lamb to the table in the roasting pan, so I use a nice clay baking dish, which also holds the potatoes in one layer. Baked lamb is traditionally accompanied by a green salad, like the fragrant, finely shredded Mixed Green Salad from Lesbos (page 179).

With slices of leftover cold roast lamb, Jim Botsacos, the chef of Molyvos restaurant, creates a wonderful wrap sandwich, intermingling the slices with arugula, lettuce and baby spinach and serving it with a dollop of refreshing Yogurt, Garlic, Cucumber and Fennel Dip (page 26).

2 tablespoons coarsely chopped garlic (about 6 cloves)

2 tablespoons dried savory or 1 tablespoon dried oregano plus 1 tablespoon dried thyme, crumbled

1 teaspoon salt

1 teaspoon Aleppo pepper or a pinch of crushed red pepper flakes or plenty of freshly ground black pepper

1/4 cup olive oil

1 5-to-6-pound bone-in leg of lamb

1/4 cup freshly squeezed lemon juice

1/3 cup white wine, plus more if needed

2–2 1/2 pounds small new potatoes, scrubbed, or medium potatoes, peeled and cut into 1-inch cubes

In a small bowl, mix the garlic with the herbs, salt, pepper or pepper flakes and 2 tablespoons of the oil. Make 8 or 9 deep slits all over the lamb and insert the garlic mixture, reserving about 1$\frac{1}{2}$ teaspoons.

Stir the remaining 2 tablespoons oil into the reserved garlic mixture and rub it over the surface of the meat. Cover and let stand for 1 hour at room temperature or, preferably, refrigerate for at least 5 hours, or overnight. Bring to room temperature before roasting.

Preheat the oven to 450°F.

Place the leg of lamb fat side down in a roasting pan large enough to hold the potatoes in a single layer and roast for 20 minutes.

Meanwhile, mix the lemon juice and $\frac{1}{3}$ cup wine in a small bowl. Turn the meat and pour the lemon-juice mixture over it. (If you are roasting the lamb in a clay dish, warm the mixture first, because cold liquid can cause the clay to break.) Reduce the oven temperature to 375°F and roast for 35 minutes, basting every 10 to 15 minutes with the pan juices. If the pan dries out, add a little more wine.

Transfer the lamb to a plate and add the potatoes to the pan, tossing them well to coat them with the pan juices. Place the lamb on the potatoes and continue roasting, basting often, for another 30 minutes, or until an instant-read thermometer inserted into the thickest part of the meat reaches 135°F. Transfer the meat to a heated platter, cover with a double layer of aluminum foil and set aside. (Leave the oven on.)

If the pan juices are watery, transfer most of them to a saucepan and cook briefly to reduce. Meanwhile, return the pan to the oven and continue baking the potatoes until tender, with crusty tops.

Turn the oven to broil. Place the lamb on the potatoes again and broil for 2 to 3 minutes, or until the surface is deep brown and crackling. Carve the lamb and serve, passing the pan juices in a bowl or sauceboat at the table.

YOUVETSI

Baked Lamb with Pasta in Tomato Sauce

MAKES 8 SERVINGS

IN THIS dish, lamb shanks are marinated overnight in olive oil and lemon, seasoned with plenty of garlic and savory, then slowly baked in a wine-and-tomato sauce accented with cinnamon. Finally, the pasta is cooked in the flavorful pan juices, and the lamb is served on top of the pasta.

Jim Botsacos, the chef of Molyvos restaurant, adapted the recipe for the larger American or New Zealand lamb shanks. You can stagger the preparation of this dish by partially cooking the meat up to 2 days in advance, but the finished dish must be served immediately when it comes out of the oven. Traditionally, it is cooked in a special clay baking dish, also called a *youvetsi*, which is taken directly to the table.

1 cup extra-virgin olive oil
Juice of 2 lemons
2 tablespoons dried savory, crumbled
3/4 cup sliced garlic cloves (about 2 heads)
8 lamb shanks (about 1 pound each)

Salt and freshly ground black pepper
1/2 cup extra-virgin olive oil
3 large onions, diced
1 tablespoon dried savory, crumbled
1/2 teaspoon Aleppo pepper or pinch crushed red pepper flakes
4 cups dry red wine
1 32-ounce can whole tomatoes, drained
1 1/2 quarts Chicken Stock (page 267), or more if needed
3 bay leaves
2 cinnamon sticks
1 pound orzo, cooked in plenty of boiling salted water for 2 minutes and drained
2 tablespoons chopped fresh flat-leaf parsley
1/2 cup coarsely grated hard myzithra, kefalotyri, pecorino Romano or Parmigiano-Reggiano cheese

The day before you plan to serve the lamb, combine the oil, lemon juice, savory and garlic in a large bowl. Add the lamb shanks and stir to coat. Transfer the lamb and marinade to large zipper-lock bags, press to force out the air and seal. Refrigerate overnight.

Preheat the oven to 375°F.

Remove the lamb from the marinade and set aside. Strain the marinade, discard the liquid, then chop the garlic. Season the lamb well with salt and pepper.

Place a Dutch oven over medium-high heat and, when it is hot, add ¼ cup of the olive oil. Add the lamb, 2 or 3 shanks at a time, and brown well on all sides, about 15 minutes. Set the lamb aside.

Reduce the heat to medium and add the remaining ¼ cup oil. Add the onions and sauté until translucent, about 5 minutes. Add the garlic and cook for 1 minute more. Stir in the savory and pepper or pepper flakes. Add the wine, scraping the bottom of the skillet to release the browned bits, and cook until reduced by half.

Return the lamb to the Dutch oven and boil over medium heat, until the liquid is again reduced by half. Add the tomatoes, crushing them between your fingers, the stock, bay leaves and cinnamon sticks, stir and bring to a boil. Cover and cook for 5 minutes. (You can prepare the meat to this point 1 or 2 days in advance; cool, cover and refrigerate. Bring the liquid to a boil before proceeding.)

MAKING MACARONI ON CHIOS

Cover the Dutch oven, or transfer the lamb to a deep baking dish with a cover, place in the oven and bake for 2½ hours, or until the lamb is tender.

Transfer the meat to a platter. Add the orzo to the pan and stir to coat with the cooking juices. If the pan seems a little dry, add about ¼ cup stock. Bake, uncovered, for about 15 minutes, or until most of the liquid has been absorbed. Place the lamb on top of the orzo and bake for another 10 minutes. Remove from the oven and discard the bay leaves and cinnamon sticks. Serve immediately on heated plates, placing a few tablespoons of orzo on each plate and setting a lamb shank on top. Drizzle with the cooking juices and sprinkle with the parsley and cheese.

ARNI RIGANATO

Braised Lamb Chops in Olive Oil, Garlic and Lemon Sauce

MAKES 4 TO 6 SERVINGS

1/3 cup olive oil

2 1/2 pounds shoulder lamb chops (5–6 chops), trimmed of most fat

1 cup warm water

1/2 cup dry white wine

4–5 garlic cloves, slivered

1 tablespoon dried oregano, crumbled

1/3 cup freshly squeezed lemon juice

1 teaspoon salt

Freshly ground black pepper

A few sprigs of fresh oregano

In a large, deep skillet with a lid, heat the oil over medium-high heat and sauté the lamb in batches, turning, until no longer pink in the center, about 10 minutes. Add the water, wine, garlic and dried oregano, reduce the heat to low, cover and simmer for 30 minutes.

Add the lemon juice, the salt and pepper to taste, turn the lamb and cook for 30 minutes more. Turn the lamb again and simmer for 20 to 30 minutes more, or until the meat is very tender. Taste and adjust the seasonings. Garnish with the oregano sprigs and serve.

FRAGRANT with garlic and oregano, these lamb chops cook slowly in olive oil, wine and lemon juice. Almost any kind of meat can be made into a *riganato:* My mother usually cooks young goat, and veal, chicken and turkey can also be prepared the same way, with the cooking times adjusted accordingly.

There is plenty of sauce, which can be served with pasta, such as egg noodles or tagliatelle. You could also serve mashed potatoes or follow my mother's example: Fry quartered medium-sized potatoes in olive oil until they are almost tender, and finish them off in the tasty sauce.

TO CHIRINO TIS ANNAS

Oven-Baked Pork Loin with Olive Oil, Garlic, Thyme and Oregano

MAKES 8 TO 10 SERVINGS

4–5 tablespoons olive oil

4 garlic cloves, finely chopped

1 tablespoon dried thyme, crumbled

1 tablespoon dried oregano, crumbled
(see Note)

1–2 teaspoons Aleppo pepper or pinch of
crushed red pepper flakes

1 teaspoon salt

1 4-to-5-pound boneless pork loin roast
or top leg (fresh ham), trimmed of
most fat

THIS IS my sister Anna's signature dish, the one she always bakes for parties. We usually make it with meat we buy on Kea, the island my mother comes from, which is famous for its tasty pork and veal. The meat cooks in its own juices, and there is plenty of delicious sauce at the end of cooking. If you like, you can carefully remove the fat from the surface before serving.

In the old days, pieces of meat in covered pots were probably taken to a communal oven for baking or baked on special occasions in the wood-burning bread oven of the house. Since wood is not plentiful on the bare Greek islands, these ovens were fired only once a week to bake bread, then other foods were cooked in the cooling oven after the bread was removed.

Serve with Roasted Potatoes with Garlic, Lemon and Oregano (page 202). Freeze any leftover sauce to use with pasta.

In a small bowl, combine the oil, garlic, thyme, oregano, pepper or pepper flakes and salt. Rub the garlic mixture all over the pork. Place the pork in a Dutch oven just large enough to hold it snugly, cover with aluminum foil and then the lid and refrigerate overnight, or up to 24 hours.

Preheat the oven to 400°F.

Remove the aluminum foil from the Dutch oven, replace the lid and bake for 30 minutes. Reduce the oven temperature to 375°F and bake for 1 hour more, basting twice with the pan juices. Uncover, baste again and bake, uncovered, for 20 to 30 minutes more, or until an instant-read meat thermometer inserted into the thickest part registers 155 to 165°F.

Remove the pork from the oven, cover and let rest for 1 hour to develop the flavors. Reheat in a 375°F oven for about 20 minutes and serve.

NOTE: Instead of oregano, you can use 1 tablespoon Hot Pepper and Herb Mix (page 270); halve the amount of Aleppo pepper or pepper flakes.

REVITHIA ME ARNI STO FOURNO

Baked Chickpea and Lamb Stew

MAKES 6 TO 8 SERVINGS

THIS HEARTY one-pot meal comes from the island of Lesbos, in the eastern Aegean, although similar dishes can be found on Crete and other islands. It is a delicious variation on Baked Lamb with Pasta in Tomato Sauce (page 100), a classic dish throughout Greece.

1 pound dried chickpeas, soaked overnight in water and drained

4 cups beef stock or Chicken Stock (page 267)

2 bay leaves

1 cup olive oil

1 3-to-3½-pound boneless lamb shoulder, trimmed of most fat and cut into 6–8 slices

2 cups chopped onions

4 tomatoes, cored, peeled and chopped

1½ cups dry red wine

10 garlic cloves: 5 minced and 5 cut into slivers

1 tablespoon tomato paste

1–2 teaspoons Aleppo pepper or ½–1 teaspoon crushed red pepper flakes

1 tablespoon dried oregano, crumbled

1 pound spicy garlic sausage, cut into bite-sized pieces

Salt and freshly ground black pepper

3 tablespoons chopped fresh flat-leaf parsley for garnish

CHICKPEA BAKING POTS

Place the chickpeas in a large pot and add cold water to cover by at least 4 inches. Bring to a boil, remove from the heat and set aside for at least 6 hours. (This extra step considerably reduces the discomfort many people experience from eating dried beans, but you may omit it if you don't have time.)

Drain the chickpeas and return to the pot. Add the stock and bay leaves and bring to a boil. Reduce the heat to low and simmer for 45 minutes to 1 hour, or until tender.

Meanwhile, preheat the oven to 325°F.

In a large skillet, heat $\frac{1}{2}$ cup of the oil over medium-high heat and brown the lamb, in batches, until golden brown on all sides, about 10 minutes. With a slotted spoon, transfer the lamb to a large bowl and set aside.

Add the onions to the skillet and sauté for 4 to 5 minutes, or until soft. Add the tomatoes, wine, minced garlic, tomato paste and pepper or pepper flakes and cook over high heat for 2 minutes, or until the juices have reduced slightly and thickened. Remove from the heat.

Make several slits in each piece of lamb and insert the garlic slivers. Place the lamb in a large roasting pan, sprinkle with the oregano and pour the tomato sauce over it. Bake for 1 hour, basting the lamb frequently with the sauce. Transfer the lamb to a plate, cover and keep warm.

Drain the chickpeas, reserving the cooking liquid. Add the chickpeas, sausage, 1 cup of the reserved cooking liquid, the remaining $\frac{1}{2}$ cup oil and salt and pepper to taste to the roasting pan and stir well. Season the lamb with salt to taste and return to the pan, spooning the chickpeas over it. Bake for 40 to 50 minutes longer, adding more reserved cooking liquid if the chickpeas begin to dry out, until the lamb is tender. Sprinkle with the parsley and serve.

VARIATION
FASSOLIA ME ARNI STO FOURNO

Baked Beans and Lamb Stew

Substitute large dried lima beans or Greek *gigantes* (giant white beans) for the chickpeas and cook as directed.

AGINARES ME KREAS

Braised Lamb (or Pork) Chops with Artichokes

MAKES 4 SERVINGS

LAMB CHOPS cooked together with artichokes take on a delicate sweetness that is complemented by the tartness of the lemon juice. In many parts of Greece, the sauce is thickened with egg, making it an avgolemono (egg-lemon sauce). But I prefer this much lighter version of the dish, based on a recipe given to me by Claire Ksida from Chios. Claire and her husband own the tiny Perleas Hotel, which they created by restoring an old Genoese villa, beautifully situated among extensive orange and tangerine groves, in Kambos, just outside the island's capital. Claire prepares this dish for her guests in the spring, with the fresh tender artichokes she grows in her garden. "I have plenty of artichokes, so I freeze some because I like to be able to continue making the dish throughout the summer," she told me.

This dish is usually served on its own, but it can be accompanied by egg noodles or Pasta Squares (page 173), tossed in the lemony sauce.

1/2 cup olive oil

2 1/2 pounds shoulder lamb chops, trimmed of most fat, or 1 1/2 pounds boneless pork loin, cut into 2-inch cubes

1 1/2 cups coarsely chopped onions

1 1/2 cups Chicken Stock (page 267) or water

2 lemons, halved

8 medium artichokes

1/4 cup freshly squeezed lemon juice, or more to taste

1 1/2 cups chopped fresh dill

Salt and freshly ground black pepper

In a large, deep skillet or a Dutch oven, heat the oil over medium-high heat and sauté the meat in batches, turning often, until golden on both sides, about 10 minutes. Add the onions and sauté for 3 to 5 minutes more, or until they are soft. Add the stock or water and bring to a boil. Reduce the heat to low and simmer for 30 to 40 minutes.

Meanwhile, fill a large bowl with cold water and squeeze the juice of the 2 lemons into it (reserve the lemon halves). Snap off several layers of leaves from each artichoke, pulling them downward to break them off at the base. Rub the cut parts often with the lemon halves as you work to prevent discoloration. Cut off the top of each artichoke and trim the broken parts of leaves around the stem with a sharp knife, again rubbing the cut surfaces with lemon. Halve the artichokes and remove the center chokes with a knife or grapefruit spoon; drop each prepared artichoke into the bowl of lemon water.

With a slotted spoon, remove the artichokes from the lemon water and add to the meat with ¾ cup of the dill, the lemon juice and salt and pepper to taste. If necessary, add a little water—the liquid should almost cover the meat and artichokes. Place an inverted heatproof plate over the meat and artichokes to keep them submerged. Cover and simmer for 20 to 30 minutes, or until the artichokes are tender.

If the sauce is too thin, remove the plate, increase the heat to high and boil for 3 to 4 minutes to reduce slightly. Taste and adjust the seasonings, adding more lemon juice, salt and/or pepper if necessary. Stir in the remaining ¾ cup dill and serve.

VARIATION
HIRINO ME SELINO
Braised Pork with Celery

In the winter, a similar meat and vegetable dish is made using large celery root, peeled and sliced, along with bunches of the wild celery that is common in Greece and the rest of the Mediterranean. This fragrant celery can be found in Asian markets under the name *kun choi* or *kin tsai*, or sometimes, chinese celery.

Substitute 4 halved celery hearts for the artichokes and cook as directed.

HIRINO ME LAHANO
Pork with Cabbage

MAKES 4 SERVINGS

~~~~~~~~~~~~~~~~~~~~~~~~~~~~~~~~~~~~~

THIS DISH is called *kapuska* in Olympi, an unspoiled medieval village on the island of Chios, where the recipe comes from. The word is probably Slavic, and it is also used in Turkey for a similar dish. During the last century, many Chians, especially people from this particular village, lived and prospered in Istanbul. *Kapuska* was most likely one of the dishes they brought with them when they returned to their island. The dish is flavored with a homemade fragrant spice mixture called *aspetsa* (page 266), which contains mainly hot peppers and dried herbs, including oregano, basil and mint, along with dried orange peel. The recipe has probably survived in this village—the only place I have seen it—since the time of the Genoese.

1   2-pound boneless pork shoulder or roast leg (fresh ham), trimmed of most fat

1   large onion, coarsely chopped

1/3   cup olive oil

1   teaspoon sugar

1½   cups grated ripe tomatoes (see page 27) or 1½ cups canned diced tomatoes with their juice

1   cup dry red wine

1   teaspoon Hot Pepper and Herb Mix (page 270; optional)

1½–2   teaspoons Aleppo pepper or 2/3–1 teaspoon crushed red pepper flakes (the smaller amount if using the Hot Pepper and Herb Mix above)

1   cinnamon stick

Salt

1   large cabbage (about 2 pounds), preferably savoy, cored, quartered and sliced into thick ribbons

3   tablespoons chopped fresh flat-leaf parsley (optional)

Place the pork, onion, oil and sugar in a large pot and add enough water to come two-thirds of the way up the sides of the meat. Bring to a boil and skim off the foam that rises to the top. Cover and simmer for 30 minutes, turning the pork once. Remove from the heat and let stand for 1 hour, or until cool, then refrigerate overnight.

Remove the pork from the pot and slice it or cut it into 2-inch cubes. Bring the cooking liquid to a boil and boil over high heat until reduced to a little less than 2 cups. Return the pork to the pot and cook for 2 minutes, turning to coat it with the sauce. Add the tomatoes, wine, hot pepper mix (if using), pepper or pepper flakes, cinnamon stick, salt to taste and enough water, if needed, to come two-thirds up the sides of the pork. Bring to a boil, then reduce the heat to low, cover and simmer for 30 minutes, turning once.

Meanwhile, cook the cabbage in a large pot of boiling salted water for 12 minutes, or until it starts to soften. Drain and rinse under cold running water.

Add the cabbage to the pork mixture and return to a boil. Reduce the heat to low and simmer for 20 to 30 minutes, or until the pork and cabbage are tender. Taste and adjust the seasonings, and discard the cinnamon stick.

Serve hot, sprinkling each serving with parsley, if using.

OLYMPI, CHIOS

YAPRAKIA TIS KERKYRAS

Cabbage Leaves Stuffed with Meat and Rice from Corfu

MAKES 6 TO 8 SERVINGS

ON CORFU, cabbage leaves are stuffed with equal amounts of rice and meat, flavored with pancetta, cheese and tomatoes.

This recipe is based on the description Ninetta Laskari gives in her book about her childhood years on Corfu, along with some of the history of the island. I first made this dish using the large blue-green leaves from the shoots that grow around the cabbage head. These leaves are similar to collards but somewhat thicker, and they have more flavor than the leaves of the common white cabbage. Here, I suggest using a combination of savoy cabbage and collards instead. The pink tomato-avgolemono sauce is my variation on the traditional recipe, and its lemony taste goes well with the sweetness of the stuffed cabbage leaves.

As with most stews, it's better to make this dish a day in advance and let the flavors develop overnight. Since it contains meat, greens and rice, all you need to accompany it is a simple side dish of steamed carrots or turnips—pour some of the avgolemono sauce over them as well.

Salt

1 large savoy cabbage (about 1³/4 pounds)

1 bunch collard greens

STUFFING

¹/4 pound pancetta, finely diced

3 tablespoons olive oil

1¹/2 cups finely chopped onions

1 pound lean ground pork

1¹/2 cups grated ripe tomatoes (see page 27) or canned diced tomatoes with their juice

²/3 cup medium-grain rice, such as Arborio

¹/2 cup dry red wine

1 teaspoon Aleppo pepper or pinch of crushed red pepper flakes

Salt

1 cup chopped fresh flat-leaf parsley

²/3 cup grated hard myzithra, kefalotyri or pecorino Romano cheese

5 scallions (white and most of the green parts), finely chopped

Freshly ground black pepper

About 1¹/2 cups beef stock or Chicken Stock (page 267)

About ¹/₂–1 cup beef stock or Chicken
    Stock (page 267)

¹/₂ cup tomato juice

1 large egg

2–4 tablespoons freshly squeezed lemon
    juice

¹/₄ cup water

2 tablespoons cornstarch
    Freshly ground black pepper

1 tablespoon chopped fresh flat-leaf
    parsley

Bring a large pot of water to a boil and add 2 ta-blespoons salt. Using a sharp knife, cut out the core of the cabbage, and separate the leaves. Fill a large bowl with cold water. Blanch the leaves in batches, in the boiling water, letting the larger leaves cook for about 5 minutes and the smaller ones for about 3 minutes, or until just tender. Transfer each batch to the bowl of cold water to stop the cooking, then transfer to a colander to drain. Repeat with the collard greens, cooking them for about 3 minutes, or until just tender. You can prepare the cabbage and collard leaves a day in advance. Stack them carefully on a large plate, cover and refrigerate.

MAKE THE STUFFING: In a large skillet, sauté the pancetta over medium-high heat until lightly browned, about 5 minutes. Add the oil and onions and sauté until the onions are soft, about 5 minutes. Add the pork and sauté, stirring often, for 5 minutes more, or until no longer pink. Add the tomatoes, rice, wine, Aleppo pepper or pep-per flakes and salt to taste and bring to a boil. Re-move from the heat and stir in the parsley, cheese, scallions and black pepper to taste. Taste and adjust the seasonings.

STUFF THE LEAVES: Cut off the hard stems from the cabbage leaves and collard greens, and make a layer of the stems in the bottom of a large pot to prevent the stuffed cabbage from sticking. Lay 1 cabbage leaf on a work surface, and place about ¹/₃ cup stuffing in the middle of the wider end of the leaf. Fold the sides over the filling and roll up the leaf to enclose the stuffing. Squeeze the stuffed leaf over a medium bowl to extract most of the excess liquid and place the stuffed leaf in the pot, seam side down. Continue stuffing the remaining leaves, overlapping 2 smaller cabbage leaves or 1 cabbage leaf and 1 collard leaf when you've used all the larger leaves, and arranging the stuffed leaves close together in the pot; make a second layer of stuffed leaves on top of the first. Place an inverted heatproof plate over the stuffed leaves to prevent them from moving during cook-ing, and pour in the collected liquid from the bowl and enough stock to just cover. Bring to a boil, reduce the heat to low, cover and simmer for 35 to 40 minutes, or until the leaves are very tender and the rice is cooked. Check from time to time to see if a little more stock is needed. Let cool completely. (If you have time, refrigerate the leaves overnight to allow the flavors to develop.)

About 30 minutes before serving, reheat the stuffed cabbage leaves: Bring the liquid just to a boil over medium heat, cover, reduce the heat to low and simmer for about 15 minutes. Transfer the stuffed leaves to a heated platter, cover and keep warm while you prepare the sauce.

MAKE THE SAUCE: In a medium saucepan, bring to a boil the stuffed-cabbage cooking liquid and enough stock to equal 2 cups. Add the tomato juice, reduce the heat to low and simmer for 5 minutes.

Meanwhile, in a medium bowl, whisk the egg, 2 tablespoons of the lemon juice and 2 tablespoons of the water. In a small bowl, whisk the cornstarch with the remaining 2 tablespoons water, then whisk into the egg mixture.

Whisking constantly, slowly pour $1\frac{1}{2}$ cups of the hot stock mixture, $\frac{1}{2}$ cup at a time, into the egg mixture. Pour the egg mixture into the saucepan and simmer, stirring gently, until the sauce thickens. Taste and adjust the seasonings, adding pepper and more lemon juice if you like.

Pour some of the sauce over the stuffed cabbage, sprinkle with the parsley and serve, with the remaining sauce on the side.

SOUTZOUKAKIA LEMONATA

Meatballs with Rice and Herbs in Lemon Broth

MAKES ABOUT 26 MEATBALLS; 4 TO 6 SERVINGS

1 pound lean ground beef, veal, lamb or pork, or a combination

$^1/_2$ cup medium-grain rice, such as Arborio

3–4 scallions (white and most of the green parts), finely chopped

1 cup finely chopped fresh flat-leaf parsley

$^1/_2$ cup finely chopped fresh dill

$^1/_2$ cup chopped fresh cilantro

$^1/_3$ cup chopped fresh mint

1 large egg, lightly beaten

$^1/_3$ cup olive oil

Salt and freshly ground black pepper

1 large onion, chopped

1 cup dry white wine

$2^1/_2$–$3^1/_2$ cups Chicken Stock (page 267) or beef stock

3–4 tablespoons freshly squeezed lemon juice

Sprigs of fresh flat-leaf parsley, dill, mint and/or cilantro

MEATBALLS similar to these are cooked all over Greece, but only on Cyprus are you likely to find cilantro mixed with the other herbs. This recipe is my own version, based on an exceptional one of my friend Despina Drakaki, from Paros.

In a large bowl, combine the meat, rice, scallions, parsley, dill, cilantro, mint, egg, 2 tablespoons of the oil, salt and pepper to taste. Knead well, cover and refrigerate for at least 1 hour.

Shape 2-tablespoon-sized portions of the meat mixture into balls. Place on a plate, cover and refrigerate.

In a large, deep skillet with a lid or a Dutch oven, heat the remaining 3 tablespoons oil and sauté the onion over medium-high heat for 2 to 3 minutes, or until soft. Add the wine and simmer for 1 minute. Add 2 cups of the stock and salt to taste. Add the meatballs to the skillet; they should be completely covered. Bring to a boil, reduce the heat to low, cover and simmer for 15 minutes.

Add $^1/_2$ cup of the stock and 3 tablespoons lemon juice and cook for 10 minutes more, or until the meatballs are cooked through and the liquid is reduced to 1 cup. If the meatballs are not cooked, add more stock and cook briefly. Taste and adjust the seasonings with lemon juice, salt and/or pepper. Serve in soup bowls, garnished with herb sprigs.

VARIATION

If you like, thicken the sauce with an egg-lemon sauce: Add only half the lemon juice to the broth. When the meatballs are cooked, remove with a slotted spoon and keep warm. In a small bowl, beat 1 large egg with 3 tablespoons water. Gradually whisk in the remaining lemon juice and the sauce from the pan. Return the sauce to the pan and gently reheat over very low heat, stirring constantly. Pour over the meatballs and serve.

KEFTEDES RODITIKI
Meatballs from Rhodes

MAKES ABOUT 30 MEATBALLS; 6 TO 8 SERVINGS

4 ounces Savory Barley and Wheat Biscuits (see page 281) or $^2/_3$ cup dried whole wheat bread crumbs

$2^1/_2$ cups coarsely chopped onions

$1^1/_2$ cups coarsely chopped fresh flat-leaf parsley

$^1/_2$ cup grated ripe tomato (see page 27) or canned diced tomatoes with their juice

1 tablespoon Aleppo pepper or pinch of crushed red pepper flakes or plenty of freshly ground black pepper

1 tablespoon dried oregano, crumbled

1 teaspoon salt, or to taste

$^1/_2$ cup packed fresh mint leaves

$2^1/_2$ pounds ground lamb or beef, or a combination

$^1/_4$ cup ouzo, vodka or water

1 cup all-purpose flour

Olive oil and safflower oil for frying

WHEN MY family makes *keftedes*, we always prepare a large quantity, since we eat them not only hot but also at room temperature—and even directly from the refrigerator. They are a common and popular meat dish, served on picnics as well as at buffet dinners and children's parties.

I first came across fresh tomatoes as an ingredient in the *keftedes* mixture in the handwritten kitchen notebook of a certain late Mrs. Papastefanou. Mrs. Papastefanou, who came from Rhodes, was an excellent cook, and in her notebook, I found lots of interesting recipes for both traditional and French-inspired savory and sweet dishes. The ordinary *keftedes* with which I was familiar have a little vinegar and some wine added to the ground-meat mixture, but never tomato.

Tomatoes are native to the Americas, and they were not incorporated into the Greek diet until the late nineteenth century, probably by way of Italy, but they have become an indispensable ingredient in many Greek dishes. Tomatoes seem to be ubiquitous in the foods of the Dodecanese islands, perhaps because they were under Italian occupation from 1911 to 1947.

I came upon a similar recipe in a marvelous book called *Recipes from Rhodes*, a collection of old local recipes published on the island in the mid-1980s by a women's organization. Theonie Mark, who is from Rhodes, also includes a recipe for *keftedes* with tomatoes in her *Greek Island Cooking*, published in the United States in the 1970s.

Fry some of the mixture as meatballs, as the recipe describes, and use the rest to make hamburgers or shape into sausages—we call them *biftekia*—and serve in pita bread with Yogurt, Garlic, Cucumber and Fennel Dip (page 26) and tomato (see the variation).

Wrap the biscuits, if using, in a clean kitchen towel and hit it with your hand to break them up. In a food processor, combine the biscuits or bread crumbs, onions, parsley, tomato, pepper or pepper flakes, oregano and salt. Pulse to chop, scraping the sides of the bowl, just until the mixture is uniform; do not overprocess. Add the mint and pulse a few more times to chop.

In a large bowl, combine the meat, onion mixture and ouzo, vodka or water. Knead with your hands to mix. Cover and refrigerate for 1 to 3 hours.

Spread the flour on a large plate. Shape 1/4-cup portions of the meat mixture into large meatballs. Flatten them slightly, dredge in the flour and place on a sheet of aluminum foil.

In a large, deep skillet, heat 1 1/2 inches of a combination of olive and safflower oil over medium-high heat to 350°F. Add a few *keftedes* at a time—do not crowd the skillet—and fry, turning two or three times, until golden brown, about 4 minutes. Transfer to paper towels to drain. Serve hot, warm or at room temperature.

VARIATION

You can also broil *keftedes*. Or shape 1/2-cup portions of the meat mixture into 4-inch-long rolls and fry or broil. Serve with warm pita bread, arugula, chopped tomato, chopped onion and Yogurt, Garlic, Cucumber and Fennel Dip (page 26). This mixture also makes great hamburgers. I cook them in a lightly oiled nonstick skillet, then wrap them in aluminum foil and freeze, so they are ready to be reheated in the microwave for a quick lunch.

VOLI ME PLYGURI

Meatballs with Bulgur in Onion and Tomato Sauce

MAKES ABOUT 26 MEATBALLS; 4 TO 6 SERVINGS

VOLI are marbles, the multicolored little balls that were so popular with kids during my childhood. But unlike the glass versions, which were quite expensive, the ones we used to play with were made of clay and colored in various bright, glossy shades. They were fragile, and their glaze would crack, revealing their dark red insides, similar in color to these delicious meatballs with bulgur.

This recipe comes from the island of Rhodes, and bulgur is probably the grain originally used. Later, in the stewed meatballs of the mainland, it was replaced by rice.

Serve with mashed potatoes, bulgur and/or rice pilaf.

1 pound lean ground beef, veal, lamb or pork, or a combination

1 cup finely chopped fresh flat-leaf parsley

4–5 scallions (white and most of the green parts), finely chopped

1/2 cup coarse bulgur (see Sources, page 285)

1 large egg, lightly beaten

1/3 cup olive oil

4 garlic cloves: 2 minced and 2 coarsely chopped

1 teaspoon ground cumin

Salt and freshly ground black pepper to taste

1 large onion, halved lengthwise and sliced into half-moons

1/2 cup dry red wine

2 cups grated ripe tomatoes (see page 27) or canned diced tomatoes with their juice

1 cinnamon stick

1/2 cup water

In a large bowl, combine the meat, all but 2 tablespoons of the parsley, the scallions, bulgur, egg, 2 tablespoons of the oil, the minced garlic, cumin, salt and pepper to taste. Knead well, cover and refrigerate for at least 1 hour and up to 4 hours.

Shape 2-tablespoon-sized portions of the meat mixture into balls. Place on a plate, cover and refrigerate.

In a large, deep skillet with a lid, or a Dutch oven, heat the remaining 3 tablespoons oil and sauté the onion over medium-high heat for 4 to 5 minutes, or until it starts to color. Add the chopped garlic and sauté for 30 seconds. Add the wine and simmer for 1 minute. Stir in the tomatoes and cinnamon stick. Carefully add the meatballs to the skillet; the sauce should almost cover them. Add the water, bring to a boil and reduce the heat to low. Cover and simmer for 20 minutes, or until the meatballs are cooked through and the sauce has thickened. Remove the cinnamon stick, sprinkle with the remaining 2 tablespoons parsley and serve.

VARIATION
BAMIES ME KEFTEDES
Meatballs with Okra

Cook the meatballs in Baked Okra in Tomato Sauce (page 196).

KOUBEBA SYRIANI

Baked Meatballs from Syros with Walnuts, Almonds and Prunes

MAKES ABOUT 12 ROLLS; SERVES 4

1 medium onion, quartered

½ cup coarsely chopped fresh flat-leaf parsley

3 tablespoons freshly squeezed lemon juice

1 pound lean ground veal or beef

½ cup ground almonds

½ cup ground walnuts, plus 20 walnut halves

⅓ cup pine nuts

⅓ cup toasted bread crumbs

¼ cup olive oil, plus more for brushing

1 large egg, lightly beaten

1 teaspoon Aleppo pepper or pinch of crushed red pepper flakes

½ teaspoon salt

20 pitted prunes

1 cup Chicken Stock (page 267) or beef stock

⅔ cup dry red wine

2–3 tablespoons red wine vinegar
Sprigs of fresh flat-leaf parsley

COOKING meat with dried fruits and nuts brings to mind medieval or ancient dishes that have survived in North African cuisine. In this recipe from Syros, ground almonds, walnuts and pine nuts are mixed with ground meat and shaped into oblong rolls. The rolls are baked in a flavorful red-wine-and-vinegar broth, together with walnut-stuffed pitted prunes. The resulting sweet-and-sour combination can be set off by mashed potatoes, french fries or any kind of egg pasta.

The name *koubeba* comes from the almost forgotten spice *piper cubeba*, a kind of pepper from Indonesia that was never very popular in Europe but is mentioned in old Arabic cookery books, according to *The Oxford Companion to Food*.

The recipe was given to me by Eleni Prochori, the head of the Agency for the Development of the Cyclades, based on Syros. Eleni has painstakingly collected recipes from all the islands of the Cyclades, including, of course, her native Syros. She gives them to any serious cook or restaurant owner interested in the authentic tastes of the region.

Trying to find out more about the dish's origin, I queried Kostas Prekas, a remarkable man who tries to re-create traditional Cycladic preparations for his gourmet shop in Ermoupolis, Syros's capital. He told me that *koubeba* was probably one of the dishes brought to the island by sailors or merchants from the East who passed through the busy port in the mid-nineteenth century.

In a food processor or blender, combine the onion, chopped parsley and lemon juice and pulse to chop.

In a large bowl, combine the onion mixture, meat, almonds, walnuts, pine nuts, bread crumbs, oil, egg, pepper or pepper flakes and salt and knead into a homogenous mixture. Cover and refrigerate for at least 30 minutes and up to 4 hours.

Preheat the oven to 450°F.

Shape 1/4-cup portions of the meat mixture into oval rolls and arrange in a 13-x-9-inch baking dish. Brush the rolls with oil and bake for 15 minutes.

Meanwhile, insert 1 walnut half into each prune (you may need to halve the larger walnuts).

Reduce the oven temperature to 400°F. Arrange the stuffed prunes between the meat rolls, add the stock, wine and 1 to 2 tablespoons of the vinegar and bake for 15 to 20 minutes more. Baste with the pan juices, turn off the oven and leave the dish in the oven for 5 minutes.

Taste the sauce and adjust the seasonings with vinegar, salt and/or pepper or pepper flakes. Garnish with parsley sprigs and serve.

DOLMADES ME KREAS KE FASSOLIA

Meat-Filled Grape Leaves with Cannellini Beans ·

MAKES 6 SERVINGS

BEANS

- 2 cups dried cannellini beans, soaked overnight in water and drained
- 1 onion, quartered
- 1 tablespoon coarse sea salt or kosher salt
- 1 bay leaf

~~~~~~

THIS UNUSUAL combination of meat-stuffed grape leaves simmered with dried beans comes from the Sephardic cooks of the island of Rhodes. In a lovely book, *Generations of Mediterranean Sephardic Cooking*, Toddy Franco Horowitz has recorded recipes from her grandmother, mother and aunts, who prepared the foods "by feel," since they had no written recipes. I've adapted Horowitz's recipe, seasoning the beans with fennel instead of cooking them with tomato as she does. As Horowitz points out in her introduction, when the Jews were expelled from Spain in 1492, they settled in Rhodes and lived there "in relative harmony under the successive rule of Turkey, Italy and Greece." For a time, most inhabitants of Rhodes were Jewish, according to Claudia Roden's *Book of Jewish Food*.

At the beginning of World War II, there were about 2,000 Jews living in Rhodes. But on July 24, 1944, in collaboration with Hitler, Mussolini ordered Rhodes's Jews to be "transported by sea and rail to German concentration camps. And except for 151 people who survived, the Jewish population of Rhodes was brutally annihilated," writes Horowitz.

- 3 tablespoons olive oil
- 1/2 fennel bulb, thinly sliced
- 1/2 medium onion, thinly sliced
- 4 ounces pancetta (optional)
- 1/2 cup dry white wine

STUFFED GRAPE LEAVES

- 1/2 fennel bulb
- 1/2 medium onion
- 4 scallions (white and most of the green parts), coarsely chopped
- 1 pound lean ground beef
- 1 ripe tomato, grated (see page 27), or 1/4 cup canned diced tomatoes with their juice
- 3 tablespoons medium-grain rice
- 1/2 teaspoon Aleppo pepper or pinch of crushed red pepper flakes
  Salt
- 1 8-ounce jar brine-packed grape leaves or half a 16-ounce jar, drained and rinsed under hot running water for at least 5 minutes

- 2–2 1/2 cups Chicken Stock (page 267) or beef stock
- 3 tablespoons olive oil
- 1/3 cup freshly squeezed lemon juice
- 1 teaspoon cornstarch, dissolved in 2 tablespoons cold water (optional)
- 3–4 tablespoons chopped fennel fronds plus tender stalks, or fresh dill
- 6 thin lemon slices

MAKE THE BEANS: Place the beans in a large pot, add cold water to cover by at least 4 inches and bring to a boil. Remove from the heat.

Drain the beans, cover with fresh cold water, add the onion, salt and bay leaf and bring to a boil. Reduce the heat to low and simmer for 45 minutes, or until the beans are almost tender. Drain the beans and discard the bay leaf and onion.

In a large, deep skillet (see Note), heat the oil over medium-high heat and sauté the fennel, onion and pancetta, if using, until the vegetables are soft, about 4 minutes. Add the wine and bring to a simmer. Stir in the drained beans and remove from the heat.

MAKE THE STUFFED GRAPE LEAVES: In a food processor, pulse the fennel, onion and scallions until finely chopped. In a large bowl, combine the beef, fennel mixture, tomato, rice, pepper or pepper flakes and salt to taste and mix well with your hands.

Place 1 grape leaf, vein side up, on a work surface, with the stem toward you. Cut off the stem with scissors. Place 1 rounded tablespoon of the filling near the stem. Fold the two sides of the leaf over the filling. Fold over the bottom and roll up the leaf tightly like a cigar (see illustrations, page 39). Place seam side down on the beans and continue with the remaining leaves and filling. You should have 28 to 30 stuffed grape leaves.

Pour 2 cups stock and the oil over the stuffed grape leaves. If you have any leftover leaves, place them on top. Set an inverted heatproof plate over the stuffed grape leaves to prevent them from unrolling during cooking. Bring the liquid to a boil, reduce the heat to low, cover and simmer for 30 minutes.

Add the lemon juice and a little more stock if needed to almost cover the grape leaves. Cook for 30 minutes more, or until the beans are tender and the filling is cooked through.

Discard the top leaves, if any, and carefully transfer the stuffed grape leaves to a platter; cover to keep warm. With a slotted spoon, transfer the beans to a serving bowl and cover to keep warm. You should have about 1½ cups sauce remaining in the pan. If there is more, boil over high heat to reduce; if there is less, add some stock and bring to a boil. Taste and correct the seasonings. For a thicker sauce, stir the cornstarch mixture into the sauce and cook briefly, stirring, until thickened.

Place 4 *dolmades* on each plate, with 2 to 3 tablespoons of the beans on the side. Pour the sauce over the *dolmades*, sprinkle with the fennel or dill and garnish with the lemon slices. Serve warm.

NOTE: A deep, 10½-inch skillet with a lid is ideal for this dish because it will hold the stuffed grape leaves in a single tight layer.

KREMYDODOLMADES
Onions Stuffed with Ground Meat and Pine Nuts

MAKES 6 SERVINGS

THIS RECIPE comes from Lesbos, where it is also called *sogania*, from the Turkish word *sogan* (onion). Many cooks halve the onions crosswise and, after blanching them for a few minutes, take out most of the inner part, creating little cups that they fill with the stuffing. After numerous tries, I decided to separate the onion layers and roll them around the stuffing. The result is a nicer-looking dish, which also tastes better because the stuffing takes on more flavor and stays moist.

Serve with mashed potatoes, Roasted Potatoes with Garlic, Lemon and Oregano (page 202) or Baked Okra in Tomato Sauce (page 196).

6 medium onions (3½–4 pounds total), unpeeled

Salt

¼ cup olive oil

2 garlic cloves, minced

10 ounces lean ground pork or beef

1 cup chopped fresh dill

⅔ cup coarse bulgur (see Sources, page 285)

½ cup dry red wine

1 tablespoon tomato paste, dissolved in 2 tablespoons warm water

1 teaspoon Aleppo pepper or pinch of crushed red pepper flakes

½ cup grated hard myzithra, kefalotyri or pecorino Romano cheese

⅓ cup pine nuts, toasted

2 large eggs, lightly beaten

SAUCE

¼ cup olive oil

2 cups grated ripe tomatoes (see page 27) or canned diced tomatoes with their juice

1 bay leaf

1 teaspoon dried oregano, crumbled

¼ cup dry red wine

About ½ cup beef stock, Chicken Stock (page 267) or water

Salt and freshly ground black pepper

3 tablespoons chopped fresh flat-leaf parsley

Bring a large pot of water to a boil. Cut a lengthwise slit on each onion all the way to the center and add to the pot. Add 2 tablespoons salt and simmer over medium heat for 25 minutes, or until soft. With a slotted spoon, transfer the onions to a colander and rinse under cold running water.

With a very sharp knife, trim off the top and bottom of each onion and peel off and discard the skin and the second layer if it is tough. Gently push out the center of each onion, leaving about four outer layers, and chop the centers. Carefully separate the remaining onion layers and place them on paper towels to drain. (The onion layers can be covered with plastic wrap and refrigerated with the chopped-onion centers in a separate container for up to 2 days.)

In a large skillet, heat the oil and sauté the chopped-onion centers over medium heat for 3 minutes, until soft. Add the garlic and sauté for 2 minutes more. Add the pork or beef and sauté, stirring, until no longer pink, about 3 minutes. Stir in the dill, bulgur, wine, tomato-paste mixture and pepper or pepper flakes and remove from the heat. Stir in the cheese, pine nuts and salt to taste and let the filling cool slightly. Taste and adjust the seasonings, then stir in the eggs.

Preheat the oven to 400°F.

Place about 2 tablespoons filling on each onion layer and roll up to enclose the filling. (The inner layers will need less stuffing, the outer more.) Arrange the stuffed onions close together and seam side down in a 13-x-9-inch baking dish.

MAKE THE SAUCE: In a medium skillet, heat the oil over medium-high heat and sauté the tomatoes with the bay leaf and oregano for 5 minutes, until the sauce starts to thicken. Remove from the heat, add the wine and pour the sauce over the stuffed onions. Add enough stock to come two-thirds of the way up the onions and sprinkle with salt and pepper to taste.

Place the onions in the oven. Reduce the oven temperature to 375°F and bake, basting the onions frequently with the sauce, for 45 minutes, or until the onions are soft and the sauce is thickened.

Let stand, covered, at room temperature for at least 1 hour, or until cool, to let the flavors develop.

Baste the onions again with the sauce and reheat in a preheated 375°F oven for about 15 minutes, basting twice. Remove the bay leaf, sprinkle the onions with the parsley and serve.

MOSCHARI SOFRITO
Veal Stew with Garlic, Parsley and Vinegar

MAKES 4 SERVINGS

THE MEAT of this stew is flavored with a combination of garlic and parsley known as *sofrito* in Catalan and *soffrito* in Italian. But because this dish has neither the onions nor the tomatoes of the Catalan *sofrito*, it is more likely Italian in origin. (The old Venetian dialect, in fact, spells the word with one *f* rather than two.) Corfu and the other islands of the Ionian Sea were part of the Venetian Empire for more than four centuries, and the Venetian language, way of life and, of course, magnificent cuisine have forever marked the culture of these islands. In Corfu, especially, one can still find variations of old dishes that seem to have been forgotten by modern Italians.

Vinegar plays an important role in this classic Corfiot dish, balancing the intensity of the garlic. Over the years, I have sampled many kinds of *sofrito*, but none that impressed me until I tasted one made with thin, well-flattened scallopini instead of the thicker chunks of meat found in traditional versions. Using the scallopini significantly shortens the cooking time of the *sofrito*, so the sauce has a much fresher taste. As with all Corfiot dishes, this one should be quite peppery—some versions are sprinkled with hot paprika or crushed red pepper flakes. The dish yields plenty of delicious sauce for mashed potatoes or Polenta with Currants and Onions (page 162), two of the most common accompaniments to Corfiot *sofrito*.

1/3 cup olive oil

4–6 garlic cloves, thinly sliced

8 small or 4 large veal scallopini (about 2 pounds total), pounded to 7/8 inch thick

1 1/2 cups coarsely chopped fresh flat-leaf parsley, plus 4 sprigs for garnish

1–1 1/2 cups Chicken Stock (page 267) or beef stock

2/3 cup dry white wine

1/3 cup white wine vinegar

Salt and freshly ground black pepper

1/2–1 teaspoon cornstarch, dissolved in 2 tablespoons cold water (optional)

Preheat the oven to 400°F.

In a large skillet, heat half of the oil and sauté the garlic over medium heat for 2 minutes, stirring, until it starts to color. With a slotted spoon, transfer the garlic to a small bowl and set aside.

Add the veal to the skillet, in batches if necessary, and sauté, turning once, for about 2 minutes per side. Arrange the veal in overlapping layers in a 13-x-9-inch baking dish.

Add the remaining oil to the skillet, then add the garlic. When it starts to sizzle, stir in the chopped parsley, 1 cup stock, the wine, vinegar and salt and pepper to taste and cook, stirring, for 2 minutes. Taste and adjust the seasonings. Remove from the heat.

Pour the sauce over the veal, lifting the scallopini so that the sauce coats each piece. The sauce should almost cover the meat; if not, add a little more stock. Cover the dish with aluminum foil.

Bake for 30 to 35 minutes, or until the sauce is bubbly. If you wish to thicken the sauce, use a slotted spoon to transfer the veal to a serving platter. Add the cornstarch mixture to the baking dish and boil over medium heat, stirring, until thickened, and pour the sauce over the meat. Garnish with the parsley sprigs and serve.

VARIATION

Instead of veal, you can use turkey cutlets.

CORFU

MOSCHARI ME KOLOKYTHAKIA
Braised Veal with Zucchini

MAKES 4 SERVINGS

2½ pounds small zucchini, trimmed and
    cut into 2-inch-thick pieces

  Salt

⅓ cup olive oil

2 pounds boneless veal shanks or boneless
    shoulder, cut into 2-inch cubes

1¼ cups coarsely chopped onions

1½ cups Chicken Stock (page 267)
    or beef stock

2 cinnamon sticks

1½ cups grated ripe tomatoes (see page 27)
    or canned diced tomatoes with
    their juice

1 teaspoon sugar

  Freshly ground black pepper

2–3 tablespoons chopped fresh flat-leaf
    parsley

Place the zucchini in a colander and salt generously, tossing to coat all sides. Set in the sink or over a bowl and let stand for at least 1 hour and up to 3 hours.

In a large, deep skillet with a lid or a Dutch oven, heat the oil and brown the veal in batches on all sides over high heat, about 10 minutes. Add the onions and sauté, stirring, for 3 to 5 minutes more, or until soft. Add the stock and cinnamon sticks and bring to a boil. Reduce the heat to low and simmer for 40 minutes.

THIS IS a special dish that my mother makes in the summer. Cooking meat with zucchini and other seasonal vegetables (see the variations) is common throughout Greece. What makes my mother's version so light—and easy—is that instead of frying the zucchini, as most cooks do, she just rubs the chunks with salt to make them wilt a little.

Add the tomatoes, sugar and pepper to taste and simmer for 30 minutes more, or until the veal is very tender.

Dry the zucchini with paper towels and add to the skillet, along with a little water if needed so that the sauce comes two-thirds of the way up the sides. Cover and simmer for 20 minutes, shaking the skillet occasionally, until the zucchini is tender and the sauce has thickened. If the sauce is too thin, increase the heat to high and boil for 3 to 4 minutes to reduce it.

Taste and adjust the seasonings. Discard the cinnamon sticks, sprinkle with the parsley and serve.

VARIATIONS
MOSCHARI ME FASSOLAKIA
Braised Veal with Green Beans

Substitute 1$\frac{1}{2}$ pounds tender green beans, trimmed, for the zucchini. You can also use snow peas. (Neither of these vegetables requires salting.) Snow peas will need to cook for only about 5 minutes.

MOSCHARI ME BAMIES
Braised Veal with Okra

Increase the stock to about 2 cups and the tomatoes to 2 cups; omit the zucchini. When the veal is almost tender, transfer to a baking dish, add 1$\frac{1}{2}$ pounds okra, prepared as described in Baked Okra in Tomato Sauce (page 196) and bake as directed in that recipe.

STOUFADO TIS KERKYRAS

Veal and Vegetable Stew from Corfu

MAKES 4 SERVINGS

2 pounds boneless veal shoulder, cut into 1-inch cubes

1 large onion, halved lengthwise and thickly sliced into half-moons

1 1/2 cups dry red wine

1/2 cup olive oil

3 garlic cloves, thinly sliced

1 bay leaf

1 teaspoon dried rosemary, crumbled

1 teaspoon dried thyme, crumbled

Freshly ground black pepper

1 1/2 cups diced celery

1 large fennel bulb, trimmed (fronds and tender stalks reserved), halved and thinly sliced

3 large carrots, peeled and sliced

About 1 cup beef stock, Chicken Stock (page 267) or water

Salt

2 tablespoons unsalted butter

3–4 tablespoons chopped fennel fronds plus tender stalks, or fresh dill

~~~~~~

IN HER fascinating book on Corfu, Ninetta Laskari claims that this dish is part of the Venetian heritage of the island. She writes that it got its name from the *stua*—the small openings on the cooler side of the old wood-burning kitchen stoves that were used for simmering. "There, we used to cook food in covered pots for hours or overnight. On the *stua*, one cooks the *stoufado*, various meats accompanied with all sorts of vegetables or beans. In the rest of Greece, meat cooked with pearl onions and scented with bay leaves is called *stifado*," she explains.

My recipe is inspired by the many variations on Corfiot *stoufado* I found in Laskari's book.

CORFU

In a large bowl, combine the veal, onion, $^2/_3$ cup of the wine, $^1/_4$ cup of the oil, the garlic, bay leaf, rosemary, thyme and pepper to taste. Toss well, cover and refrigerate for at least 2 to 3 hours, or overnight.

Remove the veal from the marinade and pat it dry with paper towels; reserve the marinade.

In a large pot, heat the remaining $^1/_4$ cup oil and sauté the veal in batches over high heat, turning, until browned on all sides, about 10 minutes. Add the reserved marinade, celery, sliced fennel, carrots, $^1/_2$ cup stock or water and salt to taste and bring to a boil. Reduce the heat to low, cover and simmer for 1 hour, or until the veal is tender, adding more stock or water as needed. Increase the heat to high, stir in the remaining wine and reduce the liquid to a thick sauce. Remove from the heat and stir in the butter.

Sprinkle with the fennel fronds or dill and serve.

MOSCHARI KYDONATO

Veal Stew with Quinces

MAKES 4 SERVINGS

~~~~~~

THIS IS one of my favorite winter stews. Quinces are equally delicious in savory and sweet dishes, and Greek islanders cook all kinds of meats with quince. On Chios, they pair quinces with free-range chicken; on Crete, with lamb; and on Lesbos, with veal. Here, the firm, fragrant fruit, with its appealing sour taste, balances well with the sweet sugar syrup and spicy rich meat sauce.

The combination of meat with quinces is not new. In the Roman cookery of Apicius, we find similar stews, and quinces must have been quite common in old traditional Greek cooking.

This stew can be prepared almost entirely in advance and refrigerated. Then you need only simmer the meat in the sauce for a few minutes and caramelize the quinces just before serving. Leftover sauce makes an unusual but excellent pasta sauce, or it can be used in *pasticcio* (page 66).

Accompany with Polenta with Currants and Onions (page 162) or Chickpeas with Rice (page 154).

2 pounds boneless veal breast or top round roast

1 large onion, quartered

2/3 cup olive oil

3–4 teaspoons sugar

Juice of 1 lemon

4 quinces

1/2 cup sweet red wine, such as Mavrodaphne or sweet Marsala

1/2 cup dry red wine

9 pitted prunes

1 teaspoon Aleppo pepper or pinch of crushed red pepper flakes

1 cinnamon stick

1 bay leaf

1/2 teaspoon coarsely crushed allspice berries

About 1 1/2 cups beef stock or Chicken Stock (page 267)

Salt

1–2 tablespoons red wine vinegar (optional)

Freshly ground black pepper

2 tablespoons chopped fresh flat-leaf parsley

In a large pot, combine the veal, onion, $1/4$ cup of the oil, 1 teaspoon of the sugar and enough water to come two-thirds up the sides of the roast. Bring to a boil and skim off the foam that rises to the top. Cover and simmer for 45 minutes, turning the meat once. Remove from the heat and let cool, then refrigerate overnight.

Fill a medium bowl with water and add the lemon juice. Quarter and core each quince, then halve each quarter lengthwise. Drop the quince pieces into the bowl of lemon water as you work.

In a large skillet, heat the remaining 6 tablespoons oil. Pat the quince pieces dry with paper towels and sauté, in batches, stirring, for 4 minutes, or until they start to color. Transfer to a medium bowl and set aside. Discard any remaining oil and add the sweet wine to the skillet, scraping up any caramelized bits in the bottom of the pan. Remove from the heat and set aside.

Remove the veal from the pot and cut it into four $1/2$-inch-thick slices. Bring the cooking liquid to a boil and boil over high heat until it has evaporated and only fat remains in the pot, 10 to 15 minutes. Return the veal slices to the pot and sauté, turning, for 5 minutes, or until browned. Add 8 of the less attractive quince pieces, the sweet wine from the skillet, the dry wine, 5 of the prunes, the Aleppo pepper or pepper flakes, cinnamon stick, bay leaf, allspice, stock and salt to taste. Bring to a boil, reduce the heat to low, cover and simmer for 45 minutes, or until the meat is very tender.

Transfer the veal to a plate and set aside. Discard the cinnamon stick and bay leaf. Transfer the quinces, prunes and sauce to a blender and puree. Return to the pot and add the remaining 4 prunes and the remaining quince pieces to the sauce and simmer for 15 to 20 minutes, or until the quinces are soft but not mushy. Carefully transfer the quinces to a small baking pan in a single layer, cover and keep warm.

Add the vinegar, if using, and black pepper to taste to the sauce. Taste and adjust the seasonings. Return the meat to the sauce and simmer for 10 minutes more, or until heated through.

Meanwhile, preheat the broiler. Sprinkle the quinces with the remaining 2 to 3 teaspoons sugar and broil until caramelized, about 2 minutes.

Place a slice of veal, a prune and some caramelized quinces on each plate. Pour a little sauce over the meat, sprinkle with the parsley and serve, passing the remaining sauce at the table.

KREAS AFELIA
Veal Stew with Coriander Seeds

MAKES 6 SERVINGS

3 pounds veal (or lean pork) stew meat, cut into 1-inch cubes

1 cup Commandaria, Madeira or other sweet wine

1 tablespoon crushed coriander seeds

1/4 cup olive oil

1–2 teaspoons Aleppo pepper or 1/2–1 teaspoon crushed red pepper flakes

Salt

About 1 cup beef stock or Chicken Stock (page 267)

Freshly ground black pepper

3 tablespoons chopped fresh cilantro or flat-leaf parsley

In a large bowl, combine the meat, 1/2 cup of the wine and 2 teaspoons of the coriander seeds. Toss well, cover and refrigerate for at least 4 hours, or overnight.

Remove the meat from the marinade and pat it dry with paper towels; reserve the marinade.

In a large pot, heat the oil and sauté the meat, in batches, turning, until browned on all sides, 4 to 5 minutes. Return the meat to the pot and add the marinade, the remaining 1/2 cup wine, the remaining 1 teaspoon coriander seeds, the Aleppo pepper or pepper flakes and salt to taste. Add stock to come two-thirds of the way up the sides of the meat; bring to a boil. Reduce the heat to low, cover and simmer for 45 minutes, or until the meat is tender, turning occasionally and adding more stock if necessary. Add black pepper to taste, then taste and add salt and/or pepper or pepper flakes.

With a slotted spoon, transfer the meat to a warmed serving platter and cover to keep warm. Increase the heat under the pot to high and boil until the liquid is reduced to about 1 cup. Spoon a little of the sauce over the meat, sprinkle with the cilantro or parsley and serve at once, with the remaining sauce on the side.

VARIATION

While you are cooking the stew, make New Potatoes with Coriander Seeds and Wine (page 201). Shortly before the meat is done, preheat the oven to 400°F. Transfer the meat and potatoes to a baking dish, pour over the sauce, cover with foil and bake for 30 minutes, or until the meat is very tender. Sprinkle with the cilantro or parsley and serve.

THIS IS a classic Cypriot dish, usually made with pork but sometimes with veal. It is the only Greek recipe for meat that I know which contains neither onions nor garlic. The flavor and aroma of crushed coriander seeds are remarkable, and people tasting it for the first time are apt to think it is actually a different kind of oregano. As in many other island recipes, sweet wine or Commandaria, the Cypriot dessert wine, is used. Traditionally, this stew is often served with Bulgur with Onion, Tomatoes and Cheese (page 158), without the cheese. I prefer it with New Potatoes with Coriander Seeds and Wine (see the variation), as the two dishes have complementary aromas.

GALOPOULA ME FRESKA KREMYDAKIA

Braised Turkey (or Chicken) with Scallions, Lemon and Dill

MAKES 4 SERVINGS

¼ cup olive oil

4 turkey drumsticks or thighs from free-range chickens (about 2½ pounds)

3 large bunches scallions (white and most of the green parts), cut into 1-inch pieces

1 cup dry white wine

½ cup Chicken Stock (page 267) or water
Salt and freshly ground black pepper

3–4 tablespoons freshly squeezed lemon juice

¼ cup chopped fresh dill

IN THIS flavorful dish, the poultry is simmered with plenty of scallions, some wine and lemon juice and seasoned with dill at the last moment. The sauce is often thickened with egg, but I prefer the lighter version, where the broth is simply thickened by the pureed scallions. Serve it with rice or a small pasta, such as orzo, which will take on a delicious flavor tossed in the lemony sauce.

The dish is adapted from a recipe for lamb that I found in the very interesting old kitchen ledger of the Chian Choremi family, part of the Choremi-Benaki clan, a large wealthy family of cotton merchants and politicians.

In a large, deep skillet with a lid or a Dutch oven, heat the oil and sauté the drumsticks or thighs over medium-high heat, turning often until golden on all sides, about 6 minutes. Transfer to a plate and set aside. Add the scallions to the skillet and sauté, stirring, until wilted, about 5 minutes.

Arrange the drumsticks or thighs on top of the scallions. Add the wine, stock or water and salt and pepper to taste and bring to a boil. Reduce the heat to low, cover and simmer for about 30 minutes. Turn the meat over, cover and continue simmering for 20 minutes more (chicken will need less cooking time than turkey). Carefully remove the meat with tongs and set aside on a plate.

Puree the sauce in a blender or food processor and return it to the pan. Add the meat, 3 tablespoons lemon juice and all but 1 teaspoon of the dill. Simmer for 10 to 15 minutes more, or until the meat is very tender. Taste and adjust the sea-

sonings, adding more salt, pepper and lemon juice, if desired. If the sauce is too thin, cook over high heat to reduce it. Serve over rice or pasta, sprinkled with the reserved dill.

VARIATION

If you like, thicken the sauce with egg, making an avgolemono: Add only 1½ tablespoons of the lemon juice to the pan. When the drumsticks or thighs have cooked in the pureed sauce, remove them with a slotted spoon and place on a platter; keep warm. Beat 1 large egg in a bowl with 3 tablespoons water. Gradually add the remaining 2½ tablespoons lemon juice and most of the sauce from the pan, whisking constantly. Return the sauce to the pan and reheat very gently over low heat, stirring constantly. Pour over the drumsticks or thighs, sprinkle with the reserved dill and serve.

KOTOPOULO SOUPA, AVGOLEMONO

Chicken Soup with Egg-Lemon Sauce

MAKES 6 TO 8 SERVINGS AS A FIRST COURSE,
4 TO 6 SERVINGS AS A MAIN COURSE

1 3-to-4-pound free-range chicken, quartered, plus 3 pounds chicken backs, necks and/or wings

1 large onion, halved

2 medium carrots, peeled and quartered

2 bay leaves

2 tablespoons salt

10–12 whole peppercorns

2 tablespoons olive oil

5 scallions (white and most of the green parts), thinly sliced

1 cup chopped fresh dill

2/3 cup medium-grain rice, such as Arborio

2 large eggs

4–6 tablespoons freshly squeezed lemon juice

Salt and freshly ground black pepper

Place the chicken and chicken parts in a large pot and add water to cover. Bring to a boil, skim off the foam and reduce the heat to low. Add the onion, carrots, bay leaves, salt and peppercorns. Cover and simmer for 2 hours, adding a little more water as needed, until the chicken starts to fall from the bones.

Transfer the chicken quarters to a large plate. Remove the meat and cut half of it into bite-sized pieces; cover and refrigerate. Refrigerate the remaining chicken for another use. Strain the stock, discarding the solids, and refrigerate it for a few hours, or until the fat congeals on top. Remove and discard most of the fat.

THIS typically Greek variation on a much-loved theme is the traditional one-pot Christmas dish on Rhodes and the other Dodecanese islands. Christmas in the Greek islands is not the big feast celebrated in the United States or northern Europe: Easter and the Virgin Mary's Assumption (August 15) are more important island festivals.

Until the late 1960s, chicken was considered a great delicacy on the islands. It was the most expensive of all meats and, except for important feasts, was usually reserved for children and the sick.

The free-range chickens or capons of Greece need a long time to cook, and even then, their flesh can be tough and stringy. But they make the most delicious soup.

In a large pot, heat the oil and sauté the scallions over medium heat for 3 to 4 minutes, or until soft. Add ½ cup of the dill and sauté for 2 minutes more. Add the stock and bring to a boil. Add the rice, reduce the heat to low and simmer for 20 minutes, or until the rice is tender.

In a medium bowl, whisk the eggs, ¼ cup lemon juice and 2 tablespoons water. Whisking constantly, slowly pour about 3 cups of the hot stock mixture into the eggs. Slowly pour the egg mixture into the pot, whisking constantly to prevent the eggs from curdling. Add the chicken and the remaining ½ cup dill. Taste and adjust the seasonings with lemon juice, salt and/or pepper. Simmer for 2 to 3 minutes more; do not boil. Serve hot.

VARIATION

On Kea, 1 cup of grated ripe tomatoes (see page 27) is added to the broth along with the rice, making a delightful pink soup.

KOTA ME KRASI, MARATHO KE KYDONI

Chicken and Fennel Stew with Quince

MAKES 6 SERVINGS

I FOUND the description for this dish in Ninetta Laskari's book on Corfu. It's a typical example of East meeting West, for it shows the distinct influence of the Venetians, who long ruled the island. The pancetta and Marsala in this stew are classic Italian ingredients rarely found in other parts of Greece. The quince in the sauce brings to mind Eastern cooking, where fruits play an important role in meat and game dishes.

Serve with mashed potatoes.

¼ cup olive oil

3 thick slices pancetta (about 6 ounces), diced

1 4-pound free-range chicken or capon, cut into 6 pieces

2 large onions, halved and thickly sliced

3 carrots, peeled and each cut into 4–5 pieces

1 large fennel bulb, trimmed (fronds and tender stalks reserved), halved and thinly sliced

1 quince, halved, cored and cut into ½-inch-thick slices

4 garlic cloves, thinly sliced

1 cup sweet red wine, such as sweet Marsala or Mavrodaphne

1 cup dry red wine

1–2 teaspoons Aleppo pepper or ½–1 teaspoon crushed red pepper flakes

1 teaspoon dried thyme, crumbled

1 teaspoon dried rosemary, crumbled

2 bay leaves

1 teaspoon salt

3 tablespoons chopped fennel fronds and tender stalks or fresh flat-leaf parsley

In a large, deep skillet with a lid or a Dutch oven, heat the oil and sauté the pancetta over medium-high heat for 1 minute. Add the chicken, in batches, and sauté, turning once or twice, for 10 minutes, or until light golden on both sides. Transfer to a plate and set aside.

Add the onions, carrots, fennel bulb and quince and sauté for 5 minutes, or until soft. Add the garlic. When it starts to sizzle, return the chicken to the skillet and add the sweet wine, dry wine, bay leaves, Aleppo pepper or pepper flakes, thyme, rosemary and salt. The liquid should just cover the chicken—add a little water if necessary. Bring to a boil, reduce the heat to low, cover and simmer, turning twice and adding a little more water if necessary, for 1 to 1^1/$_2$ hours, or until the chicken is very tender. Taste and adjust the seasonings.

Transfer the chicken and carrots to a serving platter and cover to keep warm. Cook the sauce for about 5 minutes more, or until thickened. If you like, puree the sauce with a stick (immersion) blender or regular blender. Pour some of the sauce over the chicken, sprinkle with the fennel fronds or parsley and serve, with the remaining sauce on the side.

KOTOPOULO GEMISTO ME DOMATA KE FETA

Chicken Stuffed with Tomatoes and Feta

MAKES 4 TO 6 SERVINGS

1 4-pound free-range chicken

1 lemon, halved

Salt and freshly ground black pepper

²/₃ cup chopped ripe or canned tomatoes, well drained

¹/₄ cup chopped oil-packed sun-dried tomatoes

1 cup crumbled or diced feta cheese

¹/₃ cup olive oil

4–6 garlic cloves, coarsely chopped

1 tablespoon dried oregano, crumbled

1 teaspoon Aleppo pepper or pinch of crushed red pepper flakes

¹/₂ cup sweet red wine, such as Mavrodaphne or sweet Marsala

2–2¹/₂ pounds very small new potatoes, scrubbed, or medium new potatoes, peeled and cut into 1-inch cubes

THIS roasted stuffed chicken has all the flavors and aromas associated with the islands. Scented with plenty of garlic and oregano, the chopped-tomato-and-feta stuffing gives a wonderful taste to the chicken, while the juices from both the meat and the stuffing flavor the potatoes that roast alongside.

The recipe is adapted from one in Michalis Magoulas's book *The Cooking of Ithaca*, which includes dishes that his mother and grandmother prepared on this lovely island in the Ionian Sea. Large quantities of garlic are used in the foods of Ithaca, perhaps more than anywhere else in Greece, flavoring all kinds of meat, chicken and fish dishes. (The local version of *skordalia* contains more than two dozen garlic cloves instead of the five or six of the more common version.)

To intensify the taste of the tomatoes, I added some sun-dried ones, but you can omit them if you use organic vine-ripened red tomatoes, which are full of flavor.

Preheat the oven to 425°F.

Rub the chicken inside and out with the cut sides of the lemon. Salt lightly (not too much because the feta is salty) and sprinkle with black pepper.

In a medium bowl, mix the tomatoes, sun-dried tomatoes, feta, 3 tablespoons of the oil, the garlic, oregano and Aleppo pepper or pepper flakes. Stuff the chicken cavity with the tomato mixture and sew it closed with kitchen twine, or close with small skewers or toothpicks. Place the chicken, breast side down, in a baking dish that holds it snugly.

Roast for 20 minutes. Pour the wine over the chicken, reduce the oven temperature to 375°F and continue roasting for 20 minutes more. If the skin starts to color too much, cover loosely with aluminum foil.

Place the potatoes in a single layer in a roasting pan. Drizzle with the remaining 2 tablespoons oil and sprinkle with salt and black pepper. Carefully pour the juices from the chicken over the potatoes and toss well. Place the chicken, breast side up, on top of the potatoes and roast for 40 minutes more, or until the juices run clear when you pierce the thigh. The potatoes should be tender and crusty on top. If they are not, transfer the chicken to a heated plate, cover with aluminum foil and keep warm while you bake the potatoes for a little longer. Transfer most of the sauce to a saucepan and cook for a few minutes to reduce, then pour into a bowl or sauceboat.

Place the chicken on top of the potatoes again, and take the food to the table in the baking pan. Remove the skewers or toothpicks and carve and serve the chicken, placing several tablespoons of the stuffing and some potatoes on each plate. Pass the sauce separately.

KOTA GEMISTI STIN KATSAROLA
Stuffed Poached Chicken

MAKES 6 TO 8 SERVINGS

1 4-to-5-pound free-range chicken, giblets reserved (or substitute ¹/₂ pound chicken livers for the giblets)

¹/₂ cup olive oil

3 tablespoons unsalted butter

2 cups finely chopped red onions

4 slices stale whole wheat or multigrain bread, cubed

1 cup Zante currants

3 cups sweet wine, such as Mavrodaphne or sweet Marsala

1 cup chopped fresh flat-leaf parsley

Salt and freshly ground black pepper

1 large egg, lightly beaten

IN FOLEGANDROS, a tiny, arid but picturesque island of the Cyclades, a small stuffed kid, weighing less than eight pounds, was traditionally the festive Christmas dish. It was cooked in a special large pot on top of the stove. "We had no ovens in the homes, and even if we had, an animal that small would have dried out in the oven," Maria Primikiri told me.

Living in Athens now, Maria and other cooks from Folegandros substitute chicken for kid, stuffing it with the same simple stuffing: fried country bread, lots of onions, currants and parsley. The broth that the bird cooks in is flavored with the sweet wine that many island families produce, made from partly sun-dried grapes.

Finely chop the giblets (or chicken livers).

In a large Dutch oven, heat $\frac{1}{4}$ cup of the oil and 1 tablespoon of the butter and sauté the giblets (or livers) over medium heat for 3 to 4 minutes, or until firm. With a slotted spoon, transfer to a medium bowl and set aside.

Add the onions to the Dutch oven and sauté for 5 minutes, or until soft. With a slotted spoon, transfer to the bowl with the giblets or livers. Add the bread to the pot and sauté, turning often, for 4 minutes, or until golden brown. Transfer to a plate with a slotted spoon and set aside. Add the onion mixture and currants to the Dutch oven and cook for 1 to 2 minutes, or until they start to sizzle. Add $\frac{1}{2}$ cup of the wine and remove from the heat. Add the bread, parsley and salt and pepper to taste. Add the egg and toss well.

Stuff the cavity and neck of the chicken with the bread mixture and sew up the openings with kitchen twine or close with small skewers or toothpicks.

Wipe out the Dutch oven with paper towels and heat the remaining $\frac{1}{4}$ cup oil and the remaining 2 tablespoons butter. Cook the chicken, turning, until browned on all sides, about 12 minutes. Add the remaining $2\frac{1}{2}$ cups wine and turn the chicken to coat on all sides, then turn the chicken breast side down. Add enough water to come two-thirds of the way up the sides of the chicken and bring to a boil. Reduce the heat to low, cover and simmer for 30 minutes, turning once.

Uncover the pot, add salt to taste and simmer, turning once, for 30 minutes more, or until the chicken is very tender and the juices run clear.

Transfer the chicken to a cutting board and remove the string, skewers or toothpicks. Carve the chicken, place the stuffing in the center of a warmed serving platter and arrange the chicken around it. Cover with aluminum foil and keep warm.

Meanwhile, increase the heat under the Dutch oven to high and boil the broth for about 10 minutes to reduce it to the consistency of a sauce.

Serve the chicken and stuffing with the sauce on the side.

NOTE: On the island, the broth is usually served as soup before the chicken. If you like, instead of reducing it, skim off the fat, add more water and some *trahana* (page 148) or small pasta and simmer until the pasta is cooked.

KOTOPOULO YOUVETSI
Baked Chicken with Orzo

MAKES 6 SERVINGS

1/3 cup olive oil

1 4 1/2-pound free-range chicken or capon, cut into 6 pieces, or 6 turkey drumsticks

1 large onion, halved and thinly sliced

1/3 cup chopped oil-packed sun-dried tomatoes

1 cinnamon stick

1 teaspoon dried oregano, crumbled

1 teaspoon Aleppo pepper or pinch crushed red pepper flakes

2 cups grated ripe tomatoes (see page 27) or canned diced tomatoes with their juice

Salt

2 cups Chicken Stock (page 267), plus more if needed

1 pound orzo or elbow macaroni, cooked in plenty of boiling salted water for 2 minutes and drained

2 tablespoons chopped fresh flat-leaf parsley

1/2 cup coarsely grated hard myzithra, kefalotyri, pecorino Romano or Parmigiano-Reggiano cheese

Preheat the oven to 400°F.

In a Dutch oven, heat the oil over medium-high heat and sauté the chicken or turkey in batches until golden brown on all sides. Set aside.

Add the onion to the pot and sauté until soft, about 3 minutes. Add the sun-dried tomatoes, cinnamon stick, oregano, pepper or pepper flakes and tomatoes. Sprinkle the chicken or turkey with salt and return to the Dutch oven. Add about 1/2 cup stock, or enough to come about two-thirds of the way up the chicken or turkey. Bring to a boil, cover and transfer to the oven.

Bake for about 1 1/2 hours, or until the meat is very tender. Transfer the chicken or turkey to a platter and cover with aluminum foil to keep warm.

Meanwhile, bring the remaining 1 1/2 cups stock to a simmer.

Add the stock to the cooking liquid, stir in the pasta and bake, uncovered, for about 15 minutes, or until most of the liquid has been absorbed, adding more stock if the pasta begins to dry out.

Place the chicken or turkey on top of the pasta and bake for another 10 minutes, until the pasta is tender. Serve immediately, sprinkled with the parsley and cheese.

THIS CHICKEN DISH is a common Sunday one-pot meal of the islands. In her wonderful taverna in Avgonima, Chios, Kalliopi Delios cooks homemade macaroni in the chicken-tomato stock. Orzo, elbow macaroni, ziti and penne rigate are good alternatives. This recipe is based on Kalliopi's.

KOUNELI ME SKORDO KE FETA

Rabbit Baked in Garlic, Feta and Lemon Sauce

MAKES 4 TO 6 SERVINGS

1/3 cup olive oil

1 3 1/2-to-4-pound rabbit, cut into
    4 leg/thigh joints and the loin
    Salt and freshly ground black pepper

5–6 garlic cloves, coarsely chopped

1 cup dry white wine

1 tablespoon dried oregano, crumbled

1 cup crumbled feta cheese
    About 1 cup Chicken Stock (page 267)

3–4 tablespoons freshly squeezed lemon
    juice

1 tablespoon unsalted butter

2–3 tablespoons chopped fresh oregano
    (optional)

~~~~~~

THIS RECIPE comes from Ithaca, where hare was traditionally cooked in this fashion under a *tserepa*, a thick terra-cotta domed cover. Baking the rabbit in a snug Dutch oven produces a similar effect. Serve the rabbit with the sauce spooned over mashed potatoes, rice or pasta.

Preheat the oven to 375°F.

In a Dutch oven, heat the oil and sauté the rabbit in batches over medium-high heat, turning occasionally, until golden brown on all sides. Lightly salt the rabbit (feta is usually quite salty), sprinkle with plenty of pepper and return the rabbit to the casserole. Add the garlic and cook, stirring, for 2 minutes; do not let the garlic color.

Pour in the wine, sprinkle with the dried oregano and stir in the cheese. Add enough stock to come two-thirds of the way up the sides of the rabbit. Bring to a boil, cover and transfer the casserole to the oven. Bake, covered, for about 1 hour.

Turn the rabbit pieces, add 3 tablespoons lemon juice and bake for 30 minutes more, or until the meat is very tender. Transfer the rabbit to a heated plate and cover with aluminum foil to keep warm.

Reduce the sauce on top of the stove over high heat until thickened; taste and adjust the seasonings, adding more lemon juice if necessary; the sauce should be quite lemony. Whisk in the butter and pour the sauce over the rabbit. Sprinkle with the chopped oregano, if desired, and serve at once.

KOUNELI STIFADO

Rabbit Stew with Pearl Onions in Two-Wine Sauce

FROM
MOLYVOS
RESTAURANT

MAKES 4 TO 6 SERVINGS

STIFADO, which has its origins on Corfu, is an intensely flavored stew, usually of rabbit or hare, cooked slowly in both sweet and dry red wine with tomatoes and pearl onions. Seasoned with bay leaves, cinnamon, cloves and allspice, the fragrant stew can be served over homemade egg noodles, Pasta Squares (page 173), fettuccine or tagliatelle. It is also good with mashed potatoes or Polenta with Currants and Onions (page 162).

This recipe is adapted from Jim Botsacos's version of the classic dish.

1 3¹/₂-to-4-pound rabbit, cut into 4 leg/thigh joints and the loin, with the loin tied (have the butcher do this, or purchase the rabbit in pieces from a specialty market)

Salt and freshly ground black pepper

3 tablespoons olive oil

2 cups sliced red onions

2 garlic cloves, sliced

1¹/₂ cups dry red wine, such as Cabernet Sauvignon

1 cup sweet red wine, such as Mavrodaphne or sweet Marsala, or more if needed

1 16-ounce can whole tomatoes, drained and chopped

2 cups Chicken Stock (page 267)

Bouquet garni: 1 bay leaf, 1 cinnamon stick, 3 cloves and 1 allspice berry, tied up in a piece of cheesecloth with kitchen twine

2 teaspoons unsalted butter

1 pound pearl onions, blanched and peeled, or 1¹/₂ cups frozen

1 teaspoon sugar

¹/₄ cup water

FOR OPTIONAL GARNISH

Olive oil

1 small onion, thinly sliced

2–3 tablespoons diced and drained tomatoes

Preheat the oven to 375°F.

Season the rabbit pieces on all sides with salt and pepper. Heat 2 tablespoons of the oil in a large Dutch oven and cook the rabbit, in batches if necessary, over medium-high heat, turning frequently, until browned on all sides, about 8 minutes. Transfer the rabbit to a platter and discard the oil.

Add the remaining 1 tablespoon oil to the pot, reduce the heat to medium and sauté the red onions until wilted and lightly colored, about 4 minutes. Add the garlic and sauté for 2 minutes. Pour in both wines and boil over medium-high heat until almost all the liquid has evaporated, about 10 minutes.

Add the chopped tomatoes to the pot and stir to combine, then return the rabbit to the pot with any juices from the platter, pour in the stock and season lightly with salt and pepper. Add the bouquet garni and bring to a boil. Cover, place the pot in the oven and bake for 35 minutes.

Meanwhile, melt 1 teaspoon of the butter in a medium skillet, add the pearl onions, sprinkle with the sugar and sauté, over medium heat, shaking the pan occasionally, until the onions are golden brown on all sides, about 3 minutes. Add the water and cook for 10 minutes, or until the onions are easily pierced with a knife. Remove from the heat.

Add the onions to the Dutch oven and cook for 30 minutes more, or until the rabbit is tender when pierced with a fork. Transfer the rabbit to a warm serving platter.

Discard the bouquet garni and bring the cooking juices to a boil over medium heat. Reduce the heat to low and whisk in the remaining 1 teaspoon butter. Taste and adjust the seasonings, adding salt, pepper and/or a little more sweet wine if necessary. Ladle the sauce over the rabbit and serve.

FOR THE GARNISH, IF USING: In a small skillet, heat about 1 inch of oil until it simmers. Add the sliced onion and fry until crisp and golden, about 2 minutes. Drain on paper towels. Garnish the rabbit with the crispy onion rings and diced tomatoes.

VARIATION
STIFADO OF ITHACA

Add 3 or 4 garlic cloves, sliced, just before pouring the wines into the pot, and proceed as directed.

Just before adding the butter to the sauce, add 1 to 2 tablespoons of good-quality red wine vinegar, increase the heat to medium-high and cook for 2 minutes.

BEANS, RICE, BULGUR AND PASTA

On Saturday evenings, women on Sifnos and other Cycladic islands come to the bakery, bringing their specially marked clay casseroles filled with soaked chickpeas that have been doused in fruity olive oil and seasoned with bay leaves and oregano. Covered and sealed with a piece of dough, the casseroles are set in the communal wood-burning oven, where they cook slowly all night. On Sunday morning, as the women return to their homes from church, they collect their pots of the tender, fragrant chickpeas and serve them for lunch, accompanied by crusty bread to soak up the delicious juices. Beans— legumes of all kinds, in fact—and grains are the staple foods of Greek islanders, cooked by themselves or combined with seasonal vegetables, and sometimes small amounts of meat.

Dried favas were the traditional legume of the Mediterranean. When the more refined white beans came to Europe from the New World, they replaced dried favas, which take longer to cook. Fresh favas, which have now been rediscovered by creative chefs all over the world, have always been among the spring dishes on the islands. Like green beans, the small, tender, velvety whole fava pods are eaten in the spring and early summer, stewed with lemon juice and wild fennel. Fresh favas are also served raw as a *meze*, especially on Crete, where they are brought to the tables with raki, the unscented strong local drink.

Lentils are thought of as the most nourishing and digestible of all legumes, fed to children from an early age. Yellow split peas—dried yellow peas that are peeled and split—cook easily and need no soaking. They are made into a versatile puree that is served flavored with various herbs and sauces.

Besides giving sustenance, legumes provide organic fertilization for the poor island soil, restoring the nitrogen that was absorbed by cereal grains and garden vegetables. For that reason, they are often planted every second year, alternating with wheat, barley and other cereals.

CRACKED WHEAT, BULGUR AND RICE

Coarsely ground locally grown barley and cracked wheat and bulgur are used in stuffings, added to both savory and sweet dishes as thickening and made into pilafs and soups. Unlike bulgur, which is precooked and dried, cracked wheat requires long cooking.

One woman from Mesta, a well-preserved fortified village on southern Chios, told me that when she was a child, her mother always left her in charge of cooking the cracked wheat, which needed close attention. Each morning before leaving for the fields, her mother put a large pot on the stove and the child had to stir it often and add water until the grains puffed and the wheat was almost cooked. Throughout the day, the cracked wheat was used in various dishes. At breakfast, it was simmered in milk and served with honey or sugar. For lunch or dinner, it was sautéed in olive oil with onions, tomatoes and hot peppers and topped with the local cheese. One of the oldest festive dishes, still cooked on Samos and Lesbos, is a stew of cracked wheat and lamb (or young goat), simmered for hours in a large cauldron until the meat falls from the bones. At important church festivals, the stew is distributed among the parishioners. Bulgur pilafs flavored either with greens like purslane or Swiss chard or with meat, complemented with almonds and currants, can be served as a main course or a side dish.

Today, rice has replaced bulgur in many of the traditional dishes. But until the early twentieth century, it was imported and expensive and was considered the food of the wealthy, reserved for weddings and other special occasions. The long-grain American-type rice has now become the popular choice for pilafs, while medium-grain is used in stuffings as well as the old-fashioned rice dishes made with vegetables and greens.

HOMEMADE PASTAS

People tend to associate pasta with Italy, but all the countries around the Mediterranean are particularly fond of both plain and stuffed pasta. Homemade pastas are probably more common on the islands than on the Greek mainland, because these places remained under Venetian or Genoese rule for many years. Plain flour-and-water pasta, prepared by rolling the same dough used for phyllo pastry, is considered a convenience food. It is usually made in the winter, when few vegetables or greens are available.

Cracked wheat may be replaced by rice in most stuffings, but it is still the basis for *trahana* (also called *ksinhondros*), one of the oldest Greek pastas. This hard pasta, which resembles bread crumbs, is made by simmering or mixing cracked wheat with milk or yogurt. The pasta was once prepared with sour milk, but with the advent of refrigeration, fresh milk is used.

Although *trahana* is stored and used throughout the year, homemade flour-and-water pastas are often cooked as soon as they are made, cooked in moist risotto-like dishes, in garlicky tomato sauce or in meat, chicken or vegetable broth. These peasant pasta dishes, though different from the Italian ones, are equally good if made with penne, ziti and other commercial pasta.

Island women explained to me that pasta would traditionally be prepared for unexpected visitors when meat, fish or other foods considered suitable for guests were not available. For these more elaborate dishes, the pasta was dressed with melted clarified sheep's or goat's milk butter and homemade local cheese. The scalding butter was poured over the pasta and sizzled as it melted the cheese, infusing the dish with a delightful taste and aroma. Tomato sauce was usually served on the side or ladled over the pasta after the butter. In Turkey, all kinds of soups and stuffed pastas are similarly flavored with sheep's milk butter.

Most Greeks still prepare commercial spaghetti in this manner, although today they use margarine, regular butter or a combination. In northern Chios, homemade macaroni is topped with sizzling olive oil, in which grated local goat cheese has been toasted. The macaroni takes on the aroma of the fried cheese, without the heaviness of butter.

Island pastas come in various shapes. The Chian handmade macaroni is probably the most elaborate: Hazelnut-sized pieces of dough are rubbed between the cook's palms and rolled around a straw of Spanish broom, the spiky bush that grows all over Greece. The pasta is then slipped off, creating a hollow two-inch-long tube of macaroni. A simpler pasta is made by slicing a sheet of phyllo pastry into ribbons, like Italian tagliatelle. Cooks on Karpathos and southern Crete make longish shell-like curved pasta. A tiny pasta called *fide*—probably from the Spanish *fideos*—is made on Crete, Chios and many other islands by rolling little pieces of dough between two fingers. *Fide* is usually cooked with meat or chicken to make a thick, nourishing soup.

Egg pasta is a more festive dish, usually prepared in advance, dried and stored. *Hilopites*, pasta squares or rectangles of various sizes, ranging from $1/4$ inch to 3 inches, are the most common, made all over Greece. Stuffed egg pastas, such as the Cypriot ravioli or the *latzania* of Astypalaia—longish stuffed pasta with twisted ends that are filled with smooth and creamy fresh cheese and seasoned with threads of wild saffron—are saved for special occasions.

FAKES ME PASTOULA KE DIOSMO
Lentil Soup with Pasta and Mint

MAKES 4 SERVINGS

4 cups water

1 cup brown lentils, picked over and rinsed

1 bay leaf

3 tablespoons olive oil

1 cup chopped red onions

1/2–1 teaspoon Aleppo pepper or pinch of crushed red pepper flakes

3 cups Chicken Stock (page 267) or Vegetable Stock (page 268)

Salt

1/3 cup stellini, small orzo or other tiny pasta shape or 2/3 cup crushed vermicelli

Freshly ground black pepper

1/4 cup chopped fresh mint, plus a few leaves for garnish

Extra-virgin olive oil

Sweet Greek vinegar, such as Kalamata vinegar, or balsamic vinegar

I FIRST tasted this soup in Astypalaia, the tiny, picturesque Dodecanese island. The lentils were mixed with small, somewhat crude pieces of home-made pasta and seasoned with plenty of fresh mint. In T. F. Horowitz's book *Generations of Mediterranean Sephardic Cooking*, with recipes from the island of Rhodes—which is also in the Dodecanese—I found a similar soup: lentils with vermicelli cooked in tomato sauce. In my version of the dish, I prefer to use tiny pasta shapes such as stellini or small orzo and follow the Astypalaian recipe, which has no tomatoes.

In a large pot, combine the water, lentils and bay leaf and bring to a boil. Reduce the heat to low and simmer for 20 minutes, or until the lentils are tender. Drain, reserving 1 cup of the cooking liquid. Discard the bay leaf. Wipe out the pot with paper towels.

Heat the oil in the pot and sauté the onions with the Aleppo pepper or pepper flakes over medium heat until soft, about 5 minutes. Add the lentils and sauté for 1 minute. Add the reserved cooking liquid, the stock and salt to taste, bring to a boil, reduce the heat to low and simmer for 10 minutes.

Return the broth to boiling, add the pasta, increase the heat to medium and cook for 8 minutes, or until the pasta is al dente. Taste and adjust the seasonings, adding a few grindings of black pepper. Stir in the mint.

Ladle the soup into bowls, drizzle oil and a little vinegar over each serving and garnish with the mint leaves.

FAKI SOUPA ME SPANAKI

Lentil Soup with Spinach

MAKES 6 TO 8 SERVINGS

2 cups brown lentils, picked over and rinsed

⅓ cup olive oil

½ cup chopped onion

3 garlic cloves, thinly sliced

½ cup grated ripe tomatoes (see page 27) or canned diced tomatoes with their juice

½ cup dry red wine

1 teaspoon Aleppo pepper or pinch of crushed red pepper flakes

Salt

4 cups Vegetable Stock (page 268) or Chicken Stock (page 267)

1 teaspoon dried thyme, crumbled

1 teaspoon dry mustard

1 bay leaf

1½ pounds spinach, stemmed

Pinch of ground cumin (optional)

2–3 tablespoons red wine vinegar

Freshly ground black pepper

Place the lentils in a large saucepan and add cold water to cover. Bring to a boil, remove from the heat and let stand for 15 minutes. Drain.

In a large pot, heat the oil and sauté the onion over medium heat until just soft, about 3 minutes. Add the garlic and sauté for 1 minute more; do not let it color. Add the lentils, tomatoes, wine, Aleppo pepper or pepper flakes and salt to taste. Bring to a boil, add the stock, thyme, mustard and bay leaf and return to a boil. Reduce the heat to low, cover and simmer for 30 minutes, or until the lentils are tender.

Add the spinach and cumin, if using, and simmer for 5 to 10 minutes more, or until the spinach is wilted. Add the vinegar and black pepper to taste. Taste and adjust the seasonings. Serve hot.

FOR AS long as I can remember, my mother has cooked this lentil soup once a week in the winter. Following a recipe in Theonie Mark's book *Greek Island Cooking*, which contains recipes from Rhodes, I've added spinach leaves.

Serve with cured fish, such as smoked trout.

FASSOLIA ME SELINO

White Bean Soup with Wild Celery and Lemon

MAKES 4 SERVINGS

2 cups dried white beans, soaked overnight in water and drained

2 onions, halved, one half thinly sliced in half-moons

2 cups coarsely chopped wild celery

1 teaspoon salt

⅓ cup freshly squeezed lemon juice
Freshly ground black pepper

⅓ cup extra-virgin olive oil
Aleppo pepper or crushed red pepper flakes (optional)

2 tablespoons finely chopped fresh flat-leaf parsley

In a large pot, place the beans and the 3 onion halves and add water to cover by 4 inches. Bring to a boil, reduce the heat to low and simmer for 40 minutes. Add the sliced onion, celery and salt and simmer for 20 to 40 minutes more, adding a little more water if needed, until tender.

Add the lemon juice and black pepper to taste and simmer for 10 minutes more, or until the beans are just covered with broth. Transfer 1 cup of the soup to a blender (avoiding the onion half) and puree. Return the puree to the pot and cook for 2 minutes more.

Remove from the heat and discard the onion halves. Stir in the oil and sprinkle with the Aleppo pepper or pepper flakes, if desired. Taste and adjust the seasonings, sprinkle with the parsley and serve hot.

THIS SIMPLE SOUP really needs the strongly aromatic wild celery, the Greek *selino*, which is very different from the American or northern European variety. It has become available in Greek markets only during the past decade, but in her *Mediterranean Grains and Greens*, Paula Wolfert notes that wild celery can be found in Asian markets under the name *kun choi* or *kin tsai*. When you find it, buy it in quantity, wash it, coarsely chop it and keep it in zipperlock bags in the freezer to use as needed. You can also easily grow your own in the garden or in pots (for seeds, see Sources, page 285).

This recipe comes from Cyprus, and you can serve it accompanied with smoked fish or meats or simply with a bowl of Greek olives, as is the custom in Greece during the days of Lent.

REVITHIA STO FOURNO
Oven-Cooked Chickpeas

MAKES 6 SERVINGS

2¹/₂ cups dried chickpeas, soaked overnight in water and drained

Salt

²/₃ cup olive oil

2 cups coarsely chopped onions

1 tablespoon dried oregano, crumbled

2 bay leaves, crumbled

1–2 teaspoons Aleppo pepper or pinch of crushed red pepper flakes

1¹/₂ cups Chicken Stock (page 267), Vegetable Stock (page 268) or water

Freshly ground black pepper

Preheat the oven to 400°F.

In a medium bowl, combine the chickpeas and 1 teaspoon salt and toss well.

In a medium flameproof casserole, heat the oil and sauté the onions over medium heat for 4 minutes, or until soft. Stir in the chickpeas, oregano, bay leaves and Aleppo pepper or pepper flakes, then add the stock or water and bring to a boil. Remove from the heat. Cover the dish with a double layer of aluminum foil and then the lid.

Reduce the oven temperature to 250°F and cook for 6 hours, or until the chickpeas are very tender. Taste and adjust the seasonings, adding black pepper to taste. Serve hot, warm or at room temperature.

ON SIFNOS, the most common Lenten dish is these chickpeas, cooked slowly overnight in the communal oven. On Folegandros, the dish is also made on the eve of the Day of the Cross, September 14, the day the Saints Constantine and Helen are said to have discovered the cross on which Christ was crucified.

Perhaps because the island women had to go to church and had no time for more complicated dishes on that festive day, they chose to make this simple one, and the tradition was established. The soaked chickpeas are usually placed in an unglazed clay casserole, made in the small pottery workshops of Platis Yalos, on Sifnos, and taken to the bakery in the evening, to be picked up the next morning after church. I cook these beans under a double sheet of aluminum foil in a heavy lidded casserole. After six hours, they emerge beautifully tender.

Serve as a main dish, accompanied by smoked trout, olives or feta cheese and fresh country bread.

SIFNOS

REVITHIA ME RYZI
Chickpeas with Rice

MAKES 4 SERVINGS

2 cups cooked chickpeas (see Note)
Salt

²/₃ cup extra-virgin olive oil

1¹/₃ cups coarsely chopped onions

¹/₂ cup dry white wine

1–2 teaspoons Aleppo pepper or pinch of
crushed red pepper flakes

4 cups Chicken Stock (page 267) or water,
heated, plus extra if needed

1 cup peeled, seeded and diced ripe
tomatoes or canned diced tomatoes
with their juice

1 cinnamon stick

1 bay leaf

1 cup medium-grain rice, such as Arborio

¹/₂ cup grated hard myzithra, crumbled feta
or grated pecorino Romano cheese
(optional)

¹/₄ cup chopped fresh flat-leaf parsley

In a Dutch oven, heat ¹/₃ cup of the oil and sauté the onions over medium heat, stirring frequently, for 8 to 10 minutes, or until soft. Add the wine and pepper or pepper flakes and cook for 1 minute over high heat. Add 2 cups of the stock or water, the chickpeas, tomatoes, cinnamon stick, bay leaf and salt to taste and bring to a boil. Reduce the heat to low, cover and simmer for 10 minutes.

Add the rice and the remaining 2 cups stock or water and bring to a boil, cover, then reduce the heat to low and simmer, stirring often and adding a little more stock or water if needed, for 20 minutes, or until the rice is tender.

Add the remaining ¹/₃ cup oil and the cheese, if using. Taste and adjust the seasonings. Cover, remove from the heat and let stand for 5 minutes.

Discard the cinnamon stick and bay leaf, sprinkle with the parsley and serve.

NOTE: To cook chickpeas, place 1¹/₄ cups dried chickpeas and 2 tablespoons salt in a medium saucepan and add water to cover by 2 inches. Bring to a boil and skim off the foam that rises to the surface. Reduce the heat to low and simmer for 1 to 1¹/₂ hours, or until the chickpeas are tender. Add a little warm water, if needed, during the cooking. Drain the chickpeas and set aside.

THIS RECIPE comes from the Sephardic community of Rhodes. You can make an equally terrific dish using white or cranberry beans instead of chickpeas. The grated cheese is my own addition and can be omitted if you are serving the dish as an accompaniment to meat or poultry.

MOUKENTRA
Lentils and Rice

MAKES 4 SERVINGS

1 cup brown lentils, picked over
  and rinsed

1 bay leaf

1/3 cup olive oil

1/2 cup chopped red onion

  About 2 1/2 cups Chicken Stock (page
    267) or Vegetable Stock (page 268)

1 cup medium-grain rice, such as Arborio

1 teaspoon Aleppo pepper or pinch of
  crushed red pepper flakes

  Salt and freshly ground black pepper

  Extra-virgin olive oil (optional)

1/2 cup chopped fresh cilantro

Place the lentils and bay leaf in a large pot, add water to cover by 2 inches and bring to a boil. Reduce the heat to low and simmer for 20 minutes, or until the lentils are tender. Drain and set aside. Wipe out the pot with paper towels.

Heat the oil in the pot and sauté the onion over medium heat until soft, about 5 minutes. Add 2 cups of the stock, the rice, the lentils, Aleppo pepper or pepper flakes and salt to taste and bring to a boil. Reduce the heat to low, cover and simmer for 15 minutes, stirring occasionally and adding more stock as needed, until the rice is tender and has the consistency of risotto.

Add a few grindings of black pepper and drizzle with oil, if using. Remove from the heat, stir in the cilantro and taste and adjust the seasonings. Serve at once.

THE SIMPLE combination of rice and lentils flavored with onion and chopped cilantro makes a hearty and nourishing winter main course. On Crete and other Greek islands, the dish is simply called *fakoryzo* (lentil-rice). Nikos Psilakis, in his book *Traditional Cuisine of Crete*, explains that on this island the rice was usually added on the second day to lentil soup. This dish from Cyprus, on the other hand, is prepared from scratch with lentils and rice.

Serve with sheep's milk yogurt, Drained Yogurt (page 266) or feta cheese.

FASSOLIA ME HIRINO KE PORTOKALI

Baked White Beans with Pork and Orange

MAKES 4 TO 6 SERVINGS AS A MAIN COURSE; 8 TO 10 SERVINGS AS A MEZE

2 cups dried Greek *gigantes* (giant beans), white kidney or cannellini beans, soaked overnight in water and drained

2 bay leaves

³/4 pound boneless pork shoulder
   Peel of 1 orange

¹/2 cup olive oil

2 cups coarsely chopped onions

1 cup sweet red wine, such as Mavrodaphne or sweet Marsala

²/3 cup freshly squeezed orange juice

²/3 cup grated ripe tomatoes (see page 27) or canned diced tomatoes with their juice

1 celery rib, preferably wild (see page 275), finely chopped

1–2 teaspoons Aleppo pepper or ¹/2–1 teaspoon crushed red pepper flakes

1 teaspoon dry mustard
   Salt and freshly ground black pepper
   Sprigs of fresh flat-leaf parsley

B E A N S boiled until tender and then baked in the oven in a rich tomato sauce are a traditional dish of northern Greece. The orange peel and juice make this version special, adding a fresh fruity taste and aroma to the hearty beans. Oranges and tangerines of exceptional quality are grown on Chios and inspired local chef Stefanos Kovas to create the dish. He serves it at Loukoumi, his lively ouzo bar in the heart of Chios Town.

You can serve it as a main course, a *meze* or a side dish with meat or poultry.

Place the beans and 1 of the bay leaves in a Dutch oven, add water to cover by 2 inches and bring to a boil. Reduce the heat to low, cover and simmer for 45 minutes, or until the beans are soft but not mushy. Drain the beans, reserving 1 cup of the cooking liquid.

Meanwhile, place the pork and the remaining bay leaf in another large pot, add water to cover and bring to a boil. Skim the foam that rises to the surface, reduce the heat to medium and simmer for 30 minutes.

Drain the pork, reserving the broth. Strain the broth through a sieve. You should have about $1/2$ cup; if necessary, boil over high heat to reduce. Cut the pork into $1/2$-inch cubes and set aside.

Bring a small saucepan of water to the boil and blanch the orange peel for 1 minute. Drain and repeat two more times. Drain the peel on paper towels, then cut it into thin strips.

In the Dutch oven, heat the oil and sauté the onions over medium heat for 5 minutes, or until soft. Add the pork and sauté for 3 minutes more. Add the beans and sauté for 1 minute more. Add the wine, orange juice, reserved pork broth, tomatoes, orange peel, celery, Aleppo pepper or pepper flakes, mustard and salt to taste. Bring to a boil, cover, reduce the heat to low and simmer for 30 minutes. If more liquid is needed, add some of the reserved bean liquid.

Meanwhile, preheat the oven to 400°F.

Taste the bean mixture and adjust the seasonings, adding black pepper to taste. Bake, uncovered, for 30 to 40 minutes, or until the beans are very tender and most of the liquid has evaporated. Serve hot or warm, garnished with the parsley.

HONDROS

Bulgur with Onion, Tomatoes and Cheese

MAKES 3 OR 4 SERVINGS

3 tablespoons extra-virgin olive oil, plus more for serving

1/2 cup chopped red onion

1 cup coarse bulgur (see Sources, page 285)

1 teaspoon Aleppo pepper or pinch of crushed red pepper flakes

2 cups water, Chicken Stock (page 267) or Vegetable Stock (page 268)

1 cup grated ripe tomatoes (see page 27) or canned diced tomatoes with their juice

1 teaspoon sugar

2/3 cup crumbled feta cheese, plus more for serving

Salt and freshly ground black pepper

3 tablespoons chopped fresh flat-leaf parsley

In a large saucepan, heat the oil and sauté the onion over medium heat for 3 to 4 minutes, or until soft. Add the bulgur and Aleppo pepper or pepper flakes and sauté, stirring, until the bulgur is coated with oil. Add the water or stock, tomatoes and sugar and bring to a boil. Reduce the heat to low, cover and simmer for 10 to 12 minutes, or until the bulgur has the consistency of a very moist risotto. Remove from the heat and let stand, covered, for 3 minutes.

Stir the feta into the bulgur. Taste and add salt if necessary (feta is usually quite salty, so you may not need any) and black pepper to taste. Serve in bowls, sprinkled with feta and parsley and drizzled with oil.

TRADITIONAL Chian bulgur is not the presteamed wheat we use today but coarsely ground hard local wheat, milled in the hand-operated stone mills one still finds in use in Chian homes. For lunch or dinner, it is sautéed in olive oil with onions, tomatoes and hot peppers and topped with the local cheese and, occasionally, chopped herbs.

This recipe is an adaptation of that dish.

PLIGOURI ME ADRAKLA
Bulgur Pilaf with Greens

MAKES 4 SERVINGS

^{1}/2 cup olive oil

1^1/2 cups chopped onions

3 cups chopped purslane (keep the thicker stems separate), or see the variation

2 teaspoons Aleppo pepper or 1 teaspoon crushed red pepper flakes

1^1/2 cups coarse bulgur (see Sources, page 285)

2^1/2–3 cups water, Chicken Stock (page 267) or Vegetable Stock (page 268), heated

1 teaspoon salt

1 cup grated hard feta cheese, plus more for serving (see Note)

Extra-virgin olive oil

In a large saucepan, heat the oil and sauté the onions over medium heat for 3 to 4 minutes, or until soft. Add the thick purslane stems and the pepper or pepper flakes and sauté for 1 minute. Add the bulgur and sauté, stirring, until coated with oil. Add 2^1/2 cups water or stock and the salt, reduce the heat to low, cover and simmer for 4 minutes.

Add the remaining purslane and a little more water or stock if needed and cook for 6 to 8 minutes, or until the bulgur is tender. Remove from the heat and let stand for 3 minutes.

Stir the feta into the bulgur. Drizzle with oil, and taste and adjust the seasonings.

THIS RECIPE comes from Crete, but similar dishes can be found all over Greece. A typical meal of the poor, this pilaf uses the ubiquitous purslane, a weed that proliferates in gardens and springs up by itself in pots on the balconies of island homes. Purslane is crunchy, tart and sweet at the same time, so it is difficult to suggest a substitute. The thick stems of Swiss chard combined with some mâche will make a very different bulgur pilaf, but one I also love.

Serve hot, warm or at room temperature.

Serve hot, warm or at room temperature, passing a bowl of grated feta at the table.

NOTE: If you leave feta uncovered in the refrigerator overnight, it will dry a bit and can be easily grated.

VARIATION

Instead of the purslane, use 2 cups chopped Swiss chard stems and 1 cup chopped mâche. Sauté the stems with the onions and add the mâche at the end, with the cheese.

OMATHIES
Bulgur with Chicken Livers and Currants

MAKES 4 TO 6 SERVINGS

1/4 cup olive oil

1 1/2 cups chopped onions

2/3 pound chicken livers, finely diced

1 cup sweet red wine, such as Mavrodaphne or sweet Marsala

1 teaspoon Aleppo pepper or pinch of crushed red pepper flakes

2 cups coarse bulgur (see Sources, page 285)

1 cup Zante currants

Grated zest of 1 orange

4–4 1/2 cups Chicken Stock (page 267), heated

1 cup slivered almonds

1/2 teaspoon ground cumin

Salt

2 tablespoons unsalted butter (optional)

Freshly ground black pepper

3 tablespoons chopped fresh dill

CHOPPED chicken livers, onions and sweet red wine flavor this unusual, easy bulgur pilaf. Cumin, orange peel and dill give the dish an exquisite fragrance.

According to an old Cretan recipe, from which this one is derived, chopped pork liver mixed with bulgur and all the other ingredients made the stuffing for a thick sausage that was eaten at Christmas.

Serve as a main course with a green salad or a vegetable side dish, such as Stewed Mixed Greens from Corfu (page 192) or Baked Okra in Tomato Sauce (page 196).

In a Dutch oven, heat the oil and sauté the onions over medium heat until soft, about 4 minutes. Add the liver and sauté, stirring, until firm and no longer pink, about 3 minutes. Add 1/2 cup of the wine and the Aleppo pepper or pepper flakes and simmer for 2 minutes. Stir in the bulgur, currants and orange zest and cook for 1 minute. Add 4 cups stock, the almonds, cumin and salt to taste. Reduce the heat to low, cover and simmer for 10 minutes, or until the bulgur is tender. If it becomes too dry, add a little more stock.

Stir in the remaining 1/2 cup wine and remove from the heat. Add the butter, if using, and black pepper to taste. Taste and adjust the seasonings. Cover and let stand for 5 minutes.

Serve hot, sprinkled with the dill.

ALVANIKO BRIAMI
Albanian Baked Rice with Milk, Feta, Peppers and Dill

MAKES 6 SERVINGS

1/4 cup olive oil or unsalted butter

2 cups chopped onions

3 green bell peppers, cored, seeded and diced

2–3 hot chiles, seeded and finely chopped

1 1/2 cups medium-grain rice, such as Arborio

1 pound feta cheese, coarsely crumbled or diced

1 1/2 cups chopped fresh dill

4 1/2 cups whole milk

Preheat the oven to 400°F.

In a large skillet, heat the oil or butter and sauté the onions, bell peppers and chiles until soft, about 4 minutes. Add the rice and sauté for 1 minute more. Remove from the heat and let cool slightly, then stir in the feta and dill. Transfer to a 2 1/2-quart baking dish and stir in the milk.

Bake, stirring once, for 45 minutes, or until the rice has absorbed all the milk and is tender. Serve warm or at room temperature.

MY COUSIN Leonidas Harvalias, who lives on Kea, got the recipe for this dish from the Albanian immigrants who work on the island. It has become part of our family's permanent repertoire and is one of our favorite casseroles. The name *briami* comes from the Persian *biryan*. Maria Kaneva, in her book *The Melting Pot: Balkan Food and Cookery*, writes that there are many versions of the dish, which can be traced to the Balkans in the Middle Ages.

On Kea, where dill is often difficult to get, I make an equally delicious *briami* with chopped fennel fronds.

KEA

POULENTA OR BATZINA ME STAFIDES KE KREMEDIA

Polenta with Currants and Onions

MAKES 4 TO 6 SERVINGS

COARSE cornmeal cooked like Italian polenta in water or milk is common all over Greece. It can be drizzled with clarified goat's or sheep's milk butter and cheese or, more often, served as a sweet dish, with honey or sugar. Either way, it's enjoyed warm in deep plates or soup bowls.

Michalis Magoulas, an Athenian doctor who comes from Ithaca, gives the recipe for this version of polenta in an excellent booklet he put together featuring traditional specialties from his island. In the introduction, he writes that he included this comforting dish as a tribute to the humble people who ate it and as a reminder of the hard days during the German occupation in World War II, "when the dish was the food most often consumed during the cold winter nights, as people waited for freedom."

I've adapted the dish by appropriating Paula Wolfert's no-stir oven method for cooking polenta, as described in *Mediterranean Grains and Greens*. Serve with Veal Stew with Garlic, Parsley and Vinegar (page 124), Chicken and Fennel Stew with Quince (page 136) or any other meat or poultry stew that has plenty of sauce. I also like to serve it with Stewed Mixed Greens from Corfu (page 192).

2 quarts warm water

2 cups medium- or coarse-grind cornmeal

1/2 cup Zante currants

1/2 cup olive oil

2 teaspoons salt

1 medium onion, halved lengthwise and thinly sliced into half-moons

Freshly ground white or black pepper

Preheat the oven to 350°F. Oil a 13-x-9-inch baking dish.

Combine the water, cornmeal, currants, $1/4$ cup of the oil and the salt in the baking dish, stir well and bake for 1 hour.

Meanwhile, in a small skillet, heat the remaining $1/4$ cup oil and sauté the onion over medium heat for 5 minutes, or until soft.

Stir the onion and pepper to taste into the polenta and bake for 30 minutes more, or until the polenta is set. Let stand for 5 minutes before serving.

MICROWAVE METHOD: Cook the polenta in two batches: Put 1 cup cornmeal, 4 cups water and 1 teaspoon salt in a 3-quart microwavable dish. Microwave on high for 2 minutes, uncovered. Stir in $1/4$ cup of the currants. Microwave on high for 2 minutes, uncovered. Meanwhile, sauté the onion in a small skillet in $1/2$ cup olive oil. Stir half of the onion into the polenta. Microwave for 2 minutes more, uncovered. Stir in pepper to taste. Microwave for 2 minutes more, covered. Stir and let stand for 5 minutes. Cook the second batch in the same way.

VARIATION
POULENTA ME RIGANI KE TIRI
Polenta with Oregano and Cheese

Omit the currants and onion, reduce the oil to $1/4$ cup and add 1 teaspoon dried oregano to the cornmeal. If you bake the polenta, just as you take it out of the oven, stir in $1/2$ cup coarsely grated hard myzithra, pecorino Romano or Parmigiano-Reggiano cheese. Or, if using the microwave, stir half the cheese into each batch when you add the pepper. When you take the polenta out of the microwave, drizzle it with extra-virgin olive oil, stir and let stand for 3 to 5 minutes before serving.

TRAHANOSOUPA CHIOTIKI

Chian Pasta Soup

MAKES 4 TO 6 SERVINGS

5 cups Chicken Stock (page 267)
    or Vegetable Stock (page 268)

1/3 cup grated ripe tomato (see page 27)

2/3 cup Chian Pasta (page 174)

1/2–1 teaspoon Aleppo pepper or pinch of
    crushed red pepper flakes

1/4 cup olive oil

4–6 large eggs (optional)

2/3 cup crumbled feta cheese

1 teaspoon sugar (optional)
    Salt

2 tablespoons chopped fresh flat-leaf
    parsley

ALTHOUGH the dried pasta dough already contains tomatoes, Chians always add more to this soup. And, to make it extra nourishing, they often poach eggs in the broth.

In a large saucepan, bring the stock and tomato to a boil. Add the pasta and Aleppo pepper or pepper flakes, reduce the heat to low and simmer, stirring often, for 20 minutes, or until the pasta is very soft. Stir in the oil.

Meanwhile, if you like, about 10 minutes before the pasta is cooked, break the eggs, one at a time, into a cup and slip them into the simmering soup. Poach the eggs for about 4 minutes, or until the whites are set but the yolk is still soft. With a slotted spoon, transfer them to a plate and cover to keep warm.

Stir the feta into the soup and taste to adjust the seasonings. Add the sugar, if using, and salt. Serve in soup bowls, including 1 egg in each bowl, if using, and sprinkle with the parsley.

NOTE: For a smooth and creamy texture, puree the soup before serving.

MATSATA MAKARONIA

Plain Pasta Ribbons

MAKES 1 POUND; FOR 3 OR 4 SERVINGS

1 cup all-purpose flour

1 cup fine semolina

Salt

About 1 cup water

Grated hard myzithra, kefalotyri or pecorino Romano cheese

Basic Tomato Sauce (page 269), warmed

Place the flour, semolina and $1/2$ teaspoon salt in a food processor and pulse to blend. With the motor running, slowly pour in enough water to make a firm but not hard dough. As soon as the dough forms a ball, turn off the processor and let the dough rest for 15 minutes.

Process for 1 to 2 minutes more, or until the dough is smooth and elastic. Turn the dough out onto a floured surface, cover and let rest for 5 minutes.

Knead the dough briefly, sprinkling it with a little more flour if needed, until very smooth. Cover and let rest for about 1 hour.

Divide the dough into 4 pieces. Roll each piece out on a lightly floured surface as thin as possible. Let the pasta dry for just 5 to 10 minutes; it should still be soft enough to fold without cracking.

Sprinkle each pasta sheet lightly with flour and roll it up loosely like a cigar. Cut into $1/3$-inch-wide slices to make strands of pasta. Carefully untangle the strands and let dry on a kitchen towel for 1 to 2 hours.

Bring a large pot of salted water to a boil and add the pasta. Cook for 2 to 3 minutes, or until tender; drain.

Transfer the pasta to a serving bowl and sprinkle with the cheese. Pour the tomato sauce over the top and serve immediately.

VARIATION
KORDELIA

Pasta Ribbons

Substitute whole milk for the water; the dough will be slightly more elastic.

ON FOLEGANDROS, the most popular dish served at tavernas is ribbons of fresh pasta, rolled out on the spot with a long, thin rolling pin and served simply dressed with tomato sauce and the local cheese. Women usually make the pasta with a combination of flour from the very hard *starenio* wheat and some commercial all-purpose flour. I have used fine semolina instead of the hard-wheat *starenio* flour. The sheets do not have to be rolled very thin, so this is a pasta you can make without a machine.

MAKARONIA ME TIGANITO TYRI
Penne with Olive Oil and Toasted Cheese

MAKES 3 OR 4 SERVINGS

CHIOS

~~~~~~

KATINA KRITOULI, the owner and cook of the old taverna Makelos, at the entrance of the village of Pitios on northern Chios, makes hand-rolled hollow macaroni. With extraordinary ease, she shapes each piece of dough, first between her palms, then rolling it around a piece of *spartoksylo*—Spanish broom—to make hollow 2-inch-long tubes of macaroni. The cooked pasta is topped with sizzling olive oil in which grated hard goat cheese has been toasted.

Hard myzithra or any good-quality aged goat cheese can be used to duplicate the taste of the Chian shepherd's cheese that Katina uses.

And commercial pasta is equally delicious, as it takes on the goaty aroma of the fried cheese. You can also add tomato sauce if you like.

1 pound penne
Salt
⅓ cup olive oil
⅔ cup grated hard myzithra or pecorino Romano cheese, plus more for sprinkling
Freshly ground black pepper
2–3 tablespoons chopped fresh flat-leaf parsley
Basic Tomato Sauce (page 269), warmed (optional)

In a large pot of boiling salted water, cook the pasta until al dente; drain.

Meanwhile, in a small skillet, heat the oil. Add ⅓ cup of the cheese and fry, stirring, until golden brown.

Transfer the pasta to a heated deep platter, top with the hot oil and toasted cheese and toss to coat. Sprinkle with pepper to taste, the remaining ⅓ cup cheese and the parsley.

If you like, toss the pasta with the tomato sauce or serve it on the side. Pass a bowl of grated cheese at the table.

SKORDOMAKARONIA
Pasta Cooked in Garlicky Tomato Sauce

MAKES 3 OR 4 SERVINGS

½ cup olive oil

1 cup chopped onions

3–5 garlic cloves, chopped

1–2 teaspoons Aleppo pepper or ½–1 teaspoon crushed red pepper flakes

½ cup dry red wine

2 cups grated ripe tomatoes (see page 27) or one 16-ounce can diced tomatoes with their juice

Pinch of sugar (optional)

5 cups Chicken Stock (page 267)

Salt

1 pound penne, ziti or other hollow macaroni

⅔ cup grated hard myzithra, pecorino Romano or Parmigiano-Reggiano cheese, plus more for sprinkling

3 tablespoons chopped fresh flat-leaf parsley

IN THIS traditional dish, which is made all over the islands, the pasta is cooked like a risotto, stirred in a flavorful tomato sauce with plenty of garlic until it is al dente. Homemade pastas of all kinds and shapes are cooked this way, often in a meat or seafood broth instead of tomato sauce.

In a large skillet, heat the oil and sauté the onions over medium heat until soft, about 4 minutes. Add as much garlic as you like and stir a few times; do not let it color. Add the pepper or pepper flakes and pour in the wine. As it bubbles, add the tomatoes and sugar, if using. Bring to a boil and cook for about 5 minutes, or until the sauce starts to thicken.

Meanwhile, in a small saucepan, bring the stock to a low simmer. Add salt to taste.

Pour about 2 cups of the stock into the tomato sauce. Bring to a boil and add the pasta. Stir to coat with the sauce and cook, stirring often and adding more stock as the pasta absorbs the liquid, until it is cooked al dente, about 20 minutes (you may not need all the stock).

Add the cheese, toss and transfer to a heated bowl. Sprinkle with the parsley and serve immediately, passing more grated cheese in a bowl.

VARIATION
MAKARONIA ME KAPARI
Pasta Cooked with Capers

Instead of tomato sauce, use Stewed Capers (page 27) as a base. Heat the stock and cook the pasta as described above.

MAKAROUNES KARPATHOU NISTISIMES

Pasta with Olive Oil, Onions and Spices

MAKES 3 OR 4 SERVINGS

~~~~~~~~~~~~~~~~~~~~~~~~~~~~~~~~~~~~

THIS SAUCE is my free adaptation of the traditional spicy sautéed onions of the island of Karpathos that are the base for many local meat and vegetable dishes. On Lenten days, when served with the homemade pasta, it was eaten without cheese, and you may prefer it this way. If you do use cheese, try to get good-quality hard myzithra (see Sources, page 285).

1/2 cup olive oil, plus more for serving

2 onions, halved lengthwise and thinly sliced into half-moons

1 tablespoon coriander seeds, coarsely crushed in a mortar

1 cinnamon stick

3 allspice berries, coarsely crushed in a mortar or with a rolling pin

3 cloves

1 cup dry red wine

1/2 cup water

2 tablespoons red wine vinegar

1 1/2 teaspoons ground cumin

1 teaspoon freshly ground black pepper, plus more for serving

Pinch of freshly grated nutmeg

Salt

1 pound penne rigate, orecchiette or pasta shells

2/3 cup finely chopped fresh flat-leaf parsley

Grated hard myzithra, kefalotyri or pecorino Romano cheese for serving (optional)

In a large, deep skillet with a lid, heat the oil and sauté the onions over medium heat for 3 minutes, or until soft. Add the coriander, cinnamon stick, allspice and cloves and sauté for 2 to 3 minutes more, or until the onions start to color. Add the wine, water, vinegar, cumin and pepper. Reduce the heat to low, cover and simmer for 10 to 12 minutes, or until the onions are very soft and the sauce has thickened. Add the nutmeg and salt to taste. Taste and adjust the seasonings. Keep warm.

Meanwhile, cook the pasta according to the package directions until al dente. Just before draining the pasta, add ½ cup of the cooking liquid to the onion mixture and bring to a boil.

Drain the pasta in a colander and drizzle it with oil. Remove the cinnamon stick from the onion mixture, add the pasta and toss well. Remove from the heat, add the parsley and toss again. Cover and let stand for 3 minutes.

Sprinkle with cheese, if using, and pepper to taste and serve.

OLYMPOS, KARPATHOS

RAVIOLES
Ravioli Stuffed with Haloumi and Mint

MAKES 6 SERVINGS

THIS festive pasta from Cyprus was originally shaped into half-moons, but now most cooks prefer to make square ravioli. There are as many versions of *ravioles* as there are Cypriot cooks. This one is based on a recipe given to me by the Cyprus Dairy Producers Association.

Most commercial vacuum-packed haloumi cheese is too salty for this dish, so you will need to soak it in water for 2 to 3 hours before grating it. You'll also need dried mint for the filling (the flavor of fresh is completely different). Instead of making the ravioli with the rich dough of this recipe, you could use the dough for Cheese-Stuffed Pasta from Astypalaia (page 172).

PASTA

3–3½ cups all-purpose flour

3 large egg yolks

½ cup (8 tablespoons) unsalted butter, melted, or a combination of melted butter and safflower oil

About 1 cup milk

FILLING

2½ cups grated haloumi cheese (about 12 ounces)

2 large egg whites

1½–2 teaspoons dried mint, crumbled

Salt

3 tablespoons unsalted butter

2 tablespoons olive oil

¼ cup chopped fresh mint

Freshly ground black pepper

MAKE THE PASTA: Place 3 cups flour in a food processor. With the motor running, add the egg yolks, one at a time, and then the butter or butter and oil. Slowly pour in enough milk to make a soft dough. As soon as the dough forms a ball, stop the processor and let the dough rest for 15 minutes.

Process the dough for 1 to 2 minutes more, or until smooth and slightly sticky. Turn the dough out onto a floured surface, cover and let rest for 5 minutes.

Knead the dough briefly, sprinkling with a little more flour if needed, until very smooth. Cover and let rest for 10 to 20 minutes.

MEANWHILE, MAKE THE FILLING: In a medium bowl, combine the cheese, egg whites and dried mint and beat until smooth.

Divide the dough into 8 pieces. Roll each piece through a pasta machine as thin as possible, according to the manufacturer's instructions. Line a large tray with a kitchen towel.

Work with 1 piece of dough at a time, keeping the remaining dough covered. Place $1/2$ teaspoon of the filling about 2 inches apart and 1 inch up from the bottom edge of each pasta sheet. Fold the top half of the pasta over to cover the filling. Cut into 2-inch squares with a fluted pastry wheel or a knife. Press the edges with the tines of a fork to seal.

Place the ravioli on the towel-lined tray, leaving some room between them.

Let the ravioli dry for 2 hours, then layer them between paper towels in a container, cover tightly and refrigerate for at least 1 hour or up to 24 hours.

Bring a large pot of salted water to a rolling boil. Add the ravioli and cook for 2 to 3 minutes, or until they come to the surface. Remove from the heat and quickly pour in 2 to 3 cups cold water to stop the cooking. With a slotted spoon, carefully transfer the ravioli to a serving dish.

Meanwhile, in a small skillet, heat the butter and oil and cook the fresh mint over medium heat for 1 minute. Pour over the ravioli, sprinkle with pepper to taste and serve at once.

HALOUMI CHEESE, CYPRUS

LATZANIA
Cheese-Stuffed Pasta from Astypalaia

MAKES 6 SERVINGS

PASTA

3–3½ cups all-purpose flour

2 large eggs

⅔–1 cup water

FILLING

1 cup well-drained ricotta cheese, preferably sheep's milk

½ cup finely grated mild cheddar cheese

½ cup manouri cheese (see Sources, page 285)

1 large egg

Pinch of saffron threads, toasted in a dry skillet until fragrant, cooled and crumbled

Salt

½–1 teaspoon freshly ground black pepper

2 quarts Chicken Stock (page 267) or Vegetable Stock (page 268)

2 tablespoons unsalted butter

Grated hard myzithra or pecorino Romano cheese for serving

2 tablespoons chopped fresh flat-leaf parsley

ASTYPALAIA

TRADITIONALLY prepared during Carnival, on the last weekend before Lent, this unusual stuffed pasta is shaped like old-fashioned hard candy wrapped in cellophane, with the two ends twisted. The local goat's milk cheese is the base for the filling, which is seasoned with the wild saffron threads that the women gather in the mountains of the island. Frosso Podotas, who owns an old grocery store near the medieval castle of Astypalaia, gave me her recipe. Ricotta, mixed with cheddar and manouri, makes a fine substitute for the island cheese.

MAKE THE PASTA: Place 3 cups flour in a food processor. With the motor running, add the eggs one at a time, then slowly pour in enough water to make a soft dough. As soon as the dough forms a ball, stop the processor and let it rest for 15 minutes.

Process the dough for 1 to 2 minutes more, or until smooth and slightly sticky. Turn the dough out onto a floured surface, cover and let rest for 5 minutes.

Knead the dough briefly, sprinkling with a little more flour if needed, until very smooth. Cover and let rest for 10 to 20 minutes.

MEANWHILE, MAKE THE FILLING: In a medium bowl, blend the cheeses, egg, saffron, salt to taste and the pepper.

Divide the dough into 8 pieces. Roll each piece through a pasta machine as thin as possible, according to the manufacturer's instructions. Line a large tray with a kitchen towel.

Work with 1 piece of dough at a time, keeping the remaining dough covered. Cut the pasta into 3-x-2-inch rectangles and place 1 heaping teaspoon of the filling in the center of each rectangle. Roll up from a long side like a cigarette, moistening the edge with water to seal. Twist both ends so that the stuffed pasta looks like candy wrapped in cellophane. Place the *latzania* on the towel-lined tray, leaving some room between them.

You can cook the pasta immediately or, if you prefer, let it dry for 2 hours, then layer them between paper towels in a container, cover tightly and refrigerate for at least 1 hour or up to 24 hours.

Bring the stock to a rolling boil in a large pot and add the pasta. Cook for 2 to 3 minutes, or until the pasta comes to the surface. Add the butter and stir until it melts. Serve the *latzania* in soup bowls with some of the broth, sprinkled with cheese and parsley.

VARIATION
HILOPITES
Pasta Squares

For plain pasta, make the dough as described above, roll it out and cut it into $1/2$-inch squares or $1^1/2$-x-$^1/2$-inch rectangles. Let dry completely at room temperature, 2 to 3 days, then store in an airtight container until ready to use. Cook the *hilopites* in tomato sauce with meat or chicken, or boil them in water or stock and serve with butter and cheese.

CHIOTIKOS TRAHANA
Chian Pasta

MAKES ABOUT 2½ POUNDS (ABOUT 7 CUPS)

ON CHIOS, the local pasta, called *trahana*, is made from a dough that contains fine semolina, bread flour, yogurt and pureed cooked tomatoes and onions. Some recipes even include carrots and peppers, both hot and sweet. The most important element, according to the locals, is *trahanohorto*, a dried herb that is actually the green part of the wild carrot (*Daucus carota*), which tastes like a cross between chervil and fresh thyme. *Trahanohorto* is much more fragrant on Chios than elsewhere in Greece. When I make the pasta in Athens, I substitute dried savory.

4 pounds ripe tomatoes, cored and quartered

2 pounds onions, coarsely chopped

1 tablespoon dried savory, crumbled, or 3 ounces dried *trahanohorto*

3 pounds fine semolina (about 10 cups)
Salt

16 ounces thick sheep's milk yogurt or Drained Yogurt (page 266)

1½–2 pounds bread flour (6–8 cups)

In a large pot, combine the tomatoes, onions and savory or *trahanohorto* and bring to a boil. Reduce the heat to low and simmer until the vegetables are very soft, about 35 minutes.

If you have used *trahanohorto*, discard it. Pass the vegetables through a food mill or puree them in a food processor. Place the puree in a large bowl and stir in the semolina and salt to taste. Cover with plastic wrap and let stand for 30 minutes.

Preheat the oven to 250°F. Line two baking sheets with aluminum foil.

Stir the yogurt into the puree and add enough flour to make a firm dough. It will be very sticky. Turn out the dough onto a floured surface and knead until smooth, about 15 minutes, adding more flour if the dough is too sticky. Divide the dough into 10 pieces. Flatten each piece under your palms to ¼ inch thick and place on the baking sheets. Let dry in the oven for 2 to 3 hours. (Convection ovens work faster.)

Turn the pasta and dry for 1 hour more, or until hard enough to crumble.

Break the pasta into pieces and continue to dry in the oven until quite hard.

Grind the pasta, in batches, in a food processor. Return the crumbs to the baking sheets and continue drying in the oven until very hard, 2 to 3 hours more. (Drying times will vary greatly.) Check and stir the crumbs from time to time.

Let the *trahana* cool to room temperature, then store in airtight bags or jars. It will keep for more than 1 year.

CRACKED-WHEAT
TRAHANA

SEASONAL SALADS, VEGETABLES AND POTATOES

On the small arid islands, there is neither a great variety nor an abundance of vegetables, and people must rely on those brought in by the ferries. There are usually a few intensely flavored tomatoes, peppers and zucchini grown in the garden, but they are not enough to feed the burgeoning summer population of the islands. Crete is an exception: The fertile, sunny plains of the southern parts of the island produce quantities of tomatoes, peppers, cucumbers and green beans, which are exported not only to Athens and other parts of Greece but also to northern Europe.

Because island cooks are limited to using the same vegetables over and over for months, they have evolved a variety of ways to prepare them. They stew vegetables with aromatics, stuff them with bulgur or rice, grate them and mix them with cheese to make the filling for pies or fry them and serve them with *skordalia*, the tasty garlic sauce. Salads made with a combination of greens and raw or blanched seasonal vegetables, such as zucchini or green beans, are part of every island table and are also served as a *meze*.

The most favored of all summer dishes are vegetable stews, called *ladera* because they are cooked with *ladi*, olive oil. Green beans, okra, eggplants and zucchini are made into flavorful stews, cooked in an onion-tomato sauce, often accompanied by potatoes, bulgur or homemade pasta. Or they may be served on their own, with feta or other local cheese and plenty of crusty bread to soak up the wonderful juices, or may appear as a side dish to meat or fish. Because tomatoes were traditionally available only during summer, winter and early spring, *ladera* were usually flavored with lemon juice instead. Now that tomatoes can be bought throughout the year, the lemony versions of *ladera* are less common, but remain my favorites. Peas, artichokes, fresh favas, zucchini and carrots taste particularly delicious when cooked in a lemon and olive oil sauce seasoned with fennel or dill.

Stuffed vegetables (*gemista*) are another important group of vegetable dishes. Vegetables suitable for stuffing include tomatoes, peppers, zucchini, eggplants and onions. Stuffings may contain meat, but more often, they are meatless. Rice or bulgur are briefly cooked with onion, garlic, herbs and sometimes nuts and stuffed into the hollowed-out vegetables, which are then baked or cooked on top of the stove. Like *ladera*, these dishes are prepared during the numerous fast days of Lent, when all foods deriving from animals are prohibited, according to Greek Orthodox custom. Although few people strictly follow the religious rules today, they still prefer meatless versions of the stuffed vegetables, probably because they can be served at room temperature and are perfect for the summer table. Both *ladera* and *gemista* are usually prepared a day in advance and refrigerated so that their flavors have time to develop. They are then served at room temperature the next day.

In the absence of a large variety of cultivated vegetables, islanders turn to the wild greens that grow on the hills, from soon after the October rains up until the sun starts to dry the earth, usually in late April. Wild or cultivated greens are called *horta*. The wild ones are more interesting, but some of the cultivated varieties are also good. These greens can taste sweet, tart or bitter, and some are wonderfully aromatic. Apart from the greens collected from the hills and mountains, there are also some, like purslane, that grow as weeds among the cultivated crops. For centuries, poor islanders used these wild plants to complement their frugal menu of bread, cheese, olives and olive oil. Mothers taught their daughters which greens are healthful and which are foul-tasting or poisonous. Each generation learned from the previous one how the various greens should be cooked and which ones should be combined with one another in stews and pies. Most of the wild greens go by completely differ-ent names on the different islands. To help me with my research, islanders collected the native species and sent them to me by courier, packed in wet paper towels.

Scientists have now discovered that most of these wild plants contain antioxidants and other nutrients which promote good health. Antonia Trichopoulou, professor of public health at the University of Athens, has calculated the various nutrients in the seven different greens which are cooked in the Cretan greens pie and found that they fulfill all the daily requirements for vitamins, minerals and trace elements.

Like many islanders, my grandfather used to drink the broth in which the various greens were boiled, adding plenty of lemon juice to it. A combination of mustard greens, chard, miner's lettuce, pea shoots, orache, amaranth shoots and the outer leaves of escarole or romaine lettuce makes a tasty tonic. I drink it because I love its taste, and every time I boil greens, I put aside bottles of it in my refrigerator to enjoy during the following days.

You may not have access to all the wonderful greens that grow on the hills of the Greek islands, but there are enough cultivated leafy greens—bitter, sweet and tart—in the market to make a memorable stew or salad.

SALATA TIS LESVOU

Mixed Green Salad from Lesbos

MAKES 4 SERVINGS

3–4 tablespoons extra-virgin olive oil

2–3 tablespoons red wine vinegar
  Freshly ground black pepper

1 small head romaine lettuce, cored and
  leaves separated

1 bunch arugula, trimmed and finely
  chopped

3–4 sprigs watercress, finely chopped

3 scallions (white and most of the green
  parts), thinly sliced

4 sprigs fresh dill, finely chopped

3–4 sprigs fresh mint, tough stems removed,
  thinly sliced

3–4 sprigs borage, coarsely chopped
  (optional; see Note)

1 small fennel bulb, trimmed and very
  finely chopped or grated
  Salt

1/4 cup toasted pine nuts (optional)

In a small bowl, whisk together the oil, vinegar and plenty of pepper. Set aside.

Stack half the lettuce leaves, roll them up and cut crosswise into thin slices. Repeat with the remaining lettuce leaves.

In a large bowl, combine the lettuce and other greens, scallions, dill, mint, borage (if using) and fennel. Whisk the dressing again and pour it over the salad. Add salt to taste, toss, and sprinkle with the pine nuts, if using. Serve at once.

FROM THE first October rains up until the end of April, the greengrocers of Mytilini, the capital of Lesbos, sell each head of romaine lettuce tied together with two or three sprigs of borage (often with its little blue flowers), two or three scallions, several sprigs of peppery arugula, four or five sprigs of dill or fennel fronds, a few sprigs of peppery wild cress and either fresh mint or a little wild celery. Once home, these essential ingredients for the local green winter salad are thinly sliced and tossed with a simple vinaigrette.

It's important to cut the greens at the last moment and to slice them very thin. If they are coarsely cut, the salad will taste different.

NOTE: There is no substitute for borage — its sweet taste and crunchy texture are unique — but I have heard it compared to very tender cucumbers. If you like, add 1/2 cup coarsely grated cucumber to the salad.

HORTA KE KOLOKYTHIA VRASTA
Stewed Greens and Zucchini in Lemon Vinaigrette

MAKES 6 SERVINGS

DURING the rainy winter and early spring, there are plenty of wild mountain greens to blanch. Greeks love to dress their boiled greens with lemon and olive oil and serve them as salads. The best greens are gathered from the hills that surround the big cities on special weekend excursions, but they can also be bought from the weekly farmer's markets. In the summer, when the soil dries out and there are no more tender wild greens, Greeks buy fresh amaranth shoots cut from the easily cultivated large bush. The shoots were loved by ancient Greeks, who also used the seeds as a flavoring. Pea shoots and the young shoots from the zucchini plant are also cooked to make salads of steamed greens in the summer.

Greeks love bitter greens too, and mustard green shoots and chicory are the most common varieties steamed for salads. Their cooking liquid is often drunk as tea, and it is delicious with a generous squeeze of lemon. Steamed or boiled zucchini can complement these salads, and it is also often served by itself with a simple vinaigrette.

This garlic-and-chopped-tomato dressing comes from the island of Kythera, where it is served over a summer salad of zucchini and green amaranth.

Steamed greens don't look very pretty on a plate, so for a more attractive presentation, I suggest you press them into a small bowl or cup and invert the little green molds onto a large platter.

$^{1}/_{4}$ cup extra-virgin olive oil

2–3 tablespoons freshly squeezed lemon juice

1 garlic clove, minced
   Salt and freshly ground black pepper

1 ripe tomato, cored, peeled and diced

$1^{1}/_{2}$ pounds mixed sweet tender greens (baby spinach, Swiss chard leaves, miner's lettuce, pea shoots, orache, amaranth, outer leaves of escarole or romaine lettuce and/or beet greens)

$^{1}/_{2}$ pound mixed bitter greens (chicory, curly endive, frisée, watercress and/or turnip greens)

1 pound small tender zucchini

$^{1}/_{2}$ teaspoon dried oregano, crumbled

In a small bowl, whisk together the oil, lemon juice and garlic. Add salt to taste and plenty of pepper. Set aside.

Wash the greens and, without draining, place them in a large skillet over high heat. Cover and steam for 2 minutes. Turn the greens with tongs, cover and steam for 2 minutes more, or until completely wilted. (You may need to do this in batches.)

Meanwhile, steam the zucchini or boil them in salted water until tender, about 5 minutes. Cut into 1/2-inch-thick slices.

Drain the greens and coarsely chop them. One at a time, press individual portions of the greens into six small cups or ramekins, then unmold onto a platter. Arrange the zucchini around the greens.

Whisk the dressing, add the tomato and pour over the greens and zucchini. Sprinkle the oregano over the zucchini and serve warm or at room temperature.

LAHANO SALATA KYPRIAKI
Cabbage and Pickled Cucumber Salad

MAKES 4 TO 6 SERVINGS

4 cups finely shredded green cabbage (about ⅓ medium cabbage)

3–4 tablespoons freshly squeezed lemon juice

Salt

3–4 small dill pickles (about 2 inches long), halved lengthwise and thinly sliced

3 medium carrots, peeled and steamed or boiled in salted water until tender, halved lengthwise and thinly sliced

1 bunch arugula, trimmed and finely chopped

½ cup finely chopped fresh flat-leaf parsley, plus 3 sprigs for garnish

½ cup finely chopped fresh cilantro

3 watercress sprigs

4–5 tablespoons extra-virgin olive oil

Pinch of Aleppo pepper or crushed red pepper flakes

A few Kalamata olives

In a large bowl, combine the cabbage, 3 tablespoons lemon juice and salt to taste and rub and squeeze the cabbage with your hands until reduced in volume by half. (The salad can be prepared up to this point 3 to 4 hours in advance, covered and refrigerated.)

In a serving bowl, combine the cabbage, pickles, all but 2 tablespoons of the carrots, the arugula, parsley, cilantro and watercress. Drizzle with the oil, sprinkle with pepper and toss. Taste to adjust the seasonings, adding more lemon juice if needed. Garnish with the reserved carrots, the parsley sprigs and olives and serve.

CABBAGE is associated with winter in Greece. "You can't have tender, sweet cabbage before the winter cold," a farmer in Kea told me one October morning. The trick to turn almost any cabbage into a good salad is to "knead" the finely shredded leaves with salt and lemon juice. They wilt and shrink, becoming juicy and delicious.

Cilantro is a Cypriot touch in this lovely winter salad. Pungent arugula and sour pickles balance the sweetness of the cabbage and carrots.

FASSOLIA SALATA, ME MAYONESA ME KAPARI

Bean Salad with Lemon-Caper Mayonnaise

MAKES 4 TO 6 SERVINGS

2 cups dried white beans, soaked overnight in water and drained

⅓ cup finely diced red onion

¼ cup chopped fresh flat-leaf parsley

1 garlic clove, minced

¼ cup extra-virgin olive oil

3–4 tablespoons freshly squeezed lemon juice

Salt and freshly ground black pepper

MAYONNAISE

2 large egg yolks

1 tablespoon Dijon mustard

3 tablespoons freshly squeezed lemon juice

Pinch of salt

1 cup olive oil

¼ cup capers, drained and chopped

Freshly ground black pepper

1 cup diced tomatoes

CHEF Jim Botsacos created this variation on the popular island bean salad, which is traditionally served with a lemon vinaigrette and topped with chopped scallions or thin onion rings. He adds a little chopped garlic and diced tomatoes and dresses the beans with a thin lemony mayonnaise flavored with chopped capers.

You can serve this bean salad as a side dish or as a *meze*. Chef Botsacos pairs it with his garlic-scented crab cakes (page 44), but it would go equally well with any grilled or fried fish.

Place the beans in a large pot and add cold water to cover by 2 inches. Bring to a boil, reduce the heat to low and simmer for about 1 hour, or until tender. Drain well.

Combine the beans, onion, parsley, garlic, oil, lemon juice and salt and pepper in a large bowl and refrigerate for at least 1 hour or up to 3 hours.

MEANWHILE, MAKE THE MAYONNAISE: With an electric mixer on low speed, beat the egg yolks, mustard, lemon juice and salt in a small bowl. Increase the speed to medium and slowly add the oil in a slow, steady stream until incorporated. Stir in the capers with a wooden spoon and beat for 1 minute; the mayonnaise will be thin, like a creamy vinaigrette, not thick like regular mayonnaise. Season to taste with pepper and additional salt if necessary. Cover and refrigerate until needed.

Just before serving the beans, adjust the seasonings and fold in the tomatoes and most of the mayonnaise. Serve with the rest of the mayonnaise on the side.

PATATES KE KREMYDIA STA KARVOUNA

Baked Potato and Onion Salad

MAKES 4 TO 6 SERVINGS

~~~~~~~~~~~~~~~~~~~~~~~~~~~~~~~~~~~~~~~

WAITING to board a delayed plane to Chios early one spring morning, I started a conversation with a middle-aged woman who was going to visit her mother in Mesta, the beautifully preserved medieval village of southern Chios. Our discussion soon turned to food, and she described various "old and forgotten" dishes her mother used to cook. Among them was this exceptional salad, which her mother made by "hiding the onions and potatoes in the ashes of the wood-burning oven" that they used to bake the family's bread. The salad was dressed with olive oil and served with pungent smoked herring. "It was a much-anticipated meal," she told me.

Vegetables cooked in a fireplace or on the barbecue take on an incomparable smoky aroma, but you can achieve a similar effect if you cook them, wrapped in foil, in the oven and then let them scorch a little under the broiler or on a griddle.

Serve as a side dish with grilled meat, poultry or fish or as a main course, with juicy olives, cheese or cured fish and a mixed green salad.

6 medium baking potatoes, scrubbed

4 medium red onions, unpeeled

6 tablespoons extra-virgin olive oil

1/4 cup dry red wine

2–3 tablespoons red wine vinegar or Greek sweet vinegar (see Sources, page 285)

1 tablespoon fennel seeds, preferably freshly ground or crushed in a mortar

Freshly ground black pepper

Salt

2–3 sprigs pickled samphire or 3 tablespoons capers, preferably salt-packed, rinsed well

Preheat the oven to 400°F.

Wrap each potato and onion separately in aluminum foil. Bake for 1 hour, or until cooked through and fork-tender.

Turn the oven to broil. Carefully unwrap the potatoes and onions and place them on a baking sheet. Broil about 4 inches from the heat source for 4 minutes, or until the skins start to scorch. Turn and broil for 4 to 5 minutes more. Remove from the oven, cover the baking sheet with foil and let stand for 5 minutes.

In a small bowl, whisk together the oil, wine, vinegar, fennel and plenty of pepper. Set aside.

Carefully peel the onions and potatoes, leaving some of the charred skin intact. Halve the onions and cut each half into 3 or 4 wedges. Quarter the potatoes lengthwise and halve each quarter crosswise. Place on a serving platter and sprinkle with salt to taste.

Whisk the dressing again and pour it over the vegetables. Add the samphire or capers, cover the platter with foil and let stand for 5 minutes to blend the flavors. Serve warm.

CHIOS

LOUVIA ME LAHANA

Warm Black-Eyed Pea and Swiss Chard Salad

MAKES 4 SERVINGS

1½ cups dried black-eyed peas, picked over and rinsed (see Note)

1 pound Swiss chard, stems chopped, leaves cut into 1-inch-wide strips (keep the stems and leaves separate)

Salt

3–4 tablespoons freshly squeezed lemon juice

Extra-virgin olive oil

Freshly ground black pepper

1 tablespoon chopped fresh oregano

Place the peas in a medium saucepan, add cold water to cover by 2 inches and bring to a boil. Cook for 5 minutes; drain. Add fresh water to just cover the peas and bring to a boil. Reduce the heat to low, cover and simmer for 20 minutes, or until the peas are tender. Check often and add a little more water if needed.

Add the chard stems and salt to taste and simmer for 4 minutes more. You should have about 1½ cups broth; if you have more, increase the heat briefly to reduce. Add the chard leaves and cook for 2 minutes more, or until wilted. Add the lemon juice, stir and remove from the heat. Drizzle with oil and sprinkle with pepper to taste. Taste to adjust the seasonings.

Serve warm in bowls, sprinkled with the oregano, if desired.

NOTE: Instead of cooking dried black-eyed peas, you can use a 16-ounce can of black-eyed peas, drained. Combine them with the chard and 1½ cups vegetable broth.

~~~~~~~~~~~~~~~~~~~~~~~~~~~~

I LOVE the simplicity of this wonderful mix of dried peas and greens. When Marios Mourtzis, a well-known Cypriot chef and cooking teacher, offered to prepare this warm salad for me in the large kitchen of his cooking school in Nicosia, I didn't think it would be anything exceptional. But the clear taste of the chard against the sweet, meaty beans, accented by the sourness of the lemon and the fruitiness of the raw olive oil, made it perfect. A classic Lenten dish, it can also be transformed into a substantial meal with the addition of some pork. Any leftover beans, Marios told me, can be sautéed with onions or garlic the next day.

Serve at the beginning of a meal or as a side dish with grilled meat or fish. The savory juices are delicious, so I like to serve this in bowls with spoons. Although it can be eaten at room temperature, I think that it is one of the few Greek dishes which really is best finished at the last moment and served warm.

MAVROMATIKA FASSOLIA SALATA

Black-Eyed Pea Salad with Herbs, Walnuts and Pomegranates

MAKES 4 TO 6 SERVINGS

2 cups dried black-eyed peas, picked over and rinsed (see Note on the previous page)

5–6 tablespoons extra-virgin olive oil

3–4 tablespoons freshly squeezed lemon juice

3 tablespoons coarsely ground walnuts

1 garlic clove, minced

Salt and freshly ground black pepper

^{1}/$_2$ cup torn purslane (optional; see Note)

^{1}/$_2$ cup coarsely chopped fresh flat-leaf parsley

^{1}/$_2$ cup coarsely chopped arugula

^{1}/$_4$ cup pomegranate seeds

PURSLANE

Place the peas in a medium saucepan, add cold water to cover by 2 inches and bring to a boil. Cook for 5 minutes; drain. Add fresh water to just cover the peas and bring to a boil, then reduce the heat to low, cover and simmer for 20 to 30 minutes, or until the peas are tender. Drain and let cool to room temperature.

In a small bowl, whisk together the oil, lemon juice, walnuts, garlic and salt and pepper to taste.

In a serving bowl, combine the peas, purslane (if using), parsley and arugula. Pour the dressing over them and toss well. Taste to adjust the seasonings, sprinkle with the pomegranate seeds and serve.

NOTE: If omitting the purslane, increase the amount of parsley and arugula to ^{3}/$_4$ cup each.

THIS SALAD, accented by crunchy, slightly sour purslane and sweet pomegranates, comes from the island of Chios. It probably originated in Turkey, where more than a million Greeks lived up until 1922, when they had to abandon their homes and return to the mainland as refugees after the last Greek-Turkish war.

PATZARIA KE AMBELOFASSOLIA ME SKORDALIA

Beets and Green Beans with Skordalia

MAKES 4 SERVINGS

THIS garlic-scented combination of beets and green beans is served on many islands during Lent. On other occasions, you will find it accompanying fried salt cod, fried anchovies or other humble fish. The *skordalia* (garlic sauce) in this particular version is quite mild and creamy, like garlicky mashed potatoes. Traditionally, this salad is made with *ambelofassolia*, young black-eyed peas in their pods, which are much prized in Greece because of their meaty flavor. Unfortunately, they are not readily available in the United States, although you can occasionally get them in Asian markets, so I have substituted green beans or Chinese long beans.

Serve as a first course or as a side dish with grilled or fried fish.

3 large potatoes, halved

GARLIC SAUCE

2 ½-inch-thick slices sturdy white bread, crusts removed, soaked in water until softened, and squeezed dry

½ cup blanched whole almonds, soaked in water for at least 2–3 hours, or preferably overnight, and drained

3–5 tablespoons freshly squeezed lemon juice

3 garlic cloves
  Salt

¼ cup extra-virgin olive oil
  Freshly ground black pepper

5 beets, cooked in boiling salted water until tender, peeled and sliced

1 pound green beans or Chinese long beans, cooked in boiling salted water until just tender, and drained

2–3 tablespoons red wine vinegar or Greek sweet vinegar (see Sources, page 285)

Extra-virgin olive oil

3 scallions (green parts only), thinly sliced

In a large saucepan of boiling water, cook the potatoes until tender, about 30 minutes. Drain and mash the potatoes. Set aside.

MEANWHILE, MAKE THE GARLIC SAUCE: Place the bread, almonds, 1 to 2 tablespoons of the lemon juice, the garlic and salt to taste in a food processor and process into a smooth paste.

In a medium bowl, combine the almond mixture, potatoes, oil, the remaining 1 to 2 tablespoons of the lemon juice and pepper to taste. Taste and adjust the seasonings. If the sauce is too thick, stir in a few tablespoons of water.

TO ASSEMBLE: Mound the garlic sauce in the middle of a serving platter and arrange the beet slices around one side of it and the beans on the other. Sprinkle the vegetables with the vinegar and drizzle oil over the garlic sauce. Sprinkle with the scallions and serve.

VARIATION

Instead of beans, you can use steamed broccoli.

ASTYPALAIA

KOLOKYTHIA ME SKORDO KE LADI

Braised Zucchini with Garlic and Olive Oil

MAKES 4 TO 6 SERVINGS

16 very small, tender zucchini (about
  1$\frac{1}{2}$ pounds total)
  Salt
$\frac{1}{3}$ cup olive oil
4–5 garlic cloves, slivered
$\frac{1}{2}$ cup water
$\frac{1}{4}$ cup dry white wine
1 teaspoon freshly ground black pepper
$\frac{1}{2}$–1 teaspoon dried oregano, crumbled

THIS simple dish, flavored with lots of garlic, comes from the island of Corfu. It should be made only when fresh, tender zucchini are available. Serve with any kind of grilled or roasted meat or poultry. I also love to eat the zucchini by themselves, with fresh crusty bread to dip in the sauce and some good feta cheese.

Trim the zucchini, halve them lengthwise and cut crosswise in half. Salt them generously and let drain in a colander for at least 30 minutes. Pat dry with a paper towel.

In a large skillet, heat the oil and sauté the garlic and zucchini over high heat for 5 minutes, tossing often. Add the water, wine, pepper and salt to taste, reduce the heat to medium and cook for 15 minutes, shaking the pan a few times, until the zucchini is tender and the liquid has evaporated. Taste and adjust the seasonings.

Sprinkle with the oregano and serve warm or at room temperature.

FAGITO ME MARATHO
Stewed Fennel and Onions

MAKES 4 TO 6 SERVINGS

About ³/4 cup olive oil

4 cups diced stale whole wheat, sourdough or multigrain bread

2 large onions, halved and thickly sliced into half-moons

4 fennel bulbs, trimmed (fronds and tender stalks reserved), halved and cut into ¹/4-inch-thick slices

¹/2 cup sweet white wine, such as Samos or any sweet Muscat

¹/2 cup water

1 tablespoon fennel seeds, preferably freshly ground or crushed in a mortar

Salt and freshly ground black pepper

1 cup chopped fennel fronds plus tender stalks, or fresh dill

WHEN Maria Primikiri from Folegandros gave me the recipe for this wild fennel stew, which is served over fried bread, I immediately loved the idea. The fragrant wild fennel that grows all over the Greek islands is mostly used as an herb to add aroma to various vegetable, meat and fish dishes. Because wild fennel is not easily found in the United States, I substituted regular fennel bulbs, including their tops, and added fennel seeds, creating almost the same flavorful dish.

Serve on its own, with feta cheese, or as a side dish for grilled fish.

In a large nonstick skillet, heat about ¹/4 cup of the oil and fry the diced bread in batches until golden on all sides, about 20 minutes, adding more oil if needed. Drain on paper towels. Set aside.

In a large skillet, heat the remaining ¹/2 cup oil and sauté the onions over medium heat for 5 minutes, or until soft. Add the fennel bulbs and sauté for 4 minutes more. Add the wine and simmer for 30 seconds. Add the water, fennel seeds and salt and pepper to taste. Reduce the heat to low and simmer for 10 minutes, or until the fennel is tender and most of the liquid has evaporated.

Reserve 2 tablespoons of the fennel fronds or dill for the garnish, add the remainder to the pan and cook for 2 minutes more. Taste and adjust the seasonings.

Place the fried bread on a serving platter, spoon the stewed fennel over it and sprinkle with the reserved 2 tablespoons fennel fronds or dill. Serve warm or at room temperature.

TSIGARELLI

Stewed Mixed Greens from Corfu

MAKES 4 SERVINGS

THE MAIN ingredients of this peasant dish, which is spiced with plenty of dried hot red peppers, are various seasonal wild greens gathered from the hills. You can make it with any combination of spinach and bitter greens. On Corfu, this peppery dish is called *tsigarelli*, and it also includes fresh or canned tomatoes, as does my version. It is also served as a topping for Polenta with Currants and Onions (page 162).

With the addition of Arborio rice, it becomes a delicious risotto that can be eaten warm or at room temperature.

Serve with plenty of fresh country bread and feta cheese. *Tsigarelli* can also accompany grilled meat, poultry or fish.

$2/3$ cup olive oil

2 leeks, trimmed, thinly sliced, washed well and drained

10–12 green garlic stalks (white plus most of the green parts), thinly sliced, or 4 large garlic cloves, coarsely chopped

2 pounds greens with stems (spinach and bitter greens, such as dandelion and mustard greens; sorrel and the outer green leaves of any kind of lettuce, such as romaine, butterhead or green leaf; amaranth shoots and turnip greens; or broccoli rabe, Swiss chard and frisée), leaves coarsely chopped, stems finely chopped (separate the leaves and stems)

1–3 teaspoons Aleppo pepper or $1/2$–1 teaspoon crushed red pepper flakes

2 large ripe tomatoes, cored and diced, or 1 cup canned diced tomatoes with their juice or 1 cup water

1 teaspoon salt

1 cup medium-grain rice, such as Arborio (optional)

$2^1/2$ cups boiling water or Chicken Stock (page 267; optional)

1 cup coarsely chopped fresh flat-leaf parsley

1 cup coarsely chopped arugula
Freshly ground black pepper

2 lemons, quartered

In a large, deep skillet, heat the oil and sauté the leeks and green garlic, if using, for 5 to 8 minutes, or until the leeks are soft. If you are using garlic cloves, add them now and cook for 1 minute more; do not let them color. Add the stems of the greens and the Aleppo pepper or pepper flakes. Sauté for 1 minute, stirring, then add the tomatoes or water and salt. Reduce the heat to low and simmer for 10 minutes. Add the greens and cook for 10 minutes more.

If you are using rice, add it along with the 2 1/2 cups water or stock and simmer, stirring often, until the rice is al dente, about 20 minutes.

Add 1/2 cup each of the parsley and arugula and simmer for 5 to 10 minutes more, or until most of the juices have evaporated. If the sauce is still watery, cook for 2 to 3 minutes over high heat to reduce it.

Stir in the remaining 1/2 cup each parsley and arugula, and taste and adjust the seasonings, adding a few grindings of black pepper. Serve warm or at room temperature, with the lemon wedges.

YAHNERA

Greens and Potatoes from Crete

MAKES 4 SERVINGS

½ cup olive oil

2 leeks, trimmed, thinly sliced, washed well and drained

2 medium onions, coarsely chopped

4–5 scallions (white and most of the green parts), thickly sliced

1 fennel bulb, trimmed (fronds and tender stalks reserved) and coarsely chopped

3–4 medium potatoes, cut into ¼-inch-thick slices

1 teaspoon fennel seeds, preferably freshly ground or crushed in a mortar

2 pounds spinach, sorrel, Swiss chard or other nonbitter greens

1½ cups water

1½ teaspoons salt

Freshly ground black pepper

4–5 tablespoons freshly squeezed lemon juice

1 cup chopped fennel fronds plus tender stalks, or fresh dill

Extra-virgin olive oil for drizzling (optional)

IN CRETE, a stew similar to the Corfu dish of steamed greens and tomatoes is made with sweet and tart greens, such as tender pea shoots, sow thistle, wild spinach, sorrel, wild leeks and lots of wild fennel fronds. Freshly squeezed lemon juice gives zest to the stew. Potatoes are often added. On both Crete and Corfu, artichoke bottoms and peeled artichoke stems are included when available.

In a large skillet, heat the oil over medium heat and sauté the leeks for 5 to 8 minutes, or until soft. Add the onions, scallions, fennel bulb, potatoes and fennel seeds and stir to coat with the oil, then add the greens. Sauté for 2 minutes, then add the water, salt and pepper to taste. Reduce the heat to low and simmer for 10 to 15 minutes, or until the greens and potatoes are tender and most of the juices have evaporated. If the sauce is still too watery, cook for 2 to 3 minutes over high heat to reduce it.

Add 4 tablespoons lemon juice and ½ cup of the fennel fronds or dill, and taste and adjust the seasonings. Cook for 2 to 3 minutes more, then sprinkle with the remaining ½ cup fennel fronds and drizzle with the oil, if using, and toss. Serve warm or at room temperature.

LAHANIDES ME PASPALA

Collard Greens with Pancetta

MAKES 4 TO 6 SERVINGS

Salt

2 pounds collard greens or kale

¼ cup olive oil

6 ounces pancetta, diced

3 garlic cloves, minced

1 teaspoon Aleppo pepper or pinch of crushed red pepper flakes

2–3 tablespoons Greek sweet vinegar (see Sources, page 285) or balsamic vinegar

In a large pot of boiling salted water, blanch the greens for 5 to 8 minutes, or until just tender. Drain, rinse under cold running water to stop the cooking, and drain well. Coarsely chop the greens.

In a large skillet, heat the oil and sauté the pancetta over medium heat until crisp. Add the garlic and pepper or pepper flakes and sauté for 30 seconds. Add the greens and sauté, stirring, for 3 minutes, or until coated with oil and hot. Add the vinegar, toss and taste to adjust the seasonings. Serve warm.

THE GREENS originally called for in this recipe are *lahanides*, the small green leaves with thick stems that grow around a head of cabbage. They are the cheapest vegetables in the Greek market—a certified food of the poor. But although they're very tasty, my mother would never think of buying them, because she associates them with the days of starvation during the Nazi occupation, when they were one of the few foods available.

This recipe comes from Santorini, which was once one of the poorest islands. Only in the past decade has the land on this island come to cost as much as that on New York's Park Avenue. My friend Katerina Vassiliadou, whose mother comes from the village of Kamari, described this dish to me. It's a delicious winter food, in which home-cured pork, garlic and olive oil flavor the greens. Substituting collards or kale for *lahanides* and pancetta for the pork makes the dish even better.

Serve it on its own, with feta or manouri cheese and fresh country bread, or as a side dish with grilled poultry or pork.

BAMIES ME DOMATA STO FOURNO
Baked Okra in Tomato Sauce

MAKES 4 TO 6 SERVINGS

I OWE this recipe to Christina Panteleimonitis, a wonderfully creative woman. Together with Dimitris, her husband, she has set about to preserve the old local recipes and the traditional way of milling wheat on Lesbos. The two have restored an old water mill, which they call Mylelia ("a small mill," in the dialect of Lesbos), at Ippios, a village on the southern part of the island. With the tasty flour they mill there, they make *trahana* (see page 148) and other pastas. Christina has also encouraged the village women on both Lesbos and Chios to make their best jams and pickles, which she helps distribute to Athenian gourmet shops.

This was one of the dishes served to the participants of the 1999 International Food Conference, the "Magic of the North Aegean," organized by Oldways Preservation and Exchange Trust. Christina had asked women from the nearby villages to come to the mill and prepare their specialties. This baked okra dish was my favorite.

Greek okra is tiny and tender, quite different from the American variety, so I had to make a few adaptations. To prevent it from becoming slimy, Greeks toss the okra with salt and vinegar and let it sit in the sun for a while, then rinse it off and dry it. Leaving it in a warm oven has almost the same effect.

Serve warm or at room temperature, with crusty bread and feta cheese, or as a side dish with grilled meat or poultry. You can also bake okra with chicken or veal or even with fish fillets, as people do on Crete.

1½ pounds small okra (no longer than 3 inches), tops trimmed

Salt

⅓ cup red wine vinegar

½ cup olive oil

1½ cups coarsely chopped onions

1½ cups grated ripe tomatoes (see page 27) or canned diced tomatoes with their juice

1 teaspoon Aleppo pepper or pinch of crushed red pepper flakes

1 cup chopped fresh flat-leaf parsley

Pinch of sugar

Freshly ground black pepper (optional)

Preheat the oven to 200°F.

Place the okra in a single layer in a baking dish. Sprinkle with 1½ tablespoons salt, drizzle with the vinegar and toss well.

Place in the oven and bake for 20 minutes. Rinse the okra under cold running water and pat dry with paper towels. Increase the oven temperature to 400°F.

In a large skillet, heat ¼ cup of the oil and sauté the okra in two batches over high heat until it starts to color, about 5 minutes. Transfer to the baking dish and set aside.

Add the remaining ¼ cup oil to the skillet and sauté the onions over medium heat until translucent, about 4 minutes. Add the tomatoes, Aleppo pepper or pepper flakes and salt to taste and cook until the mixture starts to thicken, about 10 minutes. Add all but 3 tablespoons of the parsley and the sugar. Taste and adjust the seasonings, adding some black pepper, if desired.

Pour the sauce over the okra and bake until tender, about 30 minutes. Let cool for 15 to 20 minutes. Sprinkle with the reserved 3 tablespoons parsley and serve warm or at room temperature.

BRIAMI ME MARATHO
Baked Mixed Vegetables with Fennel

MAKES 4 SERVINGS

2 medium eggplants, cut into
    1½-inch chunks

  Salt

6 zucchini, cut into 1-inch pieces

3 green bell peppers, cored, quartered,
    seeded and cut into ½-inch pieces

3 large tomatoes, cored and coarsely diced

2 large onions, coarsely diced

2 fennel bulbs, trimmed (fronds and
    tender stalks reserved) and coarsely
    chopped, or 1½ cups chopped wild
    fennel

5 garlic cloves, sliced

1 cup olive oil

1 tablespoon fennel seeds, preferably
    freshly ground or crushed in a mortar

1–2 teaspoons Aleppo pepper or ½–1
    teaspoon crushed red pepper flakes

1 teaspoon dried oregano, crumbled

  Freshly ground black pepper

3 tablespoons chopped fennel fronds
    plus tender stalks, or fresh dill

AS IN MOST of the Cyclades, wild fennel grows all over the island of Kea. Unless you grow herbs in your garden, it is the only local herb there is; parsley, dill and other herbs are brought from Athens. Sweet, fragrant wild fennel is exquisite, so I try to use it as much as I can. Living on Kea, I came up with this recipe for baked mixed vegetables that I think is better than the version with parsley.

Baked vegetables are a classic summer dish, eaten warm or at room temperature, ideal for picnics and summer buffets. In the United States, where wild fennel is not readily available, you can get almost the same taste by using a combination of fennel bulb and seeds. The vegetables need plenty of olive oil, but most of it is left at the bottom of the pan, although it is delicious with fresh crusty bread.

Serve these vegetables on their own, with bread and feta cheese, or as a side dish with grilled meat or poultry.

Place the eggplant in a colander and sprinkle generously with salt. Let stand for 30 minutes. Rinse and pat dry with paper towels.

Meanwhile, preheat the oven to 400°F.

In a large baking dish, combine the eggplant, zucchini, bell pepper, tomatoes, onions, fennel bulb or wild fennel, garlic, oil, fennel seeds, Aleppo pepper or pepper flakes, oregano and salt and black pepper to taste. Toss well.

Bake for 40 minutes, or until the vegetables are tender, tossing once after 20 minutes. The tops will probably char a little, but this caramelizes the vegetables and makes them sweeter.

Sprinkle with the fennel fronds or dill and serve warm or at room temperature.

DOMATES GEMISTES
Stuffed Tomatoes

12 medium ripe but firm tomatoes

1 cup olive oil

3 cups chopped onions

1 fennel bulb, trimmed and finely chopped

1 tablespoon fennel seeds, preferably freshly ground or crushed in a mortar

1 cup Arborio rice

1 cup chopped fresh flat-leaf parsley

1 cup chopped fresh dill

1/2 cup chopped fresh mint

1 1/2 teaspoons salt, plus more to taste

Freshly ground black pepper

1 medium potato, scrubbed, halved crosswise and each half quartered

KALLIOPI DELIOS, who, together with her husband, owns the taverna Castro in Avgonyma, Chios, makes delicious stuffed tomatoes. She uses plenty of wild fennel, along with fresh mint from her garden, as well as dill. Arborio rice is a good substitute for the medium-grain Greek rice used in all sorts of stuffings. You can prepare these tomatoes a day in advance and keep in the refrigerator, let them come to room temperature before serving.

Fragrant and sweet, stuffed tomatoes are delicious when accompanied by feta cheese and fresh crusty bread.

Preheat the oven to 375°F.

Cut off the top 1/2 inch of each tomato; set aside the tops. Using a grapefruit spoon, very carefully remove as much pulp as possible from each tomato, without piercing the skin. Chop the pulp. Measure out 2 1/2 cups; freeze the rest for another use, if desired.

In a large skillet, heat 2/3 cup of the oil and sauté the onions and fennel bulb over medium heat for 5 minutes, or until soft. Add the fennel seeds and rice and sauté, stirring, for 2 to 3 minutes. Add 2 cups of the tomato pulp, reduce the heat to low and cook, stirring, for 3 minutes more. Stir in the parsley, dill and mint and cook for 2 minutes more. Remove from the heat and add the salt and plenty of pepper.

Stuff the tomatoes with the rice mixture, leaving a little room for the stuffing to expand, and cover with the tomato tops. Place the tomatoes in a 13-x-9-inch baking dish and arrange the potato pieces in the gaps between the tomatoes. Pour the remaining 1/2 cup tomato pulp over everything and drizzle the tomatoes with the remaining 1/3 cup oil. Sprinkle with salt and pepper to taste.

Bake for 1 hour, or until the rice is tender (lift the cover of a tomato and check). Turn off the oven and let stand in the oven for 10 minutes, then let cool to room temperature. Serve 1 or 2 tomatoes and a couple of potato pieces on each plate.

AGINARES ME LEMONI KE SKORDO

Artichokes Marinated in Wine, Olive Oil, Lemon and Garlic

MAKES 8 SERVINGS

1½ quarts cold water

2 lemons, quartered, plus about ⅓ cup freshly squeezed lemon juice

20 baby artichokes with stems

½ cup extra-virgin olive oil

8 scallions (white and most of the green parts), thinly sliced

4 garlic cloves, coarsely chopped

1½ cups dry white wine

1 cup chopped fresh dill

Salt and freshly ground black pepper

IN THIS versatile dish from Tinos, the acidity of the sauce is a good contrast to the sweetness of the artichokes. You can serve these artichokes as an appetizer or as a side dish with lamb, poultry or fish. They keep very well in the refrigerator.

Fill a bowl with the water and squeeze the juice from the lemon quarters into it; reserve the lemon quarters. Trim the stem of each artichoke to about 1 inch. Snap off the bottom three rows of leaves, rubbing the cut surfaces frequently with the lemon quarters as you work. Cut off the tip of each artichoke. Halve each artichoke and rub generously with the lemon quarters. Using a knife or a grapefruit spoon, remove the choke from the center of each artichoke. Place each prepared artichoke in the bowl of lemon water.

In a large, deep skillet, heat ¼ cup of the oil and sauté the scallions over medium heat for 3 to 4 minutes, or until soft. Add the garlic and sauté for 1 minute more; do not let it color. Add the artichokes, wine, the remaining ¼ cup oil and wa-ter to cover. Bring to a boil, reduce the heat to medium and cook for 10 minutes, or until the artichokes are almost tender. Add ½ cup of the dill, 2½ tablespoons of the lemon juice and salt and pepper to taste and cook for 5 minutes more. Taste and adjust the seasonings, adding more lemon juice if necessary. The artichokes should have a distinct lemon flavor. Remove from the heat and let the artichokes cool in the liquid.

Sprinkle with the remaining ½ cup dill and serve at room temperature. (You can store the artichokes in the liquid in the refrigerator for up to 1 week. Let come to room temperature before serving.)

PATATES ANTINAKTES
New Potatoes with Coriander Seeds and Wine

MAKES 4 TO 6 SERVINGS

3 pounds waxy new potatoes

$^1/_3$ cup olive oil

1 tablespoon coriander seeds, coarsely crushed in a mortar or spice grinder

Salt

$^2/_3$ cup sweet red wine, such as Mavrodaphne or sweet Marsala

$^2/_3$ cup dry rosé or white wine

3 tablespoons chopped fresh cilantro or flat-leaf parsley

Freshly ground black pepper

SOME years ago, in Nicosia, I remember watching Marios Mourtzis, a Cypriot chef and cooking teacher, smash uncooked new potatoes with the palm of his hand as he explained how to cook this dish. Smashing raw potatoes is not easy—they may end up flying all over your kitchen. It is better to smash them half-cooked. Marios explained to me that the name *antinaktes* comes from an ancient Greek verb meaning "to throw something up in the air," describing the way the potatoes are tossed during cooking. Chefs will certainly toss the potatoes, but you don't need to.

This is an extremely simple Cypriot dish, fragrant with crushed coriander. In Cyprus, they also cook small taro roots in the same way.

Serve with grilled meat or poultry, or with Veal Stew with Coriander Seeds (page 132).

Soak the potatoes in cold water for 10 to 15 minutes. Scrub very well to clean and remove most of the skin. Dry with paper towels.

In a large, deep skillet with a lid, heat the oil. Add only as many potatoes as will fit in a single layer without crowding, cover and cook over medium heat for 10 minutes. Turn the potatoes, cover again and cook for 6 minutes more. With a slotted spoon, transfer the potatoes to a plate and cook the next batch. Set the skillet aside.

One at a time, place each potato on a cutting board and press with the side of a large knife or with a spatula just until the potato cracks—it should keep its shape.

Return all the potatoes to the skillet, set it over high heat and add the coriander seeds and salt to taste. When the potatoes begin to sizzle, add the wine—be careful, because it will bubble vigorously. Cover, reduce the heat to medium and cook for 2 to 3 minutes more. Toss or stir well, reduce the heat to low, cover and simmer for 10 to 12 minutes more, or until the potatoes are cooked through.

Add the cilantro or parsley and pepper to taste and serve at once.

PATATES RIGANATES
Roasted Potatoes with Garlic, Lemon and Oregano

MAKES 4 TO 6 SERVINGS

FEW PEOPLE can resist these potatoes, which are capable of stealing the show from any food they accompany—so make sure you have plenty for seconds. Although it is served all over Greece, this dish is particularly good on islands like Naxos, where the local potatoes have an exceptional taste. On the special days when a leg of lamb or a chicken is roasted, the potatoes are cooked in its juices.

If you want to cook this dish using small potatoes, there is no need to peel them, but I suggest that you halve them, because they taste best when they can absorb more sauce.

3 pounds baking potatoes, peeled and cut into 1½-inch cubes

½ cup olive oil

4 garlic cloves, minced

1½ teaspoons dried oregano, crumbled

1 teaspoon salt
  Freshly ground black pepper

½ cup beef stock or Chicken Stock (page 267)

⅓ cup freshly squeezed lemon juice

2–3 tablespoons chopped fresh oregano

Preheat the oven to 400°F.

Place the potatoes in a single layer in a 13-x-9-inch baking dish and pour the oil over them. Add the garlic, dried oregano, salt and pepper to taste and toss well to coat with the oil.

Bake the potatoes for 15 minutes. Add the stock, toss and bake for 10 minutes more. Add the lemon juice, toss and bake for 10 to 15 minutes more, or until the potatoes are cooked through. If you like, preheat the broiler and broil the potatoes for 2 to 3 minutes, or until golden brown.

Sprinkle with the fresh oregano and serve at once.

VARIATION

Dissolve 1 tablespoon tomato paste in the stock, and reduce the amount of lemon juice to taste. Substitute Aleppo pepper or crushed red pepper flakes for the black pepper.

ARAKAS LEMONATOS ME PATATES KE KAROTA

Peas, Potatoes and Carrots in Olive Oil–Lemon Sauce

MAKES 6 TO 8 SERVINGS

2/3 cup olive oil

1 cup coarsely chopped onions

1 fennel bulb, trimmed, quartered and thinly sliced

1 pound potatoes, cut into 1$\frac{1}{2}$-inch cubes

2 pounds fresh or three 10-ounce packages frozen green peas

2 cups Chicken Stock (page 267) or water

3 carrots, peeled and cut into 1-inch-thick slices

1 teaspoon fennel seeds, preferably freshly ground or crushed in a mortar

Salt and freshly ground black pepper

1/3 cup freshly squeezed lemon juice

1/2 cup chopped fresh dill

In a Dutch oven, heat 1/3 cup of the oil and sauté the onions over medium heat for 2 minutes. Add the fennel bulb and sauté for 5 minutes, or until soft. Add the potatoes and sauté for 4 minutes more.

Add the peas, 1$\frac{1}{2}$ cups of the stock or water, the carrots, fennel seeds and salt and pepper to taste. Bring to a boil, reduce the heat to low, cover and simmer for 15 minutes. Add the remaining 1/2 cup stock or water, the lemon juice, the remaining 1/3 cup oil and 1/4 cup of the dill and stir to distribute evenly. Cook for 10 minutes more, or until the vegetables are tender. Taste and adjust the seasonings.

If the sauce is too watery, increase the heat and boil to reduce it. Sprinkle with the remaining 1/4 cup dill and serve warm or at room temperature.

VARIATION

You can substitute fresh fava beans or green beans for the peas. You can also halve the amount of peas and add 3 or 4 artichokes (see page 200 for preparation instructions), quartered.

ON THE islands, this classic vegetable stew is seasoned with wild fennel. In this recipe, the fresh dill added at the end of cooking contributes an extra dimension to the sweet and lemony flavor of the vegetables.

Serve as a main dish, with feta or manouri cheese and fresh country bread, or as a side dish with grilled meat, poultry or fish.

DELLAGRACIANO
Eggplant and Cheese Casserole with Onions, Peppers and Tomatoes

MAKES 6 SERVINGS

DELLAGRACIA, or Posidonia, as the place is called today, is a village on the island of Syros where the wealthy inhabitants built summer villas at the end of the nineteenth century. This dish takes its name from that civilized resort, where one can still admire beautiful Italianate mansions with lovely gardens next to unsuccessful imitations of central European castles.

Probably created by a French-inspired cook at one of these summer residences, this casserole is a marriage between a cheese soufflé and eggplant Parmesan. It is important to use at least two different cheeses: the cooks of Syros prefer to mix San Michali—a hard aged cow's milk cheese, one of the best of its kind in Greece—with a smoother aged Fontina-type cheese that is also produced on the island. In this recipe, given to me by my friend Stefania Gianisi, an excellent cook from Syros, I have substituted aged cheddar, pecorino Romano and Parmigiano-Reggiano or grana for the original cheeses to achieve a similar taste. But you can also use all kinds of other leftover semi-firm or hard cheeses. I chop the hard parts near the rind in my food processor, as well as any other dried-out cheeses I may have, and store them in a plastic bag in my freezer to use in dishes like this one.

Stefania suggests basil as a seasoning, but I prefer the combination of rosemary and oregano. Choose smaller eggplants, because they are usually sweeter.

4–5 small eggplants (about 1 pound total), cut into ½-inch-thick rounds

Salt

2–3 tablespoons olive oil

SAUCE

⅓ cup olive oil

1½ cups thinly sliced onions

2 green bell peppers, cored, seeded and diced

5 garlic cloves, thinly sliced

⅔ cup sweet red wine, such as Mavrodaphne or sweet Marsala

2 cups grated ripe tomatoes (see page 27) or canned diced tomatoes with their juice

1 tablespoon fresh rosemary or 1 teaspoon dried, crumbled

1 teaspoon Aleppo pepper or pinch of crushed red pepper flakes

1 teaspoon dried oregano, crumbled

¼ cup toasted bread crumbs

1 cup finely diced aged cheddar cheese

1 cup grated pecorino Romano cheese

¼ cup grated Parmigiano-Reggiano or grana cheese

½ cup grated cheddar cheese

²/₃ cup yogurt, preferably sheep's milk

3 large eggs

¹/₃ cup whole milk

¹/₄ cup grated Parmigiano-Reggiano cheese
Freshly ground black pepper

Generously salt the eggplant and let drain in a colander for 1 hour. Rinse under cold running water and pat dry with paper towels.

Preheat the broiler.

Place the eggplants in a single layer on a baking sheet and brush on both sides with oil. Set the baking sheet about 5 inches from the heat source and broil, turning once, until golden, about 5 minutes per side. (You may need to do this in batches.)

Preheat the oven to 400°F.

MAKE THE SAUCE: In a large skillet, heat the oil and sauté the onions for 4 minutes, or until soft. Add the bell peppers and sauté for 3 minutes more. Add the garlic and sauté for 1 minute. Add the wine and simmer for 1 minute, then add the tomatoes, rosemary, pepper or pepper flakes and oregano. Reduce the heat to low and simmer until the sauce has thickened, about 12 minutes. Remove from the heat.

Oil a 9-inch-square baking dish and sprinkle the bottom with 2 tablespoons of the bread crumbs. Scatter ¹/₂ cup of the diced cheddar and ¹/₂ cup of the pecorino Romano over the crumbs. Layer half of the eggplant slices over the cheese. Pour half of the sauce over the eggplant, and scatter ¹/₄ cup of the pecorino Romano, the Parmigiano-Reggiano or grana and ¹/₄ cup of the grated cheddar over it. Make another layer with the remaining eggplant slices. Pour the rest of the sauce over the eggplant and sprinkle with the remaining ¹/₄ cup each cheddar and pecorino Romano.

MAKE THE CUSTARD TOPPING: In a medium bowl, whisk together the yogurt, eggs and milk. Add the cheese and pepper to taste. Pour over the casserole. Make several incisions with a knife all the way through the eggplant and let stand for 15 minutes to allow the custard to soak into the casserole.

Sprinkle the top of the casserole with the remaining 2 tablespoons bread crumbs and bake for 45 minutes, or until the custard is puffed and set. Turn the oven to broil and broil the casserole for 2 to 3 minutes, or until golden.

Let stand for at least 20 minutes before serving.

THE POWERFUL MYSTERIES OF BREAD

Greek women believe that bread rises by divine intervention. If you tell them that a batter of flour and water will ferment from the various airborne microorganisms if left for a few days, they refuse to believe it. They are certain that only the direct power of God can turn a mere flour batter into a leavening medium. This is the reason why *prozymi*, the natural sourdough starter used in traditional baking, is always made either on September 14—the day the Greek Orthodox Church celebrates the discovery of the cross on which Jesus was crucified—or near the end of Holy Week, preceding Easter. On both occasions, some plants or flowers are added to the flour and water mixture.

If the *prozymi* is started around Easter, the mixture contains a handful of the flowers that have been used to decorate the *Epitaphios*—a representation of Jesus' coffin decorated with flowers, which is paraded through the streets in the solemn funeral-like procession on Good Friday evening. If the dough is mixed on the Day of the Cross, a sprig of basil is included in the *prozymi* batter—not just any sprig, but one taken from the bunch the priest has used to sprinkle the congregation with holy water. According to Greek religious myths, fragrant basil was the plant growing around the Holy Cross, a sign that allowed Saints Constantine and Helen to distinguish Jesus' cross from among the many others in the area. To commemorate the event, women bring pots of aromatic small-leafed basil plants that they have grown with much care all through the summer to the church on the eve of the holiday. (Considered a sacred plant in Greece, basil is generally not used in cooking, although on the islands in the Ionian Sea, one can occasionally find it in some dishes.)

Much secrecy surrounds the making of *prozymi*. I have asked many women on various islands to describe the process and received only vague answers: "You mix a few handfuls of flour with some lukewarm tle. The dried flowers of hops, the plant used in making beer, worked wonders.

The island women who still keep the tradition and bake bread regularly will tell you that they have almost forgotten when they first started their *prozymi* or who gave them the initial piece of dough starter. They make sure to save a piece of the dough every time they make bread and usually have another one in the freezer as a backup.

Unfortunately, as bakeries spring up like mushrooms all over the islands, the quality of the bread is decreasing sharply. Very few bakers still get up early to make bread the traditional way and let it rise for 5 to 6 hours, as they once did. Even the breads baked in traditional-looking wood-burning ovens on the islands are made using premixed flours (no flowers!) and fast-acting yeasts that make the dough rise in a mere hour. The results are far from divine—tasteless, insubstantial loaves that can be enjoyed only when still warm.

With the aid of the Old Dough Starter on page 210, you can make sturdy, complexly flavored breads that keep well. In addition to these traditional breads, this chapter also contains recipes for small ricotta-stuffed sweet breads, savory cheese muffins and focaccia-like flatbreads topped with olive oil, onions and tomatoes or with olives and mint. You'll also find crunchy bread rings and savory biscuits, which make delicious snacks and can be stored for months.

water, add the blessed basil or the *Epitaphios* flowers and, because the mixture is blessed, after a while"—they never say how long exactly—"the mixture starts to develop little bubbles. Then you gradually add flour for the next couple of days, and your *prozymi* is ready."

Peasant and educated women alike insist that without the blessed additions, the mixture of flour and water will not ferment to become *prozymi*. Some of the women I talked to specified that the flour for starter is all-purpose white flour bought from the supermarket, distinguishing it from the *starenio*, used in the bread itself. *Starenio* means "wheat flour," but the term has come to mean the locally ground yellowish hard flour, once very common in the islands, especially those of the northern Aegean. The wheat for *starenio* is now grown primarily in central mainland Greece, and the flour is available at the central markets of the large cities and in some old-fashioned grocery stores all over the country.

I tried adding sprigs of basil and different flowers to the mixture of flour and water, thinking that they might speed up the process of fermentation, as do grapes. Basil made no difference, but some of the flowers did. Wild marigolds, the purple flowers of a gigantic thistle that looks like a miniature artichoke and a few others seemed to quicken the fermentation a lit-

HALOUMOTES
Savory Cheese and Mint Muffins

MAKES ABOUT 36 SMALL MUFFINS

2$\frac{1}{2}$ cups all-purpose flour

4 teaspoons baking powder

1 teaspoon ground mahlep (see page 279) or $\frac{1}{2}$ teaspoon mahlep plus $\frac{1}{2}$ teaspoon ground mastic (see page 279)

$\frac{2}{3}$ cup safflower oil

4 large eggs

1 cup milk

2 cups grated haloumi cheese (about 9 ounces)

$\frac{1}{2}$ cup grated cheddar, preferably aged

1 tablespoon dried mint or $\frac{1}{3}$ cup chopped fresh mint

$\frac{1}{2}$ teaspoon freshly ground white pepper (see Note)

Preheat the oven to 400°F. Oil three dozen mini muffin cups.

Sift the flour together with the baking powder and mahlep or mahlep and mastic into a medium bowl. In a large bowl, with an electric mixer, beat the oil and eggs until foamy. Beat in the milk, cheeses, mint and white pepper. Add the flour mixture and stir with a wooden spoon to incorporate. You will have a stiff batter.

Spoon the batter into the prepared muffin tins, filling each cup only two-thirds full. Bake for about 35 minutes, or until the muffins are puffed and golden and a toothpick inserted in the center comes out clean.

Let cool in the tins for about 10 minutes on a rack, then unmold. Serve warm or at room temperature.

THESE aromatic muffins from the beautiful island of Cyprus are extremely easy to make and illustrate the merging of various traditions. Cyprus, off the coast of Syria, has an age-old Greek heritage. Under English domination for about 100 years, until 1960, Cyprus is now an independent country, struggling to overcome its problems with Turkey, which has occupied the northern part of the island since 1974.

The foods of Cyprus are wisely spiced, mixing the best of the Eastern and Western traditions. These small savory cakes are probably based on an old recipe for cheese bread made with haloumi, the traditional and versatile cheese of Cyprus. The cheese bread evolved into muffins, no doubt inspired by the English tradition. My friend Niki Bahariou, an excellent Cypriot cook, introduced me to *haloumotes* and gave me her recipe, explaining that she and her friends like to serve them warm with afternoon tea.

You can also serve them at room temperature. They're perfect for brunch and for children's parties. Although I prefer the muffins, you can bake *haloumotes* in a regular cake pan as one long loaf.

NOTE: If you plan to serve *haloumotes* as a *meze*, with drinks, substitute 1 to 1$\frac{1}{2}$ teaspoons Aleppo pepper or $\frac{1}{2}$ to $\frac{3}{4}$ teaspoon crushed red pepper flakes for the white pepper.

PROZYMI APO PALIA ZYMI
Old Dough Starter

MAKES ABOUT 2 POUNDS, ENOUGH FOR 2 LOAVES OF BREAD

GREEK BAKERS save a piece of the raw dough each time they bake to use as the leavening for the next batch of bread. As they usually bake at least once a week, they are never without a piece of starter (*prozymi*), and in the unlikely event they run out of it, a friend or neighbor can lend them a piece.

In the old days, the starter was always kept in a special clay jar and became quite sour. It also dried out and needed to be soaked in warm water before it could be incorporated into a new dough. Today, the starter is stored in the refrigerator, well sealed, where it will keep for up to 7 days, or it can be frozen for up to 6 months.

To make a dough starter from scratch, you prepare a basic yeast dough for a white bread, divide it and keep it until needed. Because I like my starter slightly sour, I make it at least a week before I will be baking and keep it in the refrigerator. Or, if I've frozen it, I take it out of the freezer, let it rise at room temperature for 4 to 5 hours and, if I don't plan to use it immediately, I refrigerate it again for up to 2 days.

$^1/_2$ cup warm water
$1^1/_2$ teaspoons active dry yeast
$3^1/_2$ cups all-purpose flour
2 teaspoons coarse sea salt or kosher salt
   About $1^1/_4$ cups cold water

In a small bowl, combine the warm water and yeast and let stand for 5 minutes, or until frothy.

Place the flour and salt in a food processor. With the motor running, pour in the yeast mixture and enough cold water to make a soft, sticky dough. Let the dough rest for 15 minutes.

Process the dough for 1 to 2 minutes more, or until slightly sticky and elastic. Lightly oil a large bowl and a piece of plastic wrap.

Turn the dough out onto a lightly floured surface and knead it briefly. Shape the dough into a ball and transfer it to the oiled bowl. Cover with the oiled plastic wrap and let rise in a warm spot until doubled in volume, 2 to 3 hours.

Turn the dough out onto a lightly floured surface and divide it in half. Place each piece in an oiled bowl large enough to allow it to double. Cover with oiled plastic wrap and refrigerate for up to 7 days. Or flatten each piece (or just one) into a disk, wrap in aluminum foil, place in a zipper-lock bag and freeze for up to 6 months.

When you are ready to use it, take the starter out of the refrigerator and let it come to room temperature, at least 2 hours. Or let frozen starter stand at room temperature for at least 4 hours before using.

ELIOPSOMO ME DIOSMO

Olive and Mint Bread

MAKES 18 SQUARES

- 4 teaspoons active dry yeast
- 1 teaspoon sugar
- 1 cup warm water
- 3 1/2–4 cups all-purpose flour
- 1 tablespoon coarse sea salt or kosher salt
- 2 tablespoons extra-virgin olive oil
- 1/2 cup Kalamata olives, pitted and chopped
- 2 tablespoons dried mint
- 2 tablespoons chopped fresh flat-leaf parsley

TOPPING

- 3 tablespoons extra-virgin olive oil
- 1 teaspoon unsalted butter
- 1 medium onion, diced
  Coarse sea salt or kosher salt and freshly ground black pepper
- 2 tablespoons chopped fresh flat-leaf parsley
- 2 tablespoons chopped fresh mint

INSPIRED BY the traditional olive breads of Cyprus, Chef Jim Botsacos created this focaccia-like bread. Molyvos's patrons can't seem to get enough of it. It's excellent as an accompaniment to cheeses or *meze* or simply enjoyed on its own.

Combine the yeast, sugar and water in the bowl of a food processor and pulse to blend. Add 3 1/2 cups flour, salt and oil and process until well combined. Add the olives, mint and parsley and process until the dough forms a smooth ball. If it is too wet, add a little more flour; if it is too dry, add 1 to 2 tablespoons water.

Lightly oil a large bowl and a piece of plastic wrap. Place the dough in the bowl, cover with oiled plastic wrap and let rise in a warm place until almost doubled in volume, 45 minutes to 1 hour.

Turn the dough out onto a lightly floured surface and shape it into a ball. Return it to the bowl, lightly brush it with oil, cover with the oiled plastic wrap and let rise slowly in a cool place, until light and airy, about 45 minutes.

MEANWHILE, MAKE THE TOPPING: Heat 1 tablespoon of the oil in a medium skillet over medium heat. Add the butter and heat until it foams. Add the onion and cook, stirring, for 5 to 6 minutes, or until golden brown. Season with salt and pepper to taste. Remove from the heat and set aside to cool.

Place the dough in an oiled 13-x-9-inch baking pan and stretch it evenly over the bottom so it reaches the edges on all sides. Brush it lightly with the remaining 2 tablespoons oil and sprinkle it with the onion, parsley and mint. Let rise in a warm spot until nearly doubled in volume, about 1 hour.

At least 20 minutes before baking, preheat the oven to 425°F. Bake the bread on the center oven rack for 35 to 40 minutes, or until golden brown. Let cool on a rack, then cut into squares.

PSOMI NISIOTIKO
Whole Wheat and Barley Bread

MAKES 1 LOAF

$^1/_3$ cup warm water

1 teaspoon active dry yeast

$1^1/_2$ teaspoons aniseeds

1 teaspoon mahlep (see page 279)

3 cardamom pods (optional)

$^1/_2$ recipe Old Dough Starter (page 210)

$2^1/_2$–3 cups all-purpose flour

$1^1/_2$ cups whole wheat flour

1 cup barley flour (see Sources, page 285)

1 tablespoon coarse sea salt or kosher salt

About 2 cups cold water

In a small bowl, combine the warm water and yeast and let stand for 5 minutes, or until frothy.

In a mortar or spice grinder, finely grind the aniseeds, mahlep and cardamom, if using.

Place the starter, flours, salt and spice mix in a food processor and pulse to blend. With the motor running, pour in the yeast mixture and $1^2/_3$ cups cold water to make a soft, sticky dough. Let the dough rest in the food processor for 15 minutes.

BASIL

THERE are almost as many different breads on the islands as there are households. Island women never measure their ingredients when making bread, and they often vary the ingredients according to what they have available. Inspired by the breads I have tasted on Kea, Astypalaia, Limnos, Paros, Crete and many other islands, I developed this one. It is dense and quite heavy. Cardamom gives it an unusual aroma. The dough will not double in volume when it rises, but it expands in the oven. Have faith, and you will be rewarded in the end.

Process the dough for 1 to 2 minutes more, or until slightly sticky and elastic (add a little water if the dough is too stiff).

Lightly oil a large bowl and a piece of plastic wrap. Turn the dough out onto a lightly floured surface and knead it briefly, adding a little more flour as needed until the dough is soft and elastic. Shape the dough into a ball and transfer to the oiled bowl. Cover with the oiled plastic wrap and let rise until 1 1/2 times its original volume, 4 to 5 hours.

Turn the dough out onto a lightly floured surface and shape into an 8-x-11-inch oval or an 8-inch round. Place in a well-oiled oval baking dish or a 9-inch round cake pan, cover with the oiled plastic wrap and let it rise for 2 1/2 hours. (It won't rise much.)

At least 20 minutes before baking, preheat the oven to 450°F.

With a wet, very sharp knife or a baker's razor, make 3 diagonal slashes in the surface of the dough. Bake for 15 minutes, then reduce the oven temperature to 400°F. Bake for 45 minutes more. Wearing oven mitts and using a spatula, remove the bread from the pan and place it directly on the oven rack. Bake for 10 minutes more, or until the bread sounds hollow when you tap it on the bottom.

Let cool completely on a rack before slicing.

ARKATENIO OR EFTAZYMO
Chickpea-Leavened Bread from Cyprus

MAKES ONE 10-INCH LOAF

THIS DELICIOUS, fragrant bread is leavened using fermented chickpeas rather than the piece of starter dough that is part of most traditional Greek breads. The word *eftazymo* means "kneaded seven times," but it does not actually describe the process of making the bread. Many scholars believe that the first part of the word is not *efta* (seven), but instead a phonetic variation of the prefix *auto*, referring to bread that rises by itself.

The only baker who makes this chickpea starter on a large scale is Yannis Argyrakis from Chios. He invited me into his workshop there but warned me that he wasn't going to reveal his secrets. "It's like a diamond bracelet that you can't let everybody know you have," he told me.

Traditionally, the starter is made from a handful of coarsely crushed chickpeas that are soaked in warm water and kept at a more or less constant warm temperature for 7 to 12 hours, until a thick froth forms on the surface of the water. This froth—and sometimes the crushed chickpeas, depending on the cook—is mixed with flour. Village women usually begin the process in the afternoon, placing the peas in a covered clay pot that they nestle under lots of blankets. One woman from Cyprus told me that she wraps a woolen shawl around the well-sealed jar of crushed chickpeas and water and holds it between her thighs all night long. Other women get up a couple of times in the middle of the night to add warm water to the pot of chickpeas, especially during cold winter nights.

Fortunately, today we have the means to keep the chickpeas at a constant temperature—either in a low oven or under an electric blanket—and that, as I found out, is the key to the success of the starter.

STARTER

- 1½ cups chickpeas, preferably organic
- 2 cups all-purpose flour

- 2½–3 cups all-purpose flour
- ½ cup whole wheat flour
- 2 teaspoons Bread Spice Mix (page 270)
- ½ teaspoon freshly grated nutmeg
- ½ teaspoon ground ginger
- 1 teaspoon coarse sea salt or kosher salt
  About ⅔ cup warm water
  Nigella seeds (optional)

MAKE THE STARTER: Place the chickpeas in a large bowl and add water to cover by 4 inches. Let stand for at least 6 hours, or overnight.

Drain the chickpeas and pulse a few times in a food processor to coarsely grind them. Return the chickpeas to the bowl and add warm (100°F) water to cover by 2 inches. Set the oven on low (warm) and place the bowl in the oven, or surround the bowl with an electric blanket. Let stand for 12 to 18 hours, or until a thick foam forms on the surface of the liquid.

In a large bowl, combine the foam and 1½ cups of the liquid with the 2 cups white flour. Cover the bowl with plastic wrap and place in the oven set to its lowest temperature or under the blanket for about 3 hours.

Remove the starter from the oven or blanket and let stand for 4 to 5 hours more, or until tripled in size.

Place 2½ cups all-purpose flour, the whole wheat flour, spice mix, nutmeg, ginger and salt in a food processor and pulse to combine. With the motor running, pour in the starter and ½ cup of the water and process for about 30 seconds. Let the dough rest in the processor for 15 minutes.

Process the dough for about 2 minutes more, or until smooth and a little sticky (add a little water if the dough is too stiff).

Oil an 8- or 9-inch round pan and a piece of plastic wrap. Transfer the dough to a lightly floured surface and knead for 3 to 4 minutes, adding a little more all-purpose flour as needed until the dough is soft and elastic. Shape the dough into a loaf and place in the pan. If you like, place the dough in a 6-cup loaf pan and slash it deeply with a wet knife at 1-inch intervals. Cover with the oiled plastic wrap and place in the oven set to its lowest temperature. Let rise for 2 to 3 hours, or until doubled in size. Remove the plastic wrap and sprinkle the dough with the nigella seeds.

With the bread still inside, preheat the oven to 400°F.

Bake for 45 minutes. Wearing oven mitts, take the bread out of the pan and place it directly on the oven rack. Bake for 10 minutes more, or until it sounds hollow when tapped on the bottom.

Let cool on a rack before slicing.

NOTE: To make savory chickpea biscuits, break off pieces of the bread after it cools completely and place them on the oven rack. Bake for 45 minutes more in a warm (175°F) oven, or until completely dry.

KALITSOUNIA ANEVATA
Cheese-Filled Breads

DOUGH

- 1/3 cup warm water
- 2 teaspoons active dry yeast
- 4½–5 cups all-purpose flour
- 2–3 teaspoons aniseeds or fennel seeds
- 2 teaspoons coarse sea salt or kosher salt
- ¾ cup milk
- ¼ cup olive oil
- 2 large eggs, lightly beaten

FILLING

- 1 pound sheep's milk ricotta (see Sources, page 285, or see Note), drained for 1 hour in a cheesecloth-lined colander
- 2 large egg yolks
- 3 tablespoons honey, preferably thyme honey
- 1½ teaspoons ground cinnamon

Milk

- 3 tablespoons nigella seeds or a combination of nigella and sesame seeds

MAKE THE DOUGH: In a small bowl, combine the water and yeast and let stand for 5 minutes or until frothy.

In a food processor, place 4½ cups flour, aniseeds or fennel seeds and salt. Reserve 1 tablespoon of the beaten eggs for brushing the bread and, with the motor running, add the yeast mixture, milk, eggs and oil to the flour mixture. Process for 2 to 3 minutes, or until dough forms a ball and cleans the sides of the bowl.

Oil a large bowl and a piece of plastic wrap. Turn the dough out onto a lightly floured surface and knead it for 2 to 3 minutes, adding more flour as needed until the dough is soft and elastic. Shape the dough into a ball. Place it in the oiled bowl and cover with the oiled plastic wrap. Let rise until doubled in volume, 45 minutes to 1 hour.

THESE stuffed breads are a traditional Easter confection. They are prepared on Sitia, on Crete, with fresh sheep's and goat's milk myzithra. By slightly altering the filling, they can be turned from sweet to savory (see the variation).

Both kinds are excellent for breakfast or for a snack. Serve the savory cheese breads with a vegetable dish, such as Greens and Potatoes from Crete (page 194), or as part of a *meze* spread.

MAKE THE FILLING: Squeeze the cheesecloth to release all the moisture. In a food processor, place the ricotta, egg yolks, honey and cinnamon and process until combined.

Lightly oil a large baking sheet. Turn the dough out onto a lightly floured surface and divide it into 12 equal pieces. Shape each piece into a ball and flatten it with your hands into a 7-inch round. Place about 3 tablespoons of the filling in the center of each round. Fold one edge over the filling to envelop it, brush the edge with some milk and fold the opposite edge over it. Now fold over the top and bottom, brushing the edges with milk, to make a square. Place the breads seam side down on the oiled baking sheet. Brush with the reserved 1 tablespoon beaten egg and sprinkle with the seeds. Let rise for 40 minutes, until almost doubled in volume.

At least 20 minutes before baking, preheat the oven to 400°F.

Bake the breads for about 40 minutes, or until golden brown. Transfer to a rack and let cool completely before serving.

NOTE: If you can't get sheep's milk ricotta, mix 2/3 pound regular ricotta with 1/3 cup heavy cream. Line a strainer with cheesecloth and set it over a large bowl. Add the ricotta mixture and let drain for 1 hour. Gather the cheesecloth around the cheese and squeeze out the moisture.

VARIATION
ALMYRA KALITSOUNIA ANEVATA
Savory Cheese and Dill Filled Breads

Instead of the honey and cinnamon in the filling, add 1/2 cup chopped fresh dill, 1/2–1 teaspoon salt and 1/2–1 teaspoon freshly ground white pepper. If you like, sprinkle the *kalitsounia* with sesame seeds instead of nigella seeds. Shape and bake the breads as directed.

LEFKADITIKO PSOMI TOU GAMOU
Wedding Bread from Lefkas

MAKES 1 LOAF

1/2	cup warm water
3	tablespoons honey
1/2	teaspoon active dry yeast
1	tablespoon fennel seeds
2	teaspoons aniseeds
1	teaspoon coriander seeds
1/2	recipe Old Dough Starter (page 210)
3–3 1/2	cups all-purpose flour
1/4	cup olive oil or melted unsalted butter
1	large egg
1	teaspoon coarse sea salt or kosher salt
	About 2/3 cup cold water
	Milk

In a small bowl, combine the warm water, honey and yeast and let stand for 5 minutes, or until frothy.

In a mortar or spice grinder, coarsely grind the fennel seeds, aniseeds and coriander seeds.

In a food processor, combine the starter, 3 cups flour, oil or butter, egg, honey mixture, ground spices and salt. With the motor running, pour in 1/2 cup cold water to make a soft, sticky dough. Add a little more water if the dough is too stiff. Let the dough rest in the food processor for 15 minutes.

Process the dough for 1 to 2 minutes more, or until slightly sticky and elastic.

THE TASTE, aroma and especially the shape of this bread from Lefkas, one of the smaller islands in the Ionian Sea, are remarkable. Like all festive breads, it is not supposed to be cut but pulled apart. Instead of being baked in a loaf, the dough is divided into pieces, with each one shaped into a twist and baked next to one another. As the dough rises, the twists come together but, once baked, they are easily pulled apart. Serve with fresh cheese such as ricotta, manouri or Gorgonzola, or with butter and jam.

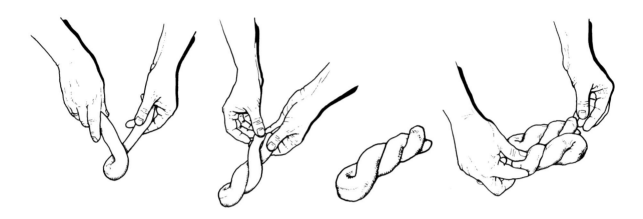

Lightly oil a large bowl and a piece of plastic wrap. Turn the dough out onto a lightly floured surface and knead briefly, adding more flour as needed until the dough is smooth and elastic. Shape the dough into a ball and transfer to the oiled bowl. Cover with the oiled plastic wrap and let rise until doubled in volume, 2 to 3 hours.

Oil a baking sheet. Turn the dough out onto a lightly floured surface and divide it into 4 pieces, then divide each piece into quarters. Roll 1 of the pieces into a 20-inch-long rope. Fold the rope in half, twist it and place on the oiled baking sheet (see illustrations). Repeat with a second piece of dough, placing the second twist next to the first, with its folded end beside the loose ends of the previous twist. Repeat with the rest of the dough to make a rectangular loaf composed of adjoining twists. Cover with oiled plastic wrap and let rise for 30 minutes.

At least 20 minutes before baking, preheat the oven to 450°F. Remove the plastic wrap and brush the dough with milk.

Bake the bread for 10 minutes. Reduce the oven temperature to 400°F and bake for 35 minutes more, or until light golden on top. Wearing oven mitts, carefully remove the bread from the baking sheet and place it directly on the oven rack. Bake for 15 to 20 minutes more, or until the bread is browned on top and sounds hollow when tapped on the bottom. Transfer to a rack and cool completely before pulling apart into pieces.

VARIATION

The same bread can be turned into delicious biscuits. Separate baked twists and rebake them on a baking sheet in a 300°F oven for 20 to 30 minutes, or until completely dry. Stored in an airtight container, they will keep for months.

ARTOS APO TA KYTHERA
Festive Bread from Kythera

MAKES 1 LARGE ROUND LOAF

~~~~~~

THIS IS one of the best breads I have ever eaten. It has a complex aromatic flavor that reminds me of one of my favorite sweets, *melomakarona*, the honey cookies prepared traditionally at Christmas. It's ideal for breakfast, spread with butter and honey or marmalade, or eaten as dessert with cheese, and it makes excellent toast and bread puddings. This recipe comes from Eleni Kalligerou, the most accomplished baker on Kythera.

In modern Greek, the word *artos* is reserved for various semi-sweet and flavored breads that are associated with religious occasions. The breads are baked at home and then taken to church to be blessed, where they are sliced and distributed to the parishioners in a special ceremony. The Kythera bread contains olive oil, some of the local red wine and orange zest, and it is sweetened with the local thyme honey and spiced with cinnamon and cloves. Since sourdough bread rises very slowly, Eleni told me that she finishes kneading it in the evening and lets the dough rise till the next morning. "But it all depends on the weather and the wind," she said, "so I get up and check during the night. Once I had to fire the oven at four in the morning."

In my recipe, the combination of dough starter and yeast makes for a completely predictable bread, so there is no need for you to bake in the wee hours.

You will need a pizza stone or unglazed oven tiles and a spray bottle, such as a plant mister. The bread keeps well for about 1 week.

SPONGE

- $1/4$ cup warm water
- $1/2$ teaspoon active dry yeast
- $2^1/2$ cups all-purpose flour or 2 cups all-purpose flour plus $1/2$ cup barley flour
- 1 teaspoon coarse sea salt or kosher salt
  About $2/3$ cup room-temperature water

BREAD

- $1/4$ cup warm water
- $1/2$ teaspoon active dry yeast
  About $2/3$ cup room-temperature water
- 4–$4^1/2$ cups all-purpose flour
- 2 tablespoons grated orange zest
- 1 tablespoon coarse sea salt or kosher salt
- 1 teaspoon ground cinnamon
- $1/4$ teaspoon ground cloves
- $1/2$ cup honey, preferably thyme honey
- $1/3$ cup dry red wine
- $1/4$ cup olive oil
  Cornmeal
- $1^1/4$ cups coarsely chopped walnuts (optional)
- $1/2$ cup chopped dried Calimyrna figs (optional)

MAKE THE SPONGE: Oil a large bowl and a piece of plastic wrap. In a small bowl, combine the warm water and yeast and let stand for 5 minutes, or until frothy.

In a large bowl or a food processor, combine the flour or flours, yeast mixture, salt and room-temperature water and stir or process, adding more water if needed, until a soft, sticky dough forms.

With floured hands, shape the dough into a ball and transfer to the oiled bowl. Cover with the oiled plastic wrap and let rise until doubled in volume, about 3 hours. The sponge is now ready to be used, but it can be refrigerated for up to 3 days. Remove from the refrigerator about 1¹/2 hours before baking. If you don't plan to bake the bread within 3 days, punch down the sponge to flatten it, wrap it in oiled plastic wrap, place in a zipperlock bag and freeze for up to 3 months. Remove from the freezer at least 4 hours before baking.

MAKE THE BREAD: In a small bowl, combine the warm water and yeast and let stand for 5 minutes, or until frothy.

In a food processor, combine the sponge, yeast mixture and ¹/2 cup room-temperature water and process until smooth. Transfer to a medium bowl.

Clean the bowl of the food processor. In the processor, combine 4 cups flour, orange zest, salt, cinnamon and cloves and process until combined. With the motor running, pour in the sponge mixture, honey, wine and oil and process until a soft, sticky dough forms, adding more water if necessary if the dough is too stiff. Do not overwork the dough.

Turn the dough out onto a lightly floured surface and knead with floured hands until smooth, elastic and only slightly sticky, about 5 minutes, adding more flour if necessary.

Oil a large bowl and a piece of plastic wrap. Shape the dough into a ball and transfer to the oiled bowl. Cover with the oiled plastic wrap and let rise until doubled in volume, about 3 hours.

Generously sprinkle a pizza peel with cornmeal. Combine the walnuts and figs in a small bowl, if using. On a floured work surface, press the dough into a 12-x-10-inch rectangle. Sprinkle the walnut mixture evenly over it. Fold the two long sides into the center, overlapping them to cover the walnut mixture. Fold the other two sides into the center and fold over to form a 6-x-5-inch rectangle, pinching the seams to seal. If not using the nuts and figs, shape the dough into a round loaf.

Transfer to the pizza peel. Cover with oiled plastic wrap and let rise until almost doubled in volume, about 2 hours.

CYPRUS

About 1 hour before baking, place a pizza stone on the bottom oven rack or line with four to six unglazed tiles and preheat the oven to 450°F.

About 15 minutes before baking, place an empty roasting pan on the bottom rack of the oven. In a medium saucepan, bring about 1½ quarts water to a boil.

With a single-edged razor blade or a very sharp knife held perpendicular to the loaf, slash an X about 5 inches long and ½ inch deep in the top of the dough, being careful not to cut too near the edge of the loaf. Sprinkle the stone or tiles with cornmeal and carefully slide the bread onto the stone or tiles. Immediately pour the boiling water into the roasting pan (it will steam vigorously) and close the oven door. After 1 minute, open the door and spray the bread three times with water. Close the door and bake for 2 minutes, then repeat the spraying. Bake for 10 minutes more, reduce the oven temperature to 375°F and bake for 35 to 45 minutes more, or until the bread is browned on top and sounds hollow when tapped on the bottom.

Transfer the bread to a rack and cool completely before slicing.

CHIOTIKO PSOMI
Chian Bread

MAKES ONE 10-INCH ROUND BREAD

2 teaspoons active dry yeast

1²/₃ cups warm water

3 cups stone-ground whole wheat bread flour

1 tablespoon coarse sea salt or kosher salt

1¹/₂ teaspoons coarsely ground aniseeds

1¹/₂ teaspoons crushed coriander seeds

2-3 teaspoons nigella seeds (optional)

In a small bowl, combine the yeast and ¹/₃ cup of the water and let stand for 5 minutes, or until frothy.

Put the flour, salt, aniseeds and coriander in a food processor and pulse to mix. With the motor running, pour in the yeast mixture and the remaining 1¹/₃ cups water. Let the dough rest for 12 to 15 minutes.

Process the dough for 2 to 3 minutes more, stopping once or twice to scrape the dough from the sides. The dough will not form a ball and will remain wet and sticky.

Generously oil a 10-inch round cake pan or a springform pan and a piece of plastic wrap. With a rubber spatula, scrape the dough into the pan. Cover with the oiled plastic wrap and let rise until 1¹/₂ times its original volume, for about 2 hours. Remove the plastic wrap and sprinkle with the nigella seeds.

At least 20 minutes before baking, preheat the oven to 450°F.

Bake the bread for 10 minutes, then reduce the heat to 375°F and continue baking for 40 minutes more. Using oven mitts, carefully remove the bread from the pan and place directly on the oven rack. Bake for 5 to 10 minutes more, or until it sounds hollow when tapped on the bottom.

Let cool completely on a rack before slicing.

THIS HEAVY, chewy bread is made entirely with stone-ground hard flour. It's a simplified version of a traditional Chian bread that I saw made by the women in Pirgi, the fortified village on southern Chios. They began not with flour but with whole wheat berries. They ground the grains in an old-fashioned grain mill and made a wet dough with the quite coarse whole wheat flour (it looked more like cake batter than bread dough). They mixed the dough with their starter and stirred in some crushed coriander seeds and aniseeds before pouring it into a round pan, then left it to rise for about six hours. It didn't rise much, but it did puff up in the oven. It was one of the tastiest breads I've ever had.

LADOKOULOURA
Crisp Savory Bread Rings

MAKES 32 BREAD RINGS

2 cups water

2 cinnamon sticks

10 cloves

2³/4 teaspoons active dry yeast

1¹/2 teaspoons aniseeds

1 tablespoon mastic (see Sources, page 285)

1 tablespoon coarse sea salt or kosher salt

4–4¹/2 cups all-purpose flour

¹/2 cup olive oil

¹/3 cup nigella seeds or sesame seeds, or a combination

In a medium saucepan, combine the water, cinnamon sticks and cloves and bring to a boil. Boil for about 5 minutes, or until reduced to about 1¹/2 cups. Let cool to barely warm; discard the spices.

In a small bowl, combine ¹/3 cup of the warm spiced water and the yeast and let stand for 5 minutes, or until frothy.

In a mortar, coarsely grind the aniseeds. Transfer them to a small bowl. Grind the mastic and salt together.

In a food processor, combine the flour, yeast mixture, aniseeds, mastic mixture and the remaining spiced water and pulse until well combined. With the motor running, add the oil and process until the dough forms a ball and cleans the sides of the bowl.

Oil a large bowl and a piece of plastic wrap. Turn the dough out onto a lightly floured surface and knead, adding more all-purpose flour if necessary, until smooth and elastic, 2 to 3 minutes. Transfer the dough to the oiled bowl, cover with the oiled plastic wrap and let rise until doubled in volume, 1¹/2 to 2 hours.

SERVE these savory bread rings with cheese or dips or on their own as snacks. They are similar to the *taralli* of southern Italy and the traditional oil cookies baked in most Sephardic Jewish communities. The original recipe is believed to have come from Sfakia, Crete. On Kalamata, in the southern Peloponnese, similar bread rings are fried in olive oil rather than baked. The dough is very easy to make, and the shaping, although somewhat time-consuming, is not complicated. For an easier, quicker version, form the dough into biscotti instead of rings, as described in the variations.

The bread rings keep well for about 6 months stored in airtight containers.

Oil two large baking sheets. Place the nigella or sesame seeds on a plate. Divide the dough into 4 pieces, then divide each piece into 8 pieces.

Work with 1 piece of dough at a time, keeping the remaining dough covered with plastic wrap. On a lightly floured surface, roll each piece of dough into a 9-inch-long rope, shape into a ring, pressing the ends together to seal, and lightly press one side of the ring into the seeds. Place the rings seeded side up and about 1 inch apart on the oiled baking sheets. Let rise for 30 minutes, until almost doubled.

At least 20 minutes before baking, preheat the oven to 375°F.

Bake the rings on the upper and lower racks of the oven for 5 minutes. Reduce the oven temperature to 350°F and bake for 10 minutes more. Switch the positions of the baking sheets and bake for 10 to 15 minutes more, or until the rings are pale golden with a hard crust.

Reduce the oven temperature to warm (175°F) and move a rack to the middle of the oven. Using oven mitts and a spatula, place the rings directly on the middle rack, overlapping them if necessary. Bake until the bread rings are completely dry, $1\frac{1}{2}$ to 2 hours. Transfer to racks and cool completely. Store in airtight containers for up to 6 months.

SAVORY BISCOTTI

Divide the dough in half and shape it into 2 logs. Place on a baking sheet and, with a metal spatula, slash them on the diagonal at $\frac{1}{2}$-inch intervals, cutting almost all the way through. Bake for 30 minutes. Cut the biscotti apart and bake in a warm oven until completely dry, about $1\frac{1}{2}$ hours.

SWEET BREAD RINGS

Reduce the amount of salt to 1 teaspoon and add $\frac{1}{3}$ cup honey to the warm spiced water. Proceed as instructed.

KOULOURIA ME MAIDANO KE MARATHO

Crisp Parsley and Fennel Bread Rings

MAKES 40 BREAD RINGS

- 1/3 cup plus 2 tablespoons olive oil
- 1 cup packed coarsely chopped fresh flat-leaf parsley
- 1/2 cup packed coarsely chopped fennel fronds plus tender stalks, or fresh dill
- About 1 cup water
- 1 tablespoon coarsely ground fennel seeds
- 2 cups all-purpose flour
- 1 teaspoon active dry yeast
- 1 teaspoon coarse sea salt or kosher salt
- 1/2 teaspoon freshly ground white pepper

I FIRST tasted these crunchy, spicy bread rings in a bakery in Chania, on Crete. They are an ideal accompaniment to wine. You can also serve them with a soft cheese, such as cottage or farmer's.

In a large skillet, heat 2 tablespoons of the oil and sauté the parsley and fennel fronds or dill over medium heat until just wilted, about 2 minutes. Transfer to a food processor, add 1/2 cup of the water and the fennel seeds and process until smooth. Transfer the parsley mixture to a medium bowl, and clean the food processor bowl.

Combine the flour, yeast, salt and pepper in the food processor and pulse to blend. With the motor running, pour in the parsley mixture and the remaining 1/3 cup oil, then slowly add enough of the remaining 1/2 cup water so a soft dough forms. Process until it forms a ball and cleans the sides of the bowl.

Oil a large bowl and a piece of plastic wrap. Turn the dough out onto a lightly floured surface and knead, adding more all-purpose flour if necessary, until smooth and elastic, about 3 minutes. Transfer the dough to the oiled bowl, cover with the oiled plastic wrap and let rise in a warm spot until doubled in volume, 1 1/2 to 2 hours.

Oil 3 or 4 baking sheets. Turn the dough out onto a lightly floured surface and divide it into 4 pieces. Divide each piece into 10 pieces. Work with 1 piece of dough at a time, keeping the remaining dough covered with plastic wrap. Roll each piece into a 7-inch-long rope and shape it into a ring, pressing the ends together to seal. Place rings on oiled baking sheets, about 1 inch apart. Let rise for 30 minutes, until almost doubled.

At least 20 minutes before baking, preheat the oven to 350°F.

Bake the rings in batches for 25 minutes, or until light golden and hard. Transfer to racks and let cool. Stored in airtight containers, they will keep for up to 3 months.

KOULOURIA TIS FOLEGANDROS
Bread Rings from Folegandros

MAKES 16 BREAD RINGS

$^1/_2$ cup warm water

$^1/_2$ teaspoon active dry yeast

$^1/_2$ recipe Old Dough Starter (page 210)

$3^1/_2$–4 cups all-purpose flour

1 tablespoon coarse sea salt or kosher salt

$^1/_2$ cup olive oil or $^1/_4$ cup olive oil plus $^1/_4$ cup safflower oil

About $^2/_3$ cup cold water

1 large egg white, lightly beaten

$^1/_2$ cup sesame seeds

THE DOUGH for these crunchy bread rings is enriched with olive oil. In Kythera, the same dough is shaped into a loaf and deeply slashed before baking; the slices are then taken apart and baked again, until completely dry, to become the famous savory olive oil biscuits of the island.

Serve these with cheese or spreads, such as Blue Cheese and Tomato (page 20) or Eggplant and Parsley (page 22). They're also fine on their own, as a snack.

In a small bowl, combine the warm water and yeast and let stand for 5 minutes, or until frothy.

Place the starter in a food processor, add $3^1/_2$ cups flour, salt, oil and the yeast mixture and pulse a few times. With the motor running, pour in $^1/_2$ cup cold water to make a soft, sticky dough. Let the dough rest for 15 minutes.

Process the dough for 1 to 2 minutes more, or until slightly sticky and elastic (add a little water if the dough is too stiff).

Lightly oil a large bowl and a piece of plastic wrap. Turn the dough out onto a lightly floured surface and knead briefly, adding a little more flour as needed until the dough is soft and elastic. Shape the dough into a ball and transfer it to the oiled bowl. Cover with the oiled plastic wrap and let rise until doubled in volume, 2 to 3 hours.

Lightly oil 3 or 4 baking sheets. Turn the dough out onto a lightly floured surface and divide it into 4 pieces. Cut each piece into quarters. Work with 1 piece of dough at a time, keeping the re-maining dough covered. Roll 1 of the pieces under your palms into a 24-inch-long rope. Press the ends together to form a ring. Transfer to an oiled baking sheet. Continue forming rings with the rest of the dough, placing them at least $^1/_2$ inch apart on the baking sheets. Brush with the egg white and sprinkle with the sesame seeds. Let rise for 30 minutes.

At least 20 minutes before baking, preheat the oven to 450°F.

Bake the rings in two batches for 10 minutes. Reduce the oven temperature to 400°F and bake for 15 minutes more, or until light golden on top. Wearing oven mitts and using a spatula, carefully remove the bread rings from the baking sheets and place them directly on the oven racks. Reduce the oven temperature to 200°F and bake for 15 to 20 minutes more, or until the bread rings are completely dry.

Transfer to racks and let cool completely. They keep for at least 3 months in a tightly covered tin.

PAXIMADIA
Savory Barley and Wheat Biscuits

MAKES SIXTEEN 4½-INCH BISCUITS

THESE crunchy, aromatic biscuits can be enjoyed on their own or served with any kind of cheese, from smooth, creamy ones like ricotta to sharp cheeses like Roquefort. Great with any kind of dip, *paximadia* can be made into a wonderful bread salad by breaking them into pieces and tossing them with chopped tomatoes, crumbled feta, some olives, onion rings, a pinch of oregano and plenty of olive oil.

An old man from Mykonos told me that not so long ago, merchant ships liked his island as a stopover, because there the sailors could stock up on *paximadia*. Similar biscuits are still baked on many islands of the Aegean, with those from Crete being the most popular. Although the generation that traditionally ate this bread has either died or switched to more refined foods, a new generation of consumers who tasted *paximadia* during their summer vacations on the islands is enthusiastically reviving them, and in most Athenian neighborhoods, one can now find them in bakeries.

The recipe is my version of the doughnut-shaped *paximadia* from Crete. They keep for up to 6 months.

About ⅔ cup warm water

2 tablespoons honey

2 tablespoons active dry yeast

1 tablespoon coarse sea salt or kosher salt

1 tablespoon aniseeds

2½ cups barley flour

2–2¼ cups all-purpose flour

½ cup olive oil

½ cup sweet red wine, such as Mavrodaphne or sweet Marsala

½ cup dry red wine

In a medium bowl, combine ⅓ cup of the water, the honey and yeast and let stand for 5 minutes, or until frothy.

In a mortar or a spice grinder, grind the salt and aniseeds into a coarse powder. Place the barley flour, 2 cups all-purpose flour and aniseed mixture in a food processor. With the motor running, pour in the yeast mixture, oil and wines, then add enough of the warm water, about ⅓ cup, to make a soft, sticky dough. Process for 1 minute, or until the dough comes together. Let rest for 15 minutes.

Process the dough for 1 to 2 minutes more, or until smooth and sticky (add more water if the dough is too stiff).

Turn the dough out onto a lightly floured surface and knead for 2 to 3 minutes, or until the dough is soft and only slightly sticky, adding more all-purpose flour as needed. Shape the dough into a ball. Oil it all over with a few drops of oil, place in a large bowl and cover with plastic wrap. Let rise until it has doubled in volume, about 1¹/₂ hours.

Oil two large baking sheets. Cut the dough in half and cut each half into quarters. Work with 1 piece of dough at a time, keeping the remaining dough covered with plastic wrap. Roll each piece into a 1-inch-thick rope, then shape each rope into a ring, overlapping the ends slightly. Pinch to seal and place 1¹/₂ inches apart on the baking sheets. Cover with plastic wrap and let rise until almost doubled, about 2 hours.

At least 20 minutes before baking, preheat the oven to 400°F.

Bake the rings for 10 minutes, then reduce the oven temperature to 375°F and bake for 20 to 30 minutes more, or until they are light golden on top and sound hollow when tapped. Remove from the oven and let cool for 10 minutes. Reduce the oven temperature to warm (175°F).

With a serrated knife, halve the circles horizontally. Place the halves cut side up directly on the oven rack in the middle of the oven, overlapping if necessary, and bake for 1¹/₂ to 2 hours, or until completely dry. Let cool completely and store in airtight containers.

KITRINA KOULOURIA ASTYPALITIKA
Saffron, Allspice and Pepper Biscuits

MAKES ABOUT 56 BISCUITS

EVER SINCE I tasted these bright yellow biscuits in a bakery in Astypalaia about fifteen years ago, I've been addicted to their slightly peppery taste and crunchy texture. When I first sampled them, I was startled by their lightness. The circles were fragrant with allspice, nutmeg and another aroma that I couldn't make out. The baker told me it was saffron that the women of the island collected from the hills each November, especially for these Easter cookies. The fat in the yeasted dough was a creamy *chlori*, the ricotta-like fresh cheese produced by shepherds from the milk of the island's semi-wild goats. It was these cookies that triggered my interest in island cooking. They were so unlike anything else I had ever tasted!

I've experimented with various soft cheeses in the dough, since it's impossible to find anything like the *chlori*. Ordinary ricotta didn't work. My best results were with a combination of yogurt, cream and butter. This baking-powder version, which is a variation on the original yeasted biscuits, produces excellent results quite quickly.

These are great as snacks, with coffee or drinks, and are an ideal accompaniment to soft cheese, both sweet and creamy ones, like manouri and ricotta, and sharp ones, like Gorgonzola, Roquefort or any other blue.

$1/2$ cup milk

$2/3$ teaspoon saffron threads, crumbled

3 tablespoons honey, preferably thyme honey

$3^{1}/2$ cups unbleached all-purpose flour, sifted

1 tablespoon baking powder

1/2 teaspoon coarse sea salt or kosher salt

$1/2$–1 teaspoon freshly ground white pepper

$1/2$ teaspoon ground allspice

$1/2$ teaspoon freshly grated nutmeg

1 cup thick sheep's milk yogurt or Drained Yogurt (page 266)

1 large egg

4 tablespoons unsalted butter ($1/2$ stick), softened

$1/2$ cup half-and-half

$1/4$ cup olive oil or safflower oil

Preheat the oven to 375°F.

In a small saucepan, combine the milk with the saffron threads and simmer gently over low heat for 1 to 2 minutes, stirring, until the milk is deep yellow (the saffron threads won't dissolve completely). Stir in the honey, remove from the heat and let cool.

Combine the flour, baking powder, salt, white pepper, allspice and nutmeg in a large bowl.

In a medium bowl, with an electric mixer, beat the yogurt with the egg and butter until creamy, about 2 minutes. Add the cooled saffron milk, the half-and-half and oil and beat for 1 minute. Add to the flour mixture, stirring with a rubber spatula, to make a soft, oily dough; do not overmix.

Divide the dough in half, and shape each half into a log about 12 inches long; don't worry if the dough isn't perfectly smooth. Place on an ungreased baking sheet about 2 inches apart, and bake for about 30 minutes, until the loaves are firm and the tops are starting to turn golden.

Reduce the heat to 200°F and leave the loaves in the oven for another 10 minutes. Remove from the oven and let cool.

As soon as the logs are cool, slice each into $1/4$-inch-thick slices, using a serrated knife. Place the slices directly on the middle rack of the oven and leave them to dry completely, 1 to $1^1/2$ hours. (You may need to do this in batches.)

Let the biscuits cool completely on racks. Stored in airtight containers, they will keep for up to 6 months.

LADENIA
Tomato and Onion Flatbread

MAKES 4 TO 6 SERVINGS

DOUGH

- ½ cup warm water
- ¼ teaspoon active dry yeast
- ½ recipe Old Dough Starter (page 210)
- 2–2½ cups all-purpose flour
  - 1 teaspoon coarse sea salt or kosher salt
    About ⅔ cup cold water
  - 1 cup whole wheat flour

TOPPING

- ¼ cup olive oil, plus more for drizzling
  - 1 large onion, halved and thinly sliced into half-moons
  - 1 cup drained grated fresh tomatoes (see page 27) or ⅔ cup drained canned diced tomatoes
- 1–2 teaspoons dried savory or oregano, crumbled
  - 1 teaspoon coarse sea salt or kosher salt
    Freshly ground black pepper

MAKE THE DOUGH: In a small bowl, combine the warm water and yeast and let stand for 5 minutes, or until frothy.

Place the starter in a food processor and add 1 cup of the all-purpose flour and the salt. Pour in the yeast mixture and ½ cup cold water and pulse to mix. Add 1 cup of the all-purpose flour and the whole wheat flour and, with the motor running, pour in enough cold water to make a sticky dough that just holds together. Let the dough rest in the food processor for 15 to 20 minutes.

Process the dough for 1 to 2 minutes more (add a little water if the dough is too stiff; it should be smooth and sticky).

WHEN women of the islands fire the oven to bake the week's bread, they also prepare flatbreads, topping them with cheese or seasonal vegetables and herbs and drizzling them with olive oil. More like focaccia than pizza, these breads are found everywhere, in many variations. *Ladenia* is the flatbread baked on Kimolos, and it is topped with onion and tomatoes.

On other islands, in the winter, people often top these flatbreads with pancetta-like cured pork or with chopped sausage. If you like, you can use the dough for Whole Wheat and Barley Bread (page 212) to make this flatbread.

CYPRUS

Transfer the dough to a lightly floured surface and knead for 2 minutes, adding a little more all-purpose flour as needed until the dough is soft and elastic. Shape the dough into a ball.

Oil a large bowl and a piece of plastic wrap. Place the dough in the bowl. Cover with the oiled plastic wrap and let rise until almost doubled in volume, 1½ to 2 hours.

Oil a 14-inch pizza pan, preferably nonstick, and transfer the dough to it. Oil your fingers and press the dough to flatten it to cover the pan, dimpling the top. Let the dough rest for 30 minutes.

MEANWHILE, MAKE THE TOPPING: In a large skillet, heat the oil and sauté the onion over medium heat until just soft, 2 to 3 minutes. Let cool.

At least 20 minutes before baking, preheat the oven to 450°F.

Distribute the onions over the dough. Top with the tomatoes, drizzle with oil and sprinkle with the savory or oregano, salt and pepper to taste.

Bake for 10 minutes. Reduce the oven temperature to 400°F and bake for 20 minutes more. Wearing oven mitts, remove the flatbread from the pan and place it directly on the oven rack. Bake for 10 minutes more. Transfer to a rack and let cool for at least 15 minutes before serving.

The flatbread can be eaten warm or at room temperature.

AETOPITA
Flatbread with Tomato, Fennel and Marinated Swordfish

MAKES 4 SERVINGS

AETOPITA, a focaccia-like bread from Syros, was usually prepared the day the week's bread was baked because the wood-burning oven was fired only once a week. Flatbreads topped with olive oil, tomato and herbs or cheese are not uncommon. "These are for the children to nibble," some island cooks told me. But *aetopita* is clearly a hearty dish for adults, needing no accompaniment other than a glass of cold fruity white wine. The juices from the fish, flavored with fennel, scallions, garlic, tomato and olive oil, seep into the thin layer of bread, making it irresistible.

Achileas Dimitropoulos, who is the head of the department of terrestrial zoology at the Goulandris Museum of Natural History in Athens, originally described the recipe to me. Achileas has spent endless hours collecting recipes from fishermen in Syros, where he was born.

DOUGH

1/4 teaspoon active dry yeast

1/2 cup warm water

1/2 recipe Old Dough Starter (page 210)

2–2 1/2 cups all-purpose flour
About 2/3 cup cold water

1 teaspoon coarse sea salt or kosher salt

1 cup whole wheat flour

TOPPING

1 pound skinless swordfish steaks
or skate, tilefish fillets with skin
or any other firm-fleshed fish
fillets, cut into 1/2-inch cubes
or 1/2-inch-wide strips

1/4 cup freshly squeezed lemon juice

2 teaspoons coarse sea salt or kosher salt

1 1/2 teaspoons fennel seeds, preferably
freshly ground or crushed in
a mortar

1/4 cup olive oil, plus more for drizzling

1 small fennel bulb, finely chopped

4 scallions (white and most of the green
parts), thinly sliced

3 garlic cloves, finely chopped

1/2 cup chopped fennel fronds plus
tender stalks, or fresh dill

2/3 cup grated ripe tomatoes (see page
27) or canned diced tomatoes with
their juice

Salt and freshly ground black pepper

MAKE THE DOUGH: In a small cup, dissolve the yeast in the warm water and let stand for 5 minutes, or until frothy.

In a food processor, place the starter, 1 cup of the all-purpose flour, the yeast mixture, $1/2$ cup cold water and the salt and pulse to mix. Add 1 more cup of the all-purpose flour and the whole wheat flour, then, with the motor running, add enough cold water to make a sticky dough that just holds together. Let rest in the processor for 15 to 20 minutes.

Process the dough for 1 to 2 minutes more (add a little water if the dough is too stiff; it should be smooth and sticky).

Turn the dough out onto a lightly floured surface and knead for 2 minutes, adding more all-purpose flour as needed, until the dough is soft and elastic. Shape the dough into a ball. Oil a large bowl and a piece of plastic wrap. Place the dough in the bowl. Cover with the oiled plastic wrap and let rise in a warm place for $1^{1}/2$ to 2 hours, or until almost doubled in volume.

MAKE THE TOPPING: Place the fish in a medium bowl and drizzle with the lemon juice. Add the salt and $3/4$ teaspoon of the ground fennel and toss well. Cover and refrigerate for at least 1 and up to 4 hours.

In a large skillet, heat the oil over medium heat and sauté the fennel bulb and scallions for 3 minutes, or until soft. Add the garlic and sauté for 1 minute more. Remove from the heat and let cool.

Oil a 14-inch pizza pan, preferably nonstick, and place the dough on it. Oil your fingers and press the dough evenly over the bottom of the pan, dimpling the top. Let the dough rest for 30 minutes.

At least 20 minutes before baking, preheat the oven to 450°F.

Transfer the fish to paper towels to drain.

In a large bowl, combine the fish, garlic mixture, $1/4$ cup of the fennel fronds or dill and the remaining $3/4$ teaspoon ground fennel. Let stand at room temperature for 5 minutes.

Spread the fish mixture over the dough, pressing the fish gently into the dough. Scatter the tomatoes over the top, drizzle with oil and sprinkle with salt and pepper to taste.

Bake for 10 minutes. Reduce the oven temperature to 400°F and bake for 25 minutes more. Carefully remove the *aetopita* from the pan and place it directly on the oven rack. Bake for 10 minutes more, or until the topping sizzles and the edges of the dough are golden. Transfer to a rack and sprinkle with the remaining $1/4$ cup fennel fronds or dill.

Let cool for at least 15 minutes before serving warm, or serve at room temperature.

ISLAND DESSERTS
HONEY, FRUITS, NUTS
AND FRESH CHEESE

CHERRY SPOON-SWEET PRESERVES 240
(Kerasi Glyko)

BAKED APPLES WITH DRIED FIGS
IN SWEET WINE AND ALMOND SYRUP 241
(Mila Psita)

BAKED QUINCES
IN SPICED SWEET WINE SYRUP 242
(Kydonia Psita)

STUFFED DRIED FIGS 243
(Syka Gemista)

TANGERINE-SCENTED ALMOND COOKIES 244
(Amygdalota me Mandarini)

"TIPSY" SWEET COOKIE RINGS
WITH ORANGE AND CINNAMON 245
(Koulourakia Methismena)

WALNUT-STUFFED HONEY COOKIES 246
(Melomakarona)

ALMOND AND YOGURT CAKE
WITH CITRUS SYRUP 248
(Tou Giaourtiou)

PISTACHIO AND DRIED FRUIT CAKE
WITH ORANGE 250
(Nistisimo Cake me Fistikia ke Ksera Frouta)

PUMPKIN AND ALMOND CAKE
FROM SIFNOS 251
(Kolokythopita tis Sifnou)

NEW YEAR'S ORANGE AND BRANDY CAKE 252
(Vassilopita)

CURRANT, WALNUT
AND CHARD TURNOVERS 253
(Seskoulopita)

FRESH CHEESE AND HONEY TART
FROM SANTORINI 254
(Melopita Santorinis)

FRESH CHEESE TART 256
(Myzithropita)

ROLLED BAKLAVA 258
(Tiliktos Baklavas)

LEMON CUSTARD IN PHYLLO 260
(Bogatsa)

MASTIC ICE CREAM 263
(Pagoto Masticha)

Sweets are not made every day on the islands, only on special occasions. Fresh fruits are the usual conclusion to lunch or dinner, with desserts served on Easter, Christmas and at family feasts. In Greece, only children celebrate their birthdays, while grown-ups feast on the day that the saint whose name they have been given is celebrated by the Church. On that occasion, a sweet is offered to the guests who visit the family to wish many happy returns to Constantine on May 21, to Maria on August 15, to Yannis (John) on January 7 and so on.

Perhaps because they are so rarely made, sweets are the only foods on the islands for which written recipes exist. Even the women who can barely write manage to record the instructions for the New Year's Orange and Brandy Cake, in which a lucky coin is hidden, or the procedure and the proportions of sugar needed for each one of the various seasonal fruit preserves.

If you ask an island cook to list some of the specialties of her region, chances are that at least two of the three dishes she mentions will be sweets. On Santorini, the women will speak about *melopita*, a honey-flavored Easter cheese tart. On Tinos, they will tell you about *seskoulopita*, an unusual pie in which rice, walnuts and cur-

rants are mixed with the leaves of Swiss chard, a ubiquitous green that is used much like rhubarb. On Lesbos, sweet pumpkin pie will certainly be mentioned, while each Chian woman will talk about her trick for preparing perfect fruit preserves. Just after introducing herself, Marionga Bobari from Avgonima gave me a detailed description of how to prick unripe pistachios with a hairpin so that they would absorb the syrup and become sweet.

Each island home always has one or two kinds of cookies in the pantry, such as crunchy ring-shaped cookies scented with cinnamon and orange, or simple almond-and-sugar-paste cookies, fragrant with rose water or tangerine juice and zest, or honey-drenched *melomakarona*, the richly aromatic Christmas cookies that are served through the holiday season to the end of January, my own favorite. These cookies are baked in large quantities and kept in tins to serve with morning or afternoon coffee and to offer to unexpected guests.

The pantry is also stocked with jars of spoon sweets, various fruit jams prepared each season. Since ancient times, cooks have preserved fruits throughout the year, conserving them submerged in honey or, before sugar became readily available on an original dessert in minutes.

Among the festive desserts, the sweets of the baking pan are the most beloved, such as Rolled Baklava and *bogatsa*, a pie filled with cinnamon-and-lemon-scented custard. There are also cakes bursting with flavor from dried fruits, grated pumpkin and almonds or walnuts.

Many of these cakes and pies, as well as most cookies, are made not with butter but with olive oil. Butter has never been an important ingredient in traditional Greek cooking, because the country is not suitable for raising cattle. Since antiquity, Greeks have used olive oil for sweet and savory dishes. Later, they learned how to use clarified sheep's milk butter from the Ottomans. The sweet butter from cows that Europeans and Americans take for granted has become readily available in Greece only during the past forty years. Margarine is still more widely used in baking than butter. But although butter is becoming more popular, cooks who observe the traditions of the Greek Orthodox Church and abstain from all animal products during Lent still rely on olive oil.

the islands, in cooked grape must. Tiny whole tangerines, rolled strips of lemon, bergamot or bitter orange peel, unripe pistachios or figs, the heavily scented citrus blossoms and the petals of pink roses, even tiny unripe eggplants and tomatoes, are cooked in thick syrup. A spoonful of the sweet is served to each guest on a special small crystal plate, together with cold water. Often, the lady of the house proudly brings more than one jar on a tray so that the guests can choose which spoon sweet they want to taste.

On Chios, where fruits of all kinds are plentiful and rich in flavor and aroma, the tradition of spoon sweets is stronger than anywhere else. There is even an entire ritual governing which spoon sweets should be offered on each occasion. At weddings, for example, the preserves offered should be white—citrus blossoms and lemon or citron peel—while at various joyous family celebrations, multicolored cherries, tangerines and pistachios are served. On the solemn days of mourning, people who visit the house will be offered dark preserves of tiny eggplant or whole unripe walnuts, with their slightly bitter flavor. Westerners sometimes feel that these fruit preserves are too sweet. But there are other uses for these wonderful sweets of the spoon besides eating them by themselves. By adding a few teaspoonfuls to a bowl of yogurt or ice cream or spooning the leftover syrup onto a simple cake, you can create

The night before making baklava or cookies, my aunt Katina used to pour some of the olive oil kept in a large tin under the sink into a saucepan. She would add half a lemon and place it over very low heat for a while. "It shouldn't boil," she would say. Then she would remove the pan from the heat, cover it with a plate and leave the oil overnight to cool and absorb the aroma of the lemon. The next day, she discarded the lemon and used the lemon-scented oil to brush phyllo sheets for her baklava.

Like my aunt, most Greeks have in their homes 17-quart tins containing the year's supply of olive oil, either pressed from olives from the family's own trees or bought from friends or relatives who produce more than they need. Up until twenty years ago, very few people bought olive

oil from gro-
cery stores or
supermarkets.
The only bottle
they would occa-
sionally buy was
of highly refined
oil, used for
Christmas honey
cookies and Lenten cakes
and sweets. It was not good quality,
but it was flavorless, for as all Greek cooks know,
fruity virgin or extra-virgin olive oil is no good for
baking. Because even the blandest olive oil has a
pronounced aftertaste, other ingredients are
added to desserts to balance the oil's flavor, such
as orange or lemon zest and often juice, as well
as cinnamon, cloves, nutmeg and brandy. The
light olive oil now available in the United States
is good for baking, and a combination of ordinary
olive oil and safflower oil works equally well.

Various sweet stuffed turnovers and squares
or ribbons of thinly rolled dough, like Cretan
phyllo, are fried in olive oil, drizzled with honey
and sprinkled with walnuts and almonds. Fried
dough puffs, called *loukoumades*, used to be
made in the home, but now they are usually
bought from special bakeries. The bakers prepare
the sourdough or yeasted dough a few hours in
advance and stand in the windows of their shops,
dropping balls of the sticky dough with remarkable dexterity into a cauldron of boiling oil. The
sizzling puffs, dripping with honey and sprinkled
with cinnamon, are transferred to small plates
and immediately served to the customers, who
patiently wait their turn.

Since ancient times, Greeks have used fresh
cheeses to make desserts. My favorite sweets of the
islands are the Easter cheese tarts, made with
creamy myzithra. These tarts were adopted by the
Romans and were probably passed on from medieval Italy to the rest of Europe, finally to evolve
into the cheesecakes everybody loves today.

In this chapter, I have included recipes that
put the local ingredients to use:
the wonderfully aromatic
thyme honey, the fresh and
dried fruits, the almonds
and the fresh shepherd's
cheeses of the islands. Most
of the ingredients for these
easy and light sweets can
be found
everywhere.

KERASI GLYKO
Cherry Spoon-Sweet Preserves

MAKES 3 CUPS

THE cornerstone of Greek sweets are the preserves made with the fruits of the seasons. Each home has several different jars of fruit in the pantry, and guests are offered a teaspoon with a glass of water as a welcome to the house.

This is one of the easiest spoon sweets. The true color is a quite unattractive murky yellow, so islanders add a few drops of red food coloring. Instead of that, I prefer to boil a red beet with the cherries, a trick I learned from Tunisian cooks.

2 pounds firm cherries, such as Rainier or Royal Ann (not pie cherries or Bing cherries), pitted

2 cups sugar

1 small red beet, peeled and quartered (optional)

1/4 cup freshly squeezed lemon juice

2–3 teaspoons pure vanilla extract

In a large bowl, combine the cherries and sugar and toss well. Cover with plastic wrap and refrigerate overnight.

Transfer the cherry mixture to a large saucepan and bring to a boil, stirring occasionally until the sugar dissolves. Boil for 3 minutes, then remove from the heat. Let cool completely. With a slotted spoon, transfer the cherries to a colander set over a large bowl.

Bring the syrup to a boil and boil for 2 minutes. Add the beet (if using), the lemon juice and the syrup from the bowl. Boil the syrup until it reaches 235°F to 240°F on a candy thermometer.

Return the cherries to the pan and boil for 2 minutes more. Remove from the heat, add the vanilla extract and let cool completely. Discard the beet and pour the cherries into clean jars. Store in the refrigerator for up to 3 months.

MILA PSITA

Baked Apples with Dried Figs in Sweet Wine and Almond Syrup

MAKES 12 SERVINGS

12 large Granny Smith apples or other firm tart apples, cored

15 dried figs, coarsely chopped

1 cup golden raisins

1½ cups walnut halves (optional)

6 pitted prunes, coarsely chopped

6 dried apricots, coarsely chopped

1 cup soumada (see Sources, page 285) or almond syrup (see Note)

1 cup sweet white wine, preferably Samos or any sweet Muscat

½ cup orange-flavored liqueur, such as Grand Marnier or Cointreau

1½ teaspoons ground cinnamon

½ teaspoon ground ginger

½ teaspoon ground cloves

½ cup sugar

MRS. KSENOU, a passionate cook and the former owner of a small family hotel in the village of Vrontados on Chios, gave me the recipe for this light fruit dessert flavored with dried fruits and almonds. Chios is famous for its almonds, which are used to produce *soumada*, a kind of thick almond syrup. It's mixed with sweet wine and orange liqueur to make the syrup for these apples. I've found an easy way to prepare it at home.

The apples taste better the day after you bake them, so make them at least one day ahead. I always prepare more than I need, because they keep well for more than a week in the refrigerator. If you like, serve with Drained Yogurt (page 266) or ice cream.

Preheat the oven to 350°F.

Place the apples in a 13-x-9-inch baking dish. Stuff with the figs and raisins, dividing them evenly. Scatter the walnuts (if using), prunes and apricots around the apples. Pour the soumada or almond syrup over the apples and pour in the wine and liqueur.

In a small bowl, combine the cinnamon, ginger and cloves and sprinkle evenly over the apples. Sprinkle ¼ cup of the sugar over the apples. Bake for 45 minutes, or until tender, basting the apples frequently with the pan juices.

Turn the oven to broil. Sprinkle the apples with the remaining ¼ cup sugar and broil for 3 to 4 minutes to caramelize the sugar. Turn off the broiler and leave the apples in the oven for 15 minutes. Let cool completely before serving.

NOTE: To make almond syrup, grind 1 cup blanched almonds with 1 cup sugar and ⅔ cup water in a food processor, adding 1 to 2 drops of almond extract. Place in a saucepan over medium heat and simmer for 10 to 15 minutes, or until the liquid starts to thicken.

KYDONIA PSITA

Baked Quinces in Spiced Sweet Wine Syrup

MAKES 6 SERVINGS

1½ cups sugar

2 cups sweet white wine, such as Samos or any sweet Muscat

2 cups sweet red wine, such as Commandaria, Mavrodaphne, or sweet Marsala

1 cup water

3 medium quinces, halved crosswise, tossed with 2 tablespoons freshly squeezed lemon juice, cores removed and reserved

6 cloves

2 tablespoons freshly squeezed lemon juice

3 cinnamon sticks

Preheat the oven to 400°F.

In a medium saucepan, combine 1 cup of the sugar, the wines, water and quince cores. Bring to a boil. Reduce the heat to low and simmer for 10 minutes. Strain into a bowl, pressing on the cores to extract all their juices.

Pierce each quince half with a clove and toss with the lemon juice to prevent discoloration. Arrange the quinces cut side up in a baking dish and add the cinnamon sticks. Pour the wine mixture over the quinces and bake for 20 minutes, or until the cut sides are lightly caramelized.

Reduce the oven temperature to 350°F. Sprinkle the remaining ½ cup sugar over the quinces and bake for 5 to 10 minutes more, or until tender. Remove from the oven and let them cool in the syrup. Refrigerate and serve cold.

THE HARD, sour quince becomes a soft and aromatic dessert when baked in sweet wine syrup scented with cinnamon and cloves. In Greece, there are as many ways of flavoring baked quinces as there are cooks. This recipe is the one prepared by Chef Jim Botsacos at Molyvos restaurant. It originates from an old recipe of the Livanos family, the owners of the restaurant.

Serve the quinces on their own or with Drained Yogurt (page 266), whipped cream or licorice-flavored Mastic Ice Cream (page 263).

SYKA GEMISTA
Stuffed Dried Figs

MAKES 6 SERVINGS

1¼ cups coarsely ground walnuts

2 tablespoons ground cinnamon

1 teaspoon ground cloves

1 teaspoon freshly grated nutmeg

1 teaspoon ground ginger

1 pound dried Calimyrna figs, washed and allowed to dry out for 2 days at room temperature

Preheat the oven to 325°F.

In a medium bowl, combine the walnuts, cinnamon, cloves, nutmeg and ginger. Make a slash in the bottom of each fig and fill them with the walnut mixture, then press them closed.

Place the figs cut side down on a baking sheet and bake for 30 minutes, or until golden. Let cool completely before serving. Store in airtight containers for up to 6 months.

TRADITIONALLY made on the island of Lesbos, these fragrant figs keep for a long time. They can be eaten on their own as a snack or soaked in sweet wine—preferably the famous one from the neighboring island of Samos—and used as a topping for ice cream, yogurt or custard.

This recipe is based on detailed instructions from Maria Koutsoumbis from Molyvos, on Lesbos, a cousin of New York restaurateur John Livanos.

AMYGDALOTA ME MANDARINI
Tangerine-Scented Almond Cookies

MAKES ABOUT 50 COOKIES

ALMOND TREES grow all over the Greek islands. They are the most common fruit trees because they can endure the dry conditions and strong sea breezes that prevent other trees from thriving. These trees are beautiful when in bloom—usually in early March—but they look thin and frail when the green leaves first appear. The almonds they produce are delicious but small. They are becoming more difficult to find in the market, even on the islands, because the cost of gathering and shelling them, which must be done by hand, is prohibitive. For that reason, in late summer, on the island hills, you can see trees full of almonds that nobody cares to harvest. People gather only what they need for their own use. To get some of the almonds from Kea, I had to be very persistent, call at people's houses more than once and be ready to pay double the market value. But it was worth it.

These tiny pear-shaped almond cookies, scented with orange flower or rose water, are traditional on most islands. On Chios, the cookies are enriched with the taste of the local fragrant tangerines. On Corfu, I found a similar recipe.

4 tangerines
1 pound blanched almonds
2 cups sugar
    Confectioners' sugar or granulated sugar

Peel the tangerines and place the peels in a small saucepan; reserve the tangerines. Add cold water to cover and bring to a boil. Drain the peels, add fresh cold water to cover and bring to a boil again. Drain, rinse under plenty of cold running water and drain again. Dry completely with paper towels.

Combine the almonds and tangerine peels in a food processor and process until finely ground. Strain the juices of the reserved tangerines through a sieve set over a bowl, pressing against the fruit to release all the juices.

In a large saucepan, combine the almond mixture, sugar and $2/3$ cup of the tangerine juice and simmer, stirring constantly, until the sugar has dissolved, about 7 minutes. Let cool.

Shape tablespoon-sized portions of the mixture into $1^1/2$-inch-high pear shapes, wetting your fingers with the remaining tangerine juice. Dredge each cookie in confectioners' or granulated sugar to coat. Wrap individually in cellophane or place in a box with a lid. Let stand for at least 3 days before serving.

KOULOURAKIA METHISMENA
"Tipsy" Sweet Cookie Rings with Orange and Cinnamon

MAKES 64 COOKIES

2½ cups all-purpose flour

½ cup whole wheat flour

1½ tablespoons grated orange zest

1½ teaspoons baking soda

1 teaspoon ground cinnamon

¼ teaspoon salt

1 cup sugar

½ cup olive oil or a combination of olive oil and safflower oil

⅔ cup freshly squeezed orange juice

½ cup grappa or vodka

CRUNCHY and aromatic, these cookies from Crete are often served with morning or afternoon coffee. In the old days, all Greek kitchens had big tins filled with cookies to serve to family members or guests who dropped in. When the supply ran out, another big batch was made. The baking was a family event where friends and neighbors and the children helped to shape the dough.

The original recipe calls for raki, the strong Cretan distilled alcoholic drink, which is not imported into the United States. Grappa is a good substitute, but vodka works equally well. If you would like to speed up the shaping process, see the variations for Crisp Savory Bread Rings (page 224) and make the dough into biscuits instead.

In a food processor, pulse together the flours, orange zest, baking soda, cinnamon and salt. In a large bowl, beat ½ cup of the sugar and the oil with an electric mixer until well blended.

With the motor running, pour the orange juice, the grappa or vodka and the sugar-and-oil mixture into the processor. Process just until a smooth, oily, elastic dough forms; do not overprocess.

Preheat the oven to 350°F.

Turn the dough out onto a lightly floured work surface and knead briefly, adding more flour if the dough is too sticky. Divide the dough into 8 pieces. Work with 1 piece of dough at a time, keeping the remaining dough covered with plastic wrap. Roll each piece of dough into a 24-inch-long rope and cut each rope into 8 lengths, then roll each slice into a 7-inch-long rope. Shape each rope into a ring, pressing the ends together to seal.

Spread the remaining ½ cup sugar on a plate. Press one side of each ring into the sugar and place about 1 inch apart, sugared side up, on ungreased baking sheets.

Bake the cookies, in batches, for 30 minutes, or until light golden and crisp. Transfer to a rack to cool. Store in airtight containers for up to 3 months.

MELOMAKARONA
Walnut-Stuffed Honey Cookies

MAKES ABOUT 40 COOKIES

~~~~~~

MADE ALL over Greece for Christmas, these cookies are my favorite sweet. This recipe is a combination of my mother's and Chryssa Livanos'. Chryssa, the wife of the owner of Molyvos restaurant, comes from the island of Kos. If you can manage to resist these, they will get even better with time.

$1\frac{1}{4}$ cups light olive oil or a combination of olive oil, canola oil and/or safflower oil

$\frac{1}{3}$ cup sugar

Grated zest of 1 orange

1 cup freshly squeezed orange juice

3–4 cups all-purpose flour

$2\frac{1}{2}$ teaspoons baking powder

$1\frac{1}{2}$ cups fine semolina

$\frac{1}{2}$ cup brandy

Grated zest of 1 lemon

1 teaspoon ground cloves

1 teaspoon ground cinnamon

FILLING

2 cups finely chopped walnuts

1 tablespoon ground cinnamon

SYRUP

1 cup sugar

1 cup honey

$1\frac{1}{2}$ cups water

INGREDIENTS FOR
MELOMAKARONA

In a large bowl, beat the oil and sugar with an electric mixer until blended. Beat in the orange zest and juice. In a medium bowl, combine 2 cups of the flour and the baking powder. Gradually beat the flour mixture into the oil mixture. Beat in the semolina, brandy, lemon zest, cloves and cinnamon.

Turn the dough out onto a lightly floured surface and knead, adding 1 cup or more flour as necessary to obtain a smooth, soft, oily dough. Cover with plastic wrap and let stand for 20 minutes.

Preheat the oven to 350°F.

MAKE THE FILLING: In a medium bowl, combine the walnuts and cinnamon.

Take pieces of dough the size of a small egg and roll with your hands into ovals, about 2½ inches long. Push three fingers into the bottom of each cookie to make an opening, and stuff with 1 teaspoon of the filling; reserve the remaining filling. Press the dough to close the opening, slightly flatten each cookie and place the cookies on ungreased baking sheets about 1 inch apart.

Bake for about 30 minutes, or until they just start to color.

MEANWHILE, MAKE THE SYRUP: In a medium saucepan, simmer the sugar, honey and water for 10 minutes. Remove from the heat.

Place the hot cookies in a large dish and pour the syrup over them. Let stand for 15 minutes.

Turn the cookies to moisten the other sides and let stand until the cookies have absorbed all the syrup.

Place the remaining filling on a plate and roll each cookie in it to coat on all sides. Place the cookies in an airtight container, with parchment or waxed paper between each layer. Let stand for at least 1 day before serving. Store for up to 1 month.

TOU GIAOURTIOU

Almond and Yogurt Cake with Citrus Syrup

MAKES ONE 10-INCH ROUND CAKE

MY GRANDMOTHER, mother and aunt used to make this cake for family feasts, often cutting it into two layers with a piece of string and filling it with sweet cream to turn it into something more elaborate and festive. Its name means "the one with the yogurt." It is also called *yaourtopita* on some islands, and there are plenty of variations on the basic formula.

The idea for the crunchy almond-and-sugar topping was given to me by Despina Drakaki, a friend and excellent cook from Paros. The syrup can be made with just sugar or with sugar and honey or with a few tablespoons of orange or lemon marmalade added to it. Greek cooks often use the leftover syrup from the various spoon sweets or seasonal fruit preserves they have on hand in the pantry. The cake tastes even better the day after it is made, when it has had time to fully absorb the syrup.

Serve the cake on its own or with vanilla or Mastic Ice Cream (page 263) or with fresh fruit like oranges, tangerines or strawberries.

1 cup sugar

3 large eggs, separated

2 tablespoons unsalted butter, softened

1 cup yogurt

1 cup fine semolina

1 cup all-purpose flour

2 teaspoons baking powder

$^1\!/_3$ cup brandy

Grated zest of 1 lemon

1 cup coarsely chopped unblanched almonds

SYRUP

$1^1\!/_2$ cups sugar, or 1 cup sugar plus 3 tablespoons honey, or 4–5 tablespoons marmalade

$1^1\!/_4$ cups water

Whole zest from $^1\!/_2$ lemon, removed in strips with a vegetable peeler

3–4 tablespoons brandy

Preheat the oven to 400°F. Grease a 10-inch round cake pan or a springform pan.

Set aside 2 tablespoons of the sugar. In a large bowl, with an electric mixer, beat the remaining sugar with the egg yolks until light-colored, 2 to 3 minutes. Beat in the butter, yogurt and semolina.

Sift together the flour and baking powder. Beat the flour mixture into the egg-yolk mixture, together with the brandy and lemon zest.

In a large bowl, with clean beaters, beat the egg whites until they form soft peaks. Fold them into the batter. Pour the batter into the prepared pan, shake it gently to even the surface, and sprinkle with the almonds. Press them lightly with a spatula so that they are almost completely submerged in the cake batter. Sprinkle with the reserved 2 tablespoons sugar.

Bake for about 40 minutes, or until the cake is golden brown on top and a toothpick inserted in the center comes out clean.

MEANWHILE, MAKE THE SYRUP: Stir the sugar or the sugar and honey (if using the marmalade, do not add it yet), water and lemon peel together in a small saucepan and bring to a boil. Reduce the heat to low and simmer for 5 minutes. Remove from the heat. If you are using marmalade, add it now. Add the brandy.

As soon as you remove the cake from the oven, remove the lemon zest from the syrup and very slowly spoon the syrup evenly over the cake, covering the entire surface. Let cool completely before serving. Store at room temperature.

SHELLING
ALMONDS
ON LIMNOS

NISTISIMO CAKE ME FISTIKIA KE KSERA FROUTA

Pistachio and Dried Fruit Cake with Orange

MAKES ONE 9-X-5-INCH LOAF CAKE

3½ cups all-purpose flour

1 tablespoon baking powder

1½ teaspoons ground cinnamon

1 teaspoon baking soda

½ teaspoon ground cloves

2 tablespoons grated orange zest

½ cup olive oil

½ cup safflower oil

⅔ cup sugar

½ cup brandy

1½ cups freshly squeezed orange juice

½ cup chopped dried figs

½ cup chopped dried apricots

½ cup chopped prunes

½ cup coarsely chopped unsalted
   pistachios or walnuts

Confectioners' sugar (optional)

MY MOTHER used to bake this cake during Lent. We were not so religious as to follow the rules of the Church, which prohibited eating any food derived from animals during the forty days before Christmas and before Easter (and on many other occasions). We were simply continuing a family tradition which dictated that various foods or sweets should be made at a particular time of year.

The flavor of this cake is rich, and its texture is dense, much like an English fruitcake. It should be made a day in advance, and it keeps for at least a week—getting better each day—if stored in an airtight container at cool room temperature.

Preheat the oven to 350°F. Oil a 9-x-5-x-3-inch loaf pan and line it with a sheet of aluminum foil that extends about 2 inches over the short ends. (This will make removing the cake from the pan easier.)

Toss together the flour, baking powder, cinnamon, baking soda and cloves in a large bowl. Stir in the orange zest. In a medium bowl, whisk the oils and sugar until well combined.

Make a well in the flour mixture and stir in the oil mixture, brandy and orange juice until smooth. Stir in the dried fruits and nuts until evenly distributed.

Spoon the batter into the prepared pan and smooth the top. Bake on the middle rack of the oven for 50 to 60 minutes, or until a skewer inserted in the center comes out almost clean. Transfer to a rack and let cool completely.

Run a thin knife or spatula along the long sides of the pan and carefully lift out the cake with the aluminum foil. Peel off the foil and place the cake on a plate. If you like, sprinkle with confectioners' sugar. Slice and serve.

KOLOKYTHOPITA TIS SIFNOU

Pumpkin and Almond Cake from Sifnos

MAKES ONE 13-X-9-INCH CAKE

2 cups grated raw pumpkin plus 1 sweet potato, baked, peeled and mashed, or 2 cups grated calabaza squash

½ cup sugar

½ cup olive oil

1½ cups fine semolina

1 tablespoon baking powder

2 large eggs

4 tablespoons honey, preferably thyme honey

1½ cups coarsely chopped almonds

1 cup Zante currants

1½ teaspoons ground cinnamon

½ teaspoon ground cloves

Freshly ground black pepper

3–4 tablespoons brandy

In a large bowl, toss the pumpkin and sweet potato or squash with the sugar and let stand for 15 minutes.

Preheat the oven to 400°F. Brush a 13-x-9-inch baking pan generously with some of the oil.

In a small bowl, combine the semolina and baking powder. Add to the pumpkin and sweet potato or squash, along with the remaining oil, the eggs, honey, 1 cup of the almonds, the currants, cinnamon, cloves and pepper to taste and stir vigorously with a wooden spoon. Pour into the prepared pan and smooth the top with a spatula. Drizzle with the brandy and sprinkle with the remaining ½ cup almonds; press down lightly to submerge the almonds in the batter almost completely.

Bake for 45 minutes, or until the top is golden brown and a toothpick inserted in the center comes out clean. Let cool completely on a rack before serving.

MOIST and fruity, this cake is easy to make. Because the pumpkin is mixed into the batter raw, the flavor is nicely discernible. I found the recipe in Eleni Troullou's book *Delicacies from Sifnos*. The cake is excellent with coffee or tea, or you can serve it with yogurt or ice cream.

ALMONDS

VASSILOPITA
New Year's Orange and Brandy Cake

MAKES ONE 10-INCH ROUND CAKE

4 large eggs, separated

1 cup plus 2 tablespoons sugar

12 tablespoons (1½ sticks) unsalted butter, melted, or a combination of butter and margarine

1¼ cups freshly squeezed orange juice

½ cup brandy

4 cups all-purpose flour

4 teaspoons baking powder

¼ teaspoon baking soda

Grated zest of 1 orange

Grated zest of 1 lemon

Whole blanched almonds

ON NEW YEAR'S EVE or after the family lunch on the first day of the New Year, the father of the family cuts into this rich and aromatic cake, which has the year written in almonds on top and a lucky coin secreted inside. A piece is distributed to each family member, starting with the older ones, and whoever gets the symbolic coin is rewarded with a gift of money and starts the year with an advantage.

The basic recipe always contains orange juice, eggs, butter (a luxury in the old days) or margarine and brandy. Like our family, most islanders bake this fragrant cake just once a year. This is my mother's recipe.

Serve on its own for breakfast or as a snack with coffee, tea or a glass of orange juice.

Preheat the oven to 375°F. Grease a 10-inch round cake pan.

In a large bowl, with an electric mixer, beat the egg yolks with the sugar until light yellow and creamy, about 3 minutes. Add the butter or butter and margarine and beat for 1 minute more. Beat in the orange juice and brandy.

Whisk together the flour with the baking powder, baking soda and the zests in another large bowl. Add to the yolk mixture and stir with a rubber spatula until incorporated.

In a large clean bowl, with clean beaters, beat the egg whites until they form soft peaks. Fold them into the batter. Pour the batter into the pan and shake gently to even the top. Decorate the top with the almonds.

Bake the cake for about 1 hour, or until it is golden brown on top and a toothpick inserted into the center comes out clean. Cool on a rack before removing from the pan and serving.

SESKOULOPITA
Currant, Walnut and Chard Turnovers

MAKES ABOUT 40 TURNOVERS

DOUGH

3½–4 cups all-purpose flour

1 teaspoon baking powder

6 tablespoons olive oil

6 tablespoons safflower oil

⅔ cup dry white wine or beer

FILLING

2 pounds Swiss chard, stemmed and coarsely chopped

1 cup water

⅓ cup medium-grain rice, such as Arborio

1½ cups coarsely ground walnuts

⅔ cup honey, preferably thyme honey

½ cup Zante currants

1 teaspoon ground cinnamon

1 large egg, beaten
Olive and safflower oil for frying
Confectioners' sugar

MAKE THE DOUGH: In a large bowl, combine 3½ cups flour and the baking powder. Add the oils and wine or beer and mix briefly with a wooden spoon or an electric mixer until a soft, oily dough forms. If it is too soft, add a little more flour. Shape the dough into a ball, cover with plastic wrap and let rest for 15 minutes.

MAKE THE FILLING: Rinse the chard and place it in a large skillet over high heat. Cover and let wilt for 2 to 3 minutes, tossing often. Add the water and rice, bring to a simmer and simmer for 15 minutes, or until the rice has absorbed the water and is almost cooked. Remove from the heat and stir in the walnuts, honey, currants and cinnamon. Let cool.

Divide the dough into 4 pieces and shape each piece into a log about 1 inch in diameter. Cut off one ½-inch-thick slice at a time and flatten the slice with your fingers to form a 4-inch round. Place 1 tablespoon of the filling in the center and fold over to make a semi-circular turnover. Brush the edges with the egg and crimp the edges to seal. Place on a platter or a baking sheet. Repeat with the remaining dough and filling.

In a large, deep skillet, heat about 1½ inches of oil to 350°F. Fry the turnovers, in batches, turning once, for 2 to 3 minutes, or until golden. Drain on paper towels, sprinkle with confectioners' sugar and serve warm or at room temperature.

COOKS on the island of Tinos use the leaves of Swiss chard the way Westerners use rhubarb, tucking them into these festive turnovers. Traditionally made for Christmas, the turnovers are fried and sprinkled with confectioners' sugar. The recipe is based on one from Nikoletta Delatolla's book *Traditional Recipes from Tinos*. If you don't want to make the phyllo dough, use wonton skins.

MELOPITA SANTORINIS
Fresh Cheese and Honey Tart from Santorini

MAKES ONE 9-INCH TART

BEEHIVE ON ASTYPALAIA

~~~~~~

INDIVIDUAL cheese tarts similar to this one are prepared in Crete and on most of the Greek islands during Easter time. The olive-oil-and-beer pastry, based on a recipe from Paros, has a very nice flavor and texture.

PASTRY

2–2½ cups all-purpose flour

1 teaspoon baking powder

¼ cup light olive oil

¼ cup safflower oil

½ cup beer

FILLING

1½ cups ricotta cheese, drained overnight in a cheesecloth-lined colander

⅓ cup honey, preferably thyme honey

About ½ teaspoon (2 pieces) ground mastic (optional; see page 279)

½ teaspoon ground cinnamon

2 large eggs

Ground cinnamon

MAKE THE PASTRY: In a large bowl, combine 2 cups flour with the baking powder. Add the oils and beer and mix briefly with a wooden spoon or an electric mixer until a soft, oily dough forms. If it is too soft, mix in a little more flour. Shape the dough into a ball, cover with plastic wrap and let rest for 15 minutes.

Preheat the oven to 375°F.

Flatten the dough with your hands. Place it in a 9-inch tart pan with a removable bottom and press it evenly over the bottom and up the sides. Line with aluminum foil, and bake for 15 minutes.

Remove the foil, prick the dough with a fork and bake for 15 to 20 minutes more, or until set but not colored. Let cool.

MAKE THE FILLING: In a food processor, combine the ricotta, honey, mastic (if using) and cinnamon. Process for 30 seconds. With the motor running, add the eggs one at a time, processing until smooth.

Pour the filling into the cooled tart shell and smooth the top with a spatula. Bake for about 30 minutes, or until the filling is golden brown and set. Sprinkle with cinnamon and let cool before serving.

VARIATION
MYZITHROPITAKIA, LIHNARAKIA or MELITINIA
Fresh Cheese and Honey Tartlets

Instead of one large tart, you can make about 30 individual tartlets.

Divide the dough into 3 pieces and shape each into a 10½-inch-long log about 1 inch in diameter. Cut each log into 10 pieces. Work with 1 piece of dough at a time, keeping the remaining dough covered with plastic wrap.

On a lightly floured surface, pat each piece into a 4½-inch round. Put 1 tablespoon of the filling in the center of each round and pinch the rim to make a star-shaped crown around the filling (see illustration). Bake on baking sheets in batches for about 25 minutes, or until light golden.

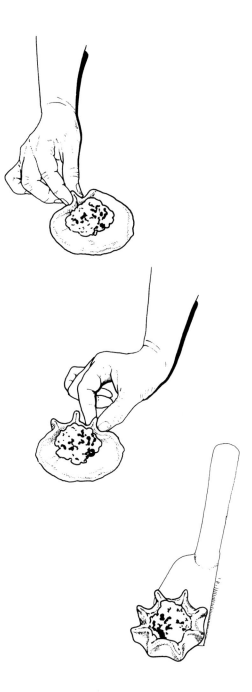

MYZITHROPITA
Fresh Cheese Tart

MAKES ONE 9-INCH TART

CRUST

2/3 cup ground Savory Barley and Wheat Biscuits (page 228; or see Sources, page 285) or dried whole wheat bread crumbs

1 large egg white

3 tablespoons melted unsalted butter or light olive oil

1 teaspoon sugar

1/2 teaspoon ground cinnamon

FILLING

2/3 cup heavy cream

2 tablespoons cornstarch

1 1/2 cups sheep's milk ricotta or regular ricotta (see Sources, page 285), drained in a cheesecloth-lined colander if watery

1 tablespoon grated orange zest

1 teaspoon ground cinnamon

1 large egg

1 large egg white

1/2 cup honey

SAUCE

1 1/2 cups sweet white wine, such as Samos or any sweet Muscat, or more as needed

5 dried figs, halved

10 pitted prunes

1/4 cup Zante currants

3–4 tablespoons honey, preferably thyme honey

A few sprigs fresh mint

THIS SIMPLE sweet tart may be the forerunner of the modern cheesecake. In ancient Greek and Roman texts, we find descriptions of desserts like this one, where a fresh farmer's cheese such as ricotta is mixed with honey, spices and sometimes dried fruits and nuts. The fresh myzithra cheese of the islands, which is traditionally the main ingredient in this tart, is made from a combination of goat and sheep's milk and is buttery and fragrant. The dessert is traditionally baked for Easter on Syros and Sifnos.

As a substitute for the fresh island cheese, I added some fresh cream to ricotta, and I made a sauce of dried fruits and sweet wine, which sets off the tart beautifully.

MAKE THE CRUST: Preheat the oven to 400°F. Oil a 9-inch pie plate.

In a medium bowl, combine the ground biscuits or bread crumbs, egg white, butter or oil, sugar and cinnamon. Transfer the crumb mixture to the pie plate, pressing it evenly over the bottom and up the sides. Bake for 8 to 10 minutes, or until the crust is set. Let cool on a rack. (Leave the oven on.)

MAKE THE FILLING: In a small bowl, combine the cream and cornstarch.

In a food processor, combine the ricotta, cream mixture, orange zest and cinnamon and pulse to blend. With the motor running, add the egg and the egg white, one at a time, and the honey. Process for a few seconds, until creamy.

Spread the filling evenly in the cooled crust. Bake for 30 to 35 minutes, or until the filling starts to color and is almost set but still a little wobbly at the center. Turn off the heat and leave the tart in the oven for 5 minutes. Cool completely on a rack.

MAKE THE SAUCE: In a medium saucepan, combine the wine, dried fruits and honey. Bring to a boil, reduce the heat to low and simmer for 5 to 8 minutes, or until the figs are soft. Transfer to a blender or a food processor and puree. If the mixture is too thick, stir in a little water or sweet wine.

To serve, cut the tart into wedges and serve with the sauce on the side, and garnish with mint sprigs.

TILIKTOS BAKLAVAS
Rolled Baklava

MAKES 30 BAKLAVA ROLLS

1/4 lemon

3 tablespoons olive oil

3 tablespoons safflower oil

1 cup almonds

1 1/2 tablespoons sugar

1/2 teaspoon ground cinnamon

1/4 teaspoon freshly grated nutmeg

1/2 pound *kataifi* (shredded phyllo)

6 thick phyllo sheets (about 1/2 pound; see page 281))

SYRUP

1 1/3 cups honey, preferably thyme honey

1 1/3 cups water

1 1/3 cups sugar

1/2 lemon

1 cinnamon stick

Preheat the oven to 350°F.

Halve the lemon quarter. In a small saucepan, heat the oils with the lemon over low heat for 5 minutes; do not boil. Let cool completely and discard the lemon.

Meanwhile, spread 1/2 cup of the almonds on a baking sheet and lightly toast, about 6 minutes. Coarsely chop the toasted almonds and the remaining 1/2 cup almonds in a food processor.

In a medium bowl, combine the almonds, sugar, cinnamon and nutmeg.

Divide the *kataifi* into thirds and place in a large plastic bag to keep it from drying out. Stack the phyllo sheets on a work surface and cover with plastic wrap and then a damp kitchen towel.

MOST baklava is now made with butter, but this lighter version with olive oil is still baked during the many Lenten days, when dairy products are forbidden. I learned to make it from Chryssa Livanos, the wife of John Livanos, the owners of Molyvos restaurant.

Oil a large baking sheet. Lay 1 sheet of phyllo on the work surface and brush lightly with the lemon oil. Lay 1 more sheet of phyllo on top and brush with oil. Sprinkle about 2$\frac{1}{2}$ tablespoons of the almond mixture evenly over the phyllo, leaving about 1$\frac{1}{2}$ inches of the short side farthest from you uncovered. Distribute one-third of the *kataifi* over the almond mixture, again leaving about 1$\frac{1}{2}$ inches of the short side farthest from you uncovered. Drizzle the *kataifi* with some oil and sprinkle about 2$\frac{1}{2}$ tablespoons of the almond mixture evenly over it.

Brush the uncovered phyllo border generously with oil. Starting with the short side nearest you, roll up the phyllo tightly like a jelly roll, brushing the outside lightly with oil as you roll. Press to seal and turn the roll seam side down on the work surface. Cut the log into 10 equal pieces and place the pieces cut side up about $\frac{1}{2}$ inch apart on the baking sheet. Make 2 more logs (20 more baklava rolls) in the same manner.

Bake the rolls on the middle rack of the oven until golden brown, about 30 minutes.

MEANWHILE, MAKE THE SYRUP: In a medium saucepan, combine the honey, water, sugar, lemon and cinnamon stick. Bring to a boil, stirring, and simmer until the sugar is completely dissolved. Let cool until warm; discard the lemon and cinnamon stick.

Transfer the hot baklava rolls to a baking dish large enough to hold them tightly in a single layer and pour the warm syrup over them, making sure to cover each roll. Let stand for 2 to 3 hours. Turn the rolls over, cover, and let stand at room temperature for at least 1 day before serving. Baklava rolls will keep in airtight containers for up to 2 weeks.

BOGATSA
Lemon Custard in Phyllo

MAKES ONE 10-INCH ROUND PASTRY OR 9 INDIVIDUAL PIES

FILLING

3 cups milk

½ cup sugar

Grated zest of 2 lemons

½ cup fine semolina

4 large eggs, each lightly beaten

4 tablespoons (½ stick) unsalted butter, melted

½ cup sugar

3 tablespoons ground cinnamon

8 tablespoons (1 stick) unsalted butter, melted

2 tablespoons olive oil

14 sheets phyllo dough

3 tablespoons confectioners' sugar

MAKE THE FILLING: In a medium saucepan, combine the milk, sugar and lemon zest and bring to a simmer over low heat. Stir in the semolina and cook, stirring, until the mixture begins to thicken, 2 to 3 minutes. Remove from the heat and stir in the eggs, one at a time. Return to the heat and cook, stirring constantly, for about 30 seconds, to cook the eggs. Remove from the heat and stir in the butter.

Preheat the oven to 350°F.

In a small bowl, combine the sugar and 1 tablespoon of the cinnamon. In another bowl, mix the butter with the oil; use a little to brush a 10-inch round baking pan. Stack the phyllo sheets on the work surface (see Note).

MY MOTHER often bakes her famous *bogatsa* on Sundays, when my sister and I, together with our husbands, have lunch at her house. It is one of the rare Greek sweets that should be eaten while still warm, so my mother makes the cream and assembles the pie just before noon, then puts the pan in the oven the minute we sit down to eat. By the time our leisurely lunch is over, the *bogatsa* is nicely browned.

Jim Botsacos, chef of Molyvos, watched my mother make the dessert and came up with the perfect adaptation: individual pastries that can be prepared well in advance (see the variation).

One at a time, lay 7 sheets of phyllo in the pan, brushing each sheet with the butter mixture and lightly sprinkling with the cinnamon-sugar mixture, letting excess dough extend over the edges of the pan. Pour in the filling and cover with another 7 sheets of phyllo, brushing each sheet with the butter mixture and sprinkling with the cinnamon sugar. Trim the dough to a 1-inch overhang. Fold the overhanging bottom phyllo over the top phyllo and pinch the edges together, crimping them to make a neat cord around the edge of the pan (see illustrations, page 262). Flatten the cord with the tines of a fork to prevent it from sticking up, or it will burn during baking.

Bake for about 40 minutes, or until the top is golden brown.

Meanwhile, mix the remaining 2 tablespoons cinnamon with the confectioners' sugar.

Sprinkle the cinnamon mixture over the pastry. Bring to the table while warm.

Individual Pastries

Make the custard filling. You will need 6 sheets of phyllo dough in all and half the butter and oil but all the cinnamon sugar. Line a 9-inch square baking pan with plastic wrap. Spread the filling evenly in it, smooth the top and cover with plastic wrap. Refrigerate until chilled and set, about 3 hours.

Remove the filling from the refrigerator, discard the plastic, invert it onto a cutting board and cut into nine 3-inch squares.

Lay 1 sheet of phyllo on the work surface and lightly brush with the butter mixture. Sprinkle with the cinnamon sugar and place another sheet of phyllo on top of the first, brushing and sprinkling as before. Cut the sheets crosswise in two and cut each half lengthwise into 3 equal strips. You now have 6 strips, each about 3 inches wide.

NOTE: When working with phyllo, keep the sheets covered and moist. To do so, stack the phyllo sheets on a work surface and cover with plastic wrap and then a damp kitchen towel.

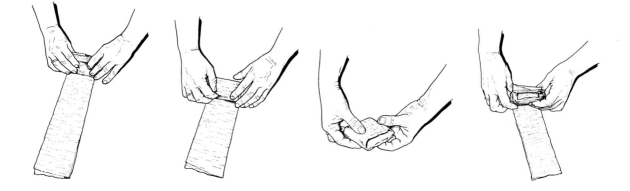

Place 1 square of custard on one end of a phyllo strip and gently roll it over to wrap it in phyllo. The wrapped piece of custard will have two exposed sides. Place it on a second strip of phyllo and roll up to completely encase the custard in phyllo (see illustrations). Repeat with the remaining custard squares. Lightly brush the tops with the butter mixture and transfer to a nonstick cookie sheet. (The *bogatsa* can be prepared to this point up to 2 days in advance and kept covered in the refrigerator. You can also freeze the wrapped *bogatsas* for up to 3 months.)

Bake for about 30 minutes (about 40 minutes if the *bogatsas* are frozen), until golden brown. Sprinkle with cinnamon and confectioners' sugar and serve warm.

PAGOTO MASTICHA
Mastic Ice Cream

MAKES 1 QUART

- 2 cups milk
- 2 cups heavy cream
- 1¼ cups plus 1 teaspoon sugar
- 2½ teaspoons mastic (see Sources, page 285)
- 15 large egg yolks

In a large saucepan, bring the milk, cream and 1¼ cups of the sugar to a boil over medium heat. Remove from the heat and set aside.

Grind the mastic together with the remaining 1 teaspoon sugar in a spice grinder.

In a medium bowl, whisk together the mastic mixture and the egg yolks.

THE GREEK equivalent of vanilla ice cream, this is uniquely flavored, scented with mastic—the crystallized sap of the wild pistachio shrub (*Pistachia lentiscus*), which grows only on the southern part of Chios. Exported to the Arab countries and the Middle East, mastic was the ancient chewing gum: hence the verb "masticate." To this day, it is still chewed to clean and sweeten the breath, while the ground crystals add their elusive licorice-like aroma to many Greek breads and cookies.

MASTIC TREE

The recipe for this ice cream was created by Jim Botsacos, who serves it with baked quinces (page 242). I also like to serve it on its own, simply topped with spoonfuls of Cherry Spoon-Sweet Preserves (page 240) or any other fruit preserves. And it goes well with Almond and Yogurt Cake with Citrus Syrup (page 248).

I still remember the wonderful ice creams we used to make in the summers, when I was a child, using a rented hand-cranked machine, to which we added ice and coarse salt. In those days, the cream was thickened not with eggs but with *salep*, a starch produced by pounding the dried tuber of a wild orchid. Ice creams thickened with *salep* form strands as you dip into them. Today, such wonderful eggless ice creams are found only in Turkey.

Gradually pour 1 cup of the hot milk mixture over the yolks, whisking constantly until well mixed. Return the remaining milk mixture to medium heat, pour the yolk mixture into the pan, and cook over medium-low heat, stirring constantly with a wooden spoon, until the mixture thickens, about 3 minutes; do not let it boil. To test it, dip the back of the spoon into the mixture and run your finger across the spoon; the line should hold.

Pass the cream through a fine-mesh sieve and transfer to an ice cream machine. Chill and then freeze according to the manufacturer's instructions.

COLLECTING MASTIC ON CHIOS (TOP)

WASHING MASTIC (MIDDLE)

MASTIC CANDY IN WATER AND COFFEE (BOTTOM)

BASIC PREPARATIONS

YIAOURTI STRAGISTO
Drained Yogurt

MAKES 1 CUP

1²/₃ cups plain whole-milk yogurt

Line a strainer with cheesecloth and set it over a large bowl. Add the yogurt, cover with plastic wrap and let drain overnight in the refrigerator.

SHEEP'S MILK yogurt is sweeter and creamier than cow's milk yogurt. Drained regular yogurt is a good approximation. I never discard the slightly sour but very tasty liquid left in the bowl after draining the yogurt; it adds flavor to vegetable stews and stocks. Keep it in a jar or, better yet, freeze it to use when you need it.

ASPETSA
Hot Pepper and Herb Mix

MAKES ABOUT 1 CUP

7 tablespoons Aleppo pepper or ¼ cup crushed red pepper flakes plus 3 tablespoons paprika

¼ cup dried oregano, crumbled

2 tablespoons fennel seeds, preferably freshly ground or crushed in a mortar

2 tablespoons chopped dried orange zest

1 tablespoon dried basil, crumbled

1 tablespoon dried mint, crumbled

In a small bowl, mix all the ingredients together. Transfer to a jar and keep in a cool, dark place for up to 6 months.

FOUND only in the unspoiled medieval village of Olympi, on southern Chios, this very unusual spicy mixture probably takes its name from the Italian word *specie* (spices). But it clearly comes from the East and has nothing to do with Italy or with the Genoese who occupied Chios for many centuries. Almost every cook makes his or her own variation, using the basic ingredients: dried hot red pepper, oregano, basil, fennel seeds and, sometimes, dried orange zest. My recipe is based on a jar of *aspetsa* given to me by Georgia Ksyderi, the beautiful daughter of the village priest.

Use it to flavor meat stews, such as Pork with Cabbage (page 108).

ZOMOS KOTAS
Chicken Stock

MAKES ABOUT 2½ QUARTS

2 tablespoons olive oil

1 large onion, halved and thickly sliced

10–12 black peppercorns, crushed in a mortar

1 cup dry white wine

4 pounds chicken backs, necks and wings

2 medium carrots, peeled and quartered

5 scallions (white and most of the green parts)

2 tablespoons coarse sea salt or kosher salt

2 bay leaves

> ∼∼∼∼∼∼∼∼∼∼∼∼∼∼∼∼∼∼∼∼∼
>
> I LEARNED to make chicken stock from my mother. This one is deeply flavored, with bay leaves rather than the celery of most American chicken stocks, and harmonizes well in traditional Greek soups and stews.

In a large pot, heat the oil and sauté the onion over medium heat for 6 minutes, or until soft. Stir in the peppercorns and cook for 1 minute more. Add the wine and bring to a simmer; remove from the heat.

Place the chicken parts in the pot and add water to cover. Bring to a boil, skimming off the foam. Reduce the heat to low. Add the carrots, scallions, salt and bay leaves and simmer, partially covered, for 2½ hours, or until the chicken meat is falling from the bones.

Strain the stock, pressing down on the solids to extract all their juices. Refrigerate until the fat congeals; scrape off and discard the fat.

Reheat the stock, let it cool again and refrigerate for up to 2 days or freeze it in measured cupfuls in heavy-duty zipperlock plastic bags or plastic containers. It will keep for up to 3 months.

ZOMOS APO LAHANIKA
Vegetable Stock

MAKES ABOUT 2½ QUARTS

2 tablespoons olive oil

1 large onion, halved and thickly sliced

½ cup dry white wine

2 fennel bulbs, trimmed and quartered

2 cups chopped Swiss chard stalks (optional)

2 ripe tomatoes, halved

2 leeks (white parts and light green parts), halved lengthwise and quartered crosswise

3 carrots, halved lengthwise

1 green bell pepper, cored, halved and seeded

1 cup coarsely chopped green beans

4–5 sprigs fresh flat-leaf parsley

2 sprigs fresh oregano

1–2 tablespoons coarse sea salt or kosher salt

In a large pot, heat the oil and sauté the onion over medium heat for 6 minutes, or until soft. Add the wine and bring to a simmer; remove from the heat.

Place the onion mixture and all the vegetables and herbs in the pot and add water to cover. Bring to a boil, then reduce the heat to low, add salt to taste and simmer, partially covered, for 1½ hours, or until all the vegetables are very soft.

Strain the stock, pressing down on the vegetables to extract all their juices. Refrigerate until cool.

THIS vegetable stock is perfect for cooking rice, bulgur, beans or lentils, for making *trahana* soup or poaching fish. To further concentrate the flavor, cook it longer to reduce it.

Refrigerate for up to 4 days or freeze measured cupfuls of the stock in heavy-duty zipperlock plastic bags or other containers. It will keep for up to 3 months.

VARIATION
ZOMOS APO LAHANIKA ME SELINO
Vegetable Stock with Celery

Omit the tomatoes and add 3 or 4 coarsely chopped celery stalks.

SALTSA DOMATA
Basic Tomato Sauce

MAKES ABOUT 3 CUPS, ENOUGH FOR 1 POUND PASTA

¹/₃ cup olive oil

1 cup finely chopped red onions

1 tablespoon tomato paste

1 cup sweet wine, such as Mavrodaphne or sweet Marsala

$1/2$–1 teaspoon Aleppo pepper or $1/4$–$1/2$ teaspoon crushed red pepper flakes

$2^1/2$ cups grated ripe tomatoes (about $1^1/2$ pounds; see page 27) or one 16-ounce can diced tomatoes with their juice

1 cinnamon stick

Salt

Sugar

In a medium saucepan, heat the oil and sauté the onions over medium heat for about 3 minutes, or until soft. Add the tomato paste and cook, stirring, for 2 minutes, or until glossy. Add the wine and pepper and simmer for 1 minute. Add the tomatoes, cinnamon stick, salt and about 1 tablespoon sugar, or to taste, and bring to a boil. Reduce the heat to low, cover and simmer for 20 minutes, or until the sauce thickens. Remove from the heat and discard the cinnamon stick.

The sauce will keep in the refrigerator for up to 4 days.

ONIONS and sweet wine are key ingredients in this well-balanced tomato sauce. Cinnamon is common in traditional Greek tomato sauce and in almost any dish that contains tomatoes. Maria Primikiri of Folegandros gave me the recipe.

This sauce freezes well, and I usually have some in my freezer in case I decide to make a quick pasta dish.

MYRODIKA GIA PSOMI
Bread Spice Mix

MAKES ABOUT ½ CUP

4½ tablespoons aniseeds

4½ tablespoons mahlep (see Sources, page 285)

1 tablespoon mastic (see Sources, page 285)

2 tablespoons sugar

In an electric spice grinder, a clean coffee grinder or a mortar, grind all the ingredients to a fine powder. Transfer to a jar and keep in the freezer for up to 6 months.

GREEK BREADS are usually seasoned with aniseeds, mahlep and mastic. It is very convenient to have a ground mixture of these spices ready for use in the freezer. Mixed with the sugar, mahlep and aniseeds, mastic can be ground in an electric spice grinder; if you try to grind it by itself, the heat may make the mastic stick to the blades.

SISSIRA
Preserved Pork Cracklings

MAKES ABOUT 2 CUPS

1½ quarts water
1 pound pork fat from the side, with
  very little meat
1 bay leaf
  Salt
1 tablespoon dried savory (optional)

In a large saucepan, bring the water to a boil.
Add the fat, return to a boil and skim the surface.
Add the bay leaf, reduce the heat to low and sim-
mer for 30 minutes.

Remove the fat and chop it, leaving the stock at
a simmer. Return the fat to the pan and add salt
to taste. Increase the heat to medium and simmer briskly for 30 minutes more, or until all the
water has evaporated and the cracklings start to
sizzle in the fat. Remove from the heat. Discard
the bay leaf and stir in 1 teaspoon salt and the savory, if using. Transfer the cracklings to a jar and
pour the fat over them. Let cool and store in the
refrigerator, where they will keep for up to 3
months.

VARIATION
PASPALAS

Savory Salted Pork Cracklings

Before boiling the pork fat, salt it generously, toss
well and let stand in a colander for 24 hours. Boil
as directed. Just before all the water has evaporated, add 1½ teaspoons dried savory.

THESE cracklings are an indispensable ingredient of island cooking, giving flavor to vegetable stews,
bean dishes, sautéed greens, omelettes and savory
pies. Tablespoons of the fat, with or without the meat,
are added to many foods as flavoring. Pancetta is a
good substitute.

On Tinos, they call the cracklings *sissira*, while
on other islands they are called *siglina*. The name is
probably derived from the sizzling sound the pork
makes as it cooks in its own fat.

MOSTARDA DOLCE
Fruit and Mustard Sauce

MAKES ABOUT 2 QUARTS

3–4 quinces (about 2 pounds), cored and cut
    into eighths (see Note)

4 cups water

5 pears (about 1 pound), halved and cored

2 Golden Delicious apples (about
    1 pound), halved and cored

1½ cups Zante currants

1½ cups sugar

3 cups Dijon mustard

¼ cup Aleppo pepper or 2 tablespoons
    crushed red pepper flakes

2 tablespoons grated orange zest or
    6 tablespoons finely chopped candied
    orange peel

AN AROMATIC and fruity relish, sweet and pungent at the same time, *mostarda dolce* is traditionally served in Corfu with the Christmas turkey. It also goes well with ham, chicken, lamb, veal and beef. Or serve it alongside cheeses like myzithra, ricotta, manouri and Gruyère.

The original recipe probably derives from the time when the Venetians ruled the islands of the Ionian Sea, although some Corfiots have told me that the sauce is related to chutney, a reminder of the English, who held the island from 1815 to 1864.

My recipe is based on one from Ninetta Laskari in her marvelous book on Corfu. Make it in large batches—*mostarda* is a great gift for friends.

In a large saucepan, simmer the quinces in 2 cups of the water over medium heat for 25 minutes, or until soft.

Meanwhile, in another large saucepan, simmer the pears in the remaining 2 cups water over medium heat for 10 minutes. Add the apples and cook for 10 minutes more, or until the fruit is soft.

Transfer all the fruit to a blender or food processor and puree; you may need to do this in batches. Pour the puree back into one of the saucepans and add the currants and sugar. Bring to a boil and simmer over medium heat, stirring with a wooden spoon, for 15 minutes more. (You should have about 6 cups.) Remove from the heat and let cool.

In a large bowl, combine the fruit mixture, mustard, Aleppo pepper or pepper flakes and orange zest or candied peel. Transfer to clean jars and store in the refrigerator for up to 2 months.

NOTE: If quinces are not available, use a total of 8 pears and 3 apples and puree them with 2 cups good-quality quince preserves. Reduce the sugar to 2 tablespoons. The result will not be exactly the same, but it will still be good.

THE INGREDIENTS
OF THE GREEK ISLANDS

The most important elements in the cuisine of the islands—good fresh vegetables and fruits, olive oil, beans and meat, poultry and fish—are available everywhere in the world. Island cooking is forgiving and flexible, and most of the recipes in this book offer alternatives so that you can make them with whatever ingredients you have on hand. For the few hard-to-find items, such as some of the cheeses, I have suggested substitutes. Authentic imported products are available in Greek and Middle Eastern grocery stores. I have also included a list of shops, mail-order sources and Internet sites where Greek spices and cheeses can be ordered (see page 285).

ALEPPO PEPPER: These crushed dried Middle Eastern red peppers, which are less hot than Mexican chiles, are close in flavor to the indigenous hot peppers of the Greek islands. Turkish Maras peppers are similar in taste to Aleppo peppers, but often hotter, while Urfas peppers, from the eponymous region of Turkey, have an exceptionally deep flavor. Aleppo and the Turkish peppers can be bought at Middle Eastern shops, where they are often simply called "Middle Eastern pepper." If you buy a large quantity, store in a sealed jar in the refrigerator.

You can substitute about half the amount of ordinary crushed red pepper flakes for Aleppo pepper or, even better, a combination of crushed

red pepper flakes and some good paprika.

ALMONDS: Raw unblanched (unpeeled) almonds are used in baklava and many other Greek cakes, as well as savory dishes. The taste of unblanched almonds is much more complex than the blanched (and scientists point out that the fibers and other components of the skin are good for you). The skin also prevents the almonds from drying out.

If blanched almonds are called for, they are easily peeled: Blanch them in boiling water for 1 minute, then drain and squeeze each one between your index finger and thumb—the almond will slip right out of its skin. If you have blanched almonds that seem too dry, soak them in cold water for 2 to 3 hours before using. Like all nuts, almonds are best stored in the freezer to retain their freshness.

BITTER ALMONDS are used in some sweets for their aroma, but it is illegal to import them into the United States. A few drops of almond extract are a good substitute.

BARLEY FLOUR: See *Flour*.

BEANS: Along with chickpeas, lentils, favas, peas and other legumes, dried beans play a very important role in the diet of the islands, simply boiled and served as a salad, with a lemon vinaigrette and some chopped onion, or cooked into soups and stews, often including meat. If you have a choice, get organically grown and freshly dried beans, with shiny, not wrinkled, outer skins, or buy them from a store with a good turnover to ensure that they are fresh. Soak beans in cold water for 4 to 6 hours, or overnight, before cooking. Drain and rinse. If you have time, you can considerably reduce the discomfort many people experience from eating dried beans by covering them with plenty of fresh water, bringing them to a boil and setting them aside for 4 to 6 hours. Drain again and cook as directed.

For most dishes, white kidney beans and cannellini beans can be used interchangeably. Greek GIGANTES (GHEE-gan-tes), Greek giant white beans, have a creamy taste.

Fresh GREEN BEANS—runner beans, *haricots verts*—are a favorite in many summer dishes, often stewed in tomato sauce or cooked together with meat.

BLACK-EYED PEAS: These are cooked by themselves or in combination with other beans. *Ambelofassolia*, tender FRESH BLACK-EYED PEAS in the pod, are used in a much-loved Greek salad and side dish. Yard-long beans, which can be substituted, are available at Chinese and other Asian markets; ordinary green beans can also be substituted.

BRANDY: See *Wines and Spirits*.

BULGUR: Bulgur is cracked wheat that has been steamed and dried. It cooks quickly, unlike *Wheat Berries*, which need long cooking. Made into pilafs and stuffings or used as a thickening in both savory and sweet dishes, bulgur was an island staple before rice became widely available. It comes in three grinds. The coarse and the medium, which are best for pilafs and stuffings, are available in Middle Eastern stores (see page 285). Fine bulgur is available in most supermarkets, usually packaged as tabbouleh mix. If you

can't get coarser bulgur, use fine (discard the herb mixture in the package, if there is one) and cook it for about 3 minutes less than instructed in the recipe. If you buy bulgur in a large quantity, store it in a sealed plastic bag in the refrigerator or in the freezer.

CALIMYRNA FIGS: See *Figs*.

CAPERS: These are the buds of the caper bushes, which grow wild in the stony soil all over the islands. They are bitter, so they are cured first and pickled in vinegar or preserved in salt. Although capers in vinegar are more common, I prefer the salted ones because they have more flavor. Both kinds need to be rinsed under lukewarm running water and dried with paper towels before using. Greeks prefer larger caper buds, because they have more flavor.

On many islands, caper buds are also dried in the sun. Dried capers need to be soaked in warm water for about 3 hours, then blanched in two or three changes of boiling water.

CAPER BERRIES, which look like a small dark green almond, are the fruits of the ca-

UNCURED CAPERS

GOAT'S MILK CHEESES

per bush. Cured in vinegar, they are meatier and have a milder taste than capers. On Chios and other islands, they are stuffed with garlic cloves and served as an appetizer. The tender shoots and leaves of the caper bush are also pickled and added to salads or served as a *meze*.

CELERY: Greek celery is the thin-stalked, dark green leafy plant that Americans call "wild celery." Although it does grow wild in Greece, most of it is cultivated. This fragrant celery has a strong taste, so a little goes a long way. It can be found in Asian markets under the name *kun choi* or *kin tsai*. You can also grow your own in the garden or in pots (for seeds, see page 285). If you come across it in the farmer's market, buy a lot, wash it well, coarsely chop it and store it in zipperlock bags in the freezer, where it will keep for about 6 months. Thick-stalked American celery

can be substituted in these recipes, but its taste is much milder. This celery has become available in Greece in the last few years, and Greeks use it as a raw vegetable in salads or serve it with dips, as Americans do.

CHEESES: The islands have a great variety of cheeses, and often even the villages on one island will have very different cheeses, since the majority of households produce their own fresh and hard cheeses. Most of the cheeses made by home cooks or shepherds can't be sold or exported and so are not seen outside the village where they are made. The majority of island cheeses are made from a combination of goat and sheep's milk, but several cow's milk cheeses are made on Tinos, Syros, Naxos and a few other islands.

Some of the most interesting island cheeses are: ladotyri, from Lesbos, which is submerged in olive oil and left to mature for a few months; the crumbly and pungent blue-type cheese *kopanisti*, which is made on Mykonos, Chios and some other islands; *gilomeni manoura* from Sifnos and *possias* from Kos, pungent, semi-hard cheeses, stored in wine sediment; and *touloumo-tyri*, another piquant cheese, which is wrapped in goat hide. Unfortunately, these are rarely available in the United States. However, even island cooks now living in Athens have had to come up with interesting and unexpected substitutes for the cheeses they can't get.

All the cheeses called for in the recipes in this book are exported and can be found in specialty cheese shops, ethnic grocery stores or even some supermarkets (see page 285). And the excellent artisanal sheep's milk cheeses produced in Vermont and other parts of the United States can often be used in these recipes in place of the Greek cheeses.

The Greek cheeses most readily available in the United States include:

FETA, a cheese of the mainland that has taken over the entire Greek market and has a slightly sour taste and a creamy texture. Authentic feta is made primarily from sheep's milk, with a small amount of goat's milk, and is naturally very white. The cheap cow's milk feta produced in northern Europe and the United States is treated with a chemical to make it white and is nothing like the real thing. Feta should be stored in its salty brine to keep it fresh; if this is not possible, buy only a small quantity at a time and store it in a covered container in the refrigerator, where it will keep for 3 to 4 days. If you want to grate feta, leave a piece uncovered overnight in the refrigerator to dry.

HALOUMI (hal-OO-mi), the most famous cheese of Cyprus, is a semi-hard, firm white cheese with a somewhat elastic texture, similar to mozzarella. It is firmer than feta and does not crumble when sliced, making it excellent for grilling and frying. It can also be coarsely grated. It can be found in Middle Eastern stores and many supermarkets (see page 285). Traditionally, haloumi was made from sheep's milk, but the commercial cheese available today is made mainly from cow's milk, with some sheep's milk added for flavor. Haloumi is usually sold sprinkled with dried mint and vacuum-packed in its brine. The longer the cheese remains in the brine, the saltier it becomes. If it is too salty, simply soak it overnight in fresh water or rinse it briefly under lukewarm running water. Unlike most cheeses, haloumi can be frozen without loosing its texture or taste.

KEFALOTYRI (kefa-lo-TEE-ri), a sharp, pungent, hard aged cheese, is made from a combination of sheep's and cow's milk, often with the addition of goat's milk. It is mostly grated, served over pasta or baked in savory pies. Good-quality pecorino Romano, Manchego or any American aged sheep's or goat's milk cheese is a good substitute.

MANOURI (man-OO-ri) is a rich and creamy cheese similar to ricotta salata made from a combination of sheep and goat's milk. It is made by adding cream to the whey, and it is often eaten as dessert, topped with quince or other fruit preserves. Manouri is available in many su-

CHEESES IN BRINE

permarkets as well as cheese shops and ethnic grocery stores (see page 285).

MYZITHRA (miz-EE-thra) is a generic name used for many different fresh cheeses. Sweet, creamy and delicious, myzithra can be drizzled with honey and eaten with *paximadia* (Savory Barley and Wheat Biscuits; page 228). The most common cheese of the islands, it is usually made by adding fresh milk to the whey left after the production of another cheese, often one that is dried. Full-fat sheep's milk ricotta is a very good substitute. If substituting the more common cow's milk ricotta, it should be drained well and mixed with some heavy cream or manouri, as instructed in the individual recipes.

When heavily salted and air-dried, these cheeses become HARD MYZITHRA, which keeps for much longer than the fresh version. It is grated over pasta or added to savory pies. To keep it from drying out further, grate it and store in an airtight container in the freezer for up to 3 months. You can substitute dry aged ricotta salata from Italy, a Spanish Queso Ibores or a hard Italian grana-type cheese for hard myzithra.

COD, SALT: See *Salt Cod.*

COMMANDARIA: see *Wines and Spirits.*

CURED FISH: On the islands, *skoubri*, a kind of mackerel, *lakerda*, a kind of small tuna, and other oily fish are sliced, salted and submerged in olive oil in jars. These cured fish are served as a *meze* or as a side dish with beans; smoked trout is a good substitute. Sardines and anchovies are also salted and eaten as a *meze*, either fresh or preserved in salt in sealed tins. Imported Italian salted sardines can be substituted. Rub them with a paper towel to get rid of most of their salt and then drizzle them with olive oil and lemon.

CURED MEAT: See *Pork, Cured.*

DAIRY PRODUCTS: See *Cheeses* or *Yogurt.*

DRIED FRUIT: Besides being important ingredients for many island sweets, grapes dried in the sun—sultanas, dark raisins or Zante currants—are also used in savory sauces as sweeteners. ZANTE CURRANTS, dried tiny, sweet seedless red grapes, are the ones most commonly used in Greek cooking and baking. They originated in Corinth, but after the Ottomans took over the mainland, the Venetians transplanted the vines to Zante (Zakynthos), an island in the Ionian Sea, west of the mainland. For a long time, they were the most important export of Greece.

FAVAS (FAH-vas): Both dried and fresh fava beans are cooked in many ways. DRIED FAVAS have a meaty, earthy and slightly bitter taste. It's best to buy them peeled and split, because their skin is quite tough and indigestible. If you get them with the skin on, soak them overnight, peel them and cut off the black sprout on top before cooking. Tender young FRESH FAVAS are shelled and stewed in olive oil and lemon juice and eaten like green beans. Favas are also eaten raw, as a *meze*, and are often added to salads and stews. In Greece, the somewhat tough skins that surround fresh fava beans are never removed. If you want to peel them, blanch the fava beans in boiling water for 1 to 2 minutes, then slip them out of their skins.

FENNEL: Wild fennel, which grows all over the islands, has a sweet aromatic licorice taste. Besides using it to flavor all kinds of dishes, Greek cooks also treat wild fennel like a wild green, cooking it in stews or frying it in patties. Chopped FENNEL BULB and tops (fronds plus tender stalks) mixed with freshly ground fennel seeds are a good substitute for the wild fennel of the islands. Fennel and fresh dill can be used interchangeably in some dishes.

FETA: See *Cheeses.*

FIGS: Figs are the trademark of the Greek summer. Both green and purple figs grow all over the islands, on semi-wild (nonirrigated) trees. They have a deeply sweet flavor that distinguishes them from figs grown in other parts of the world. Dried figs, plain or stuffed with nuts and spices (page 243), are eaten by children and grown-ups as snacks and are used in desserts, breads and cakes. The imported Greek ones are often difficult to find. California CALIMYRNA FIGS are a good substitute.

FISH, CURED: See *Cured Fish*.

FLOUR: ALL-PURPOSE FLOUR is used in most baked goods, while hard yellowish WHOLE WHEAT FLOUR is used in breads, either on its own or mixed with all-purpose and some barley flour. If you have a choice, buy unbleached organic stone-ground flour. BARLEY FLOUR: Barley grows easily in the Mediterranean climate and has been used since antiquity instead of wheat, which was much harder to grow. Made by grinding partly husked barley grains, the nutty-tasting flour is closer in texture to whole wheat flour than to all-purpose flour, but it is darker in color. Bread and *paximadia* (page 228), the twice-baked Savory Barley and Wheat Biscuits that are an island staple, were traditionally made with barley flour, and barley flour continues to be used today, in combination with wheat flour, for most island breads. It is available at most health-food stores and can also be ordered from larger mills (see page 285). Like all flours, it is best stored in the refrigerator in a sealed bag or container. SEMOLINA (also called semolina flour), coarsely ground husked hard wheat, is also used in some sweets and cookies. It comes in two grades; "fine" is the most commonly used.

All flours, if not used within a month, are best stored in sealed bags or containers in the refrigerator. Refrigerate all organic stone-ground flours.

GIANT WHITE BEANS: See *Beans*.

GRAPE LEAVES: In the United States, grape leaves from California, preserved in salt brine and sold in jars, are better than the imported Greek ones, which are usually too salty and tough. Rinse canned grape leaves under warm running water before using.

Greek cooks buy fresh grape leaves each spring and keep them in the freezer to use throughout the year. Fresh leaves add extraordinary flavor to any stuffing. If you can get them fresh—and nonsprayed—rinse and dry them carefully. Make neat stacks of about 50 leaves each, wrap in aluminum foil, seal in zipperlock bags and store in the freezer, where they will keep for more than a year. Take them out about 2 hours before you plan to use them. Fresh leaves should be blanched for 2 to 3 minutes in boiling water before using, but freezing softens the leaves so they can be rolled as they are.

HARVESTING GRAPE LEAVES

HALOUMI: See *Cheeses*.

HERBS: Oregano, savory and thyme are always used dried in Greek cooking. Only MINT is used both fresh and dried, each of the two forms having a very different taste and aroma. There are many varieties of oregano on the islands, all fabulously aromatic. GREEK OREGANO is gathered in the spring before it blooms. Its aroma is fruitier and lighter than that of SAND-COL-ORED OREGANO, which is gathered in late summer, after it has bloomed and been dried by the sun. It is delightfully aromatic, with a scent closer to that of thyme. Greek oregano is now readily available in the United States. SAVORY, which tastes like a cross between oregano and thyme, is used in sausages and other cured pork products and as a flavoring for olives. I often use it instead of oregano in tomato sauce and to flavor grilled fish or meat. THYME, the bush more closely associated with the arid landscape of the Greek islands, grows and thrives in the Cyclades. Its tiny purple flowers help the bees make their thyme-scented honey.

HONEY: Greek island honey is thyme-scented. If you want to flavor a pot of ordinary honey, wrap a teaspoon of dried thyme in a square of cheesecloth, add it to a jar of honey and set the jar in a saucepan filled with an inch or so of water. Warm it over low heat, stirring a few times, for 15 to 20 minutes. Taste, and either re-move the herb bag or leave it in the honey overnight, depending on how intensely flavored you want the honey to be.

KATAIFI (ka-ta-EE-fee): This vermicelli-like shredded phyllo pastry comes frozen in 1-pound packages. It's used in desserts and to wrap savory foods before frying to create a crunchy crust. Kataifi is sold in ethnic and Middle Eastern gro-cery stores (see page 285). Thaw following the package instructions.

KEFALOTYRI: See *Cheeses*.

KRITAMO, or rock samphire, is a slightly aro-matic bush with small fleshy leaves that grows on beaches. On Chios and in some parts of central Greece, kritamo is pickled, and the sprigs are used to flavor tomato, mixed green salads and sauces. Rock samphire is similar to marsh sam-phire, which grows in the United States. Also called pickleweed or sea bean, it is sold in Asian markets. Capers can be substituted.

MAHLEP (MAH-lehp): The small seeds of a wild cherry, the size of apple seeds, mahlep gives a sweet and smoky aroma to breads and other baked goods. The grains should be the color of café au lait; dark brown grains indicate that the spice is old and probably stale. Mahlep is sold in Middle Eastern stores (see page 285). Buy it whole, not ground. Keep it in sealed jars in the freezer, and grind small quantities as needed.

MANOURI: See *Cheeses*.

MASTIC: This is the crystallized sap of the mastic shrub (*Pistachia lentiscus*), a kind of wild pistachio that grows only on southern Chios. Very popular in the Arab countries and the Mid-dle East, mastic is used as a flavoring, mainly in sweets, ice cream, breads and drinks. Mastic was the chewing gum of ancient people, hence our word "masticate." Mastic is sold in Middle East-ern and ethnic grocery stores (see page 285); store it in the freezer. When grinding it in a spice grinder, always mix the crystals with the sugar and the other spices used in the recipe to prevent the heat of the motor from melting the mastic, which could stick to the blades of the grinder.

MAVRODAPHNE: See *Wines and Spirits*.

MYZITHRA: See *Cheeses*.

NIGELLA (nigh-JELL-a): These tiny black seeds have a licoricey flavor and aroma, similar

to aniseeds. They are used as a topping or mixed into dough for breads and the crunchy savory biscuits of the islands. Although they are sometimes called black cumin or black sesame seeds, nigella seeds come from *Nigella sativa*, a plant not related to either of the two. They are sold at Middle Eastern and Indian grocery and spice shops (see page 285). Aniseeds or caraway seeds, or a combination, can be used as a substitute.

OLIVE OIL: The taste of Greek food relies heavily on olive oil. It is used for cooking, frying and baking. Crete and Lesbos produce more olive oil than any of the other islands, but Corfu, Kythera and other islands of the Ionian Sea also produce some. Until very recently, most of the Greek extra-virgin olive oil was sold in bulk to Italian firms, which bottled and sold it all over the world under their labels. Today, more Greek producers bottle and market their own oils, though a significant amount is still sold in bulk to large multinational companies. In recent years, as international demand has grown, an increasing number of producers are making organic olive oil. Greek olive oil is now available in most American food markets, and it is well worth buying, because its flavor is excel-

lent—and it is usually cheaper than Italian oils (see page 285).

OLIVES: Greek olives are among the best in the world, but they have only recently started to be available in gourmet grocery stores in the United States (see page 285). The most well-known and popular of these is the firm-fleshed KALAMATA, but many lesser varieties are sold under the same name. Some of my favorite olives are the green slightly bitter CRACKED OLIVES, often called Nafplion in the United States. In Cyprus, these olives are flavored with crushed coriander seeds, garlic and lemon. I also like the large and juicy olives from PELION. On Chios, island cooks cure green olives with lemon and bitter orange juice and scent them with the fragrant leaves of the licorice-flavored mastic tree (see *Mastic*). The olives from the groves of ROVIES, on northern Evia, are considered to be of excellent quality. Cured and stuffed, they are exported to specialty stores in Europe but not yet to the United States.

ORANGE PEEL: Dried and ground orange peel is used as a flavoring in sausages and is part of spice mixtures such as *aspetsa* from Chios (page 266). Ground dried orange peel is sold in Chinese, Middle Eastern and ethnic grocery stores. Grated orange zest can be substituted if it is unavailable.

OREGANO: See *Herbs*.

ORZO: This small barley-shaped pasta—the word means "barley" in Italian—can be cooked for a long time without becoming mushy, so it is used in risotto-like dishes and baked in the sauce of lamb. In Greece, this pasta is called *kritharaki* (small barley).

OUZO: See *Wines and Spirits*.

PAXIMADIA (pak-see-MA-dia) are savory biscuits made with barley flour or a combination of wheat and barley flour. For centuries, they were the staple food of the islanders, and sailors took them on voyages because they keep for months. Eaten with olives, cheese, stews or soups, *paximadia* need to be briefly dunked in water to soften them; they are also used as an in-gredient in salads and sweets. In the United States, *paximadia* imported from Crete are available at specialty markets (see page 285).

PEPPER: see *Aleppo Pepper*.

PHYLLO (FEE-lo): Phyllo dough is sold frozen in most supermarkets and ethnic stores. If you have a choice, choose the thicker (#7) sheets for savory pies. If you can't get it, substitute thin phyllo, layering 7 to 8 sheets on the bottom and the top of the pie. Baklava is made with the thinner sheets. Defrost phyllo in the refrigerator according to the package instructions. Keep the sheets covered while you are working with them, to prevent them from drying out and becoming brittle and unusable. Frozen puff pastry can be substituted for homemade phyllo in many recipes.

PICKLES: See *Capers* or *Kritamo*.

PISTACHIOS: Greek pistachios are much smaller than the ones from California, but they

have more flavor. Salted and briefly toasted, pistachios are served as a snack or with drinks. Raw unsalted pistachios are used in this book. To skin them, follow the instructions for *Almonds*.

Like all nuts, pistachios should be stored in sealed bags or jars in the freezer.

PORK, CURED: Small pieces from the side of the pig—a little meat with fat—are added to all sorts of island dishes. Italian pancetta is a good substitute.

Pigs are reared by all island households, fed vegetable peelings, leftovers from the family's table and the nourishing whey from the daily production of cheeses. On some islands, particularly Kea, pigs are fed acorns from age-old oaks. Pigs are slaughtered in December, before Christmas. Small amounts are eaten fresh, while most of the meat and other parts are cured and stored for the year.

Louza or *loza*, considered a delicacy, is the most famous cured product of the Cyclades, made with the pork tenderloin, marinated in wine, spiced and smoked. On Crete, *apaki* are strips of pork spiced with salt, pepper and cumin, marinated in vinegar or bitter orange juice, or a combination, smoked with aromatic herbs and covered in pork fat. They're used to flavor beans, omelettes, greens and vegetable dishes. GLYNA, the fat from the pork's belly, is considered the best for cooking.

Island SAUSAGES are spiced with all sorts of aromatics: On the Cyclades, they are scented with dried orange peel and savory, while on the Dodecanese, they are made with cumin. Cinnamon, cloves and tangerine peel give Chian sausages their characteristic flavor. LEFKADA SALAMI, air-dried and pepper-studded, is made on a small island in the Ionian Sea and is very popular in Greece. Many lefkada–type salamis are available in Athenian grocery stores, but the authentic one is hard to get.

PUMPKIN: Growing in abundance on the islands, pumpkins are sweet and flavorful. Of the various pumpkins and squash available in the United States, the South American calabaza squash is actually closer in texture and taste to the Greek pumpkin. If you can't get it, add about 1 cup baked mashed sweet potato to each 2 to 3 cups of grated pumpkin called for in the recipe.

PURSLANE: A thick-stalked weed with small juicy leaves and a fresh taste, purslane is eaten raw in salads or used in pilafs. Often available at farmer's markets and specialized greengrocers, purslane grows wild in Greek and American gardens and can easily be grown (for seeds, see page 285).

QUINCE: This large bright yellow apple-like fruit is very firm, fragrant and sour; it is never eaten raw. Baked with sweet wine, made into preserves or cooked with meat and chicken, quinces are an invaluable ingredient of Greek winter cooking. Granny Smith apples can occasionally be used as a substitute.

RAISINS: See *Dried Fruit*.

RICE: Medium-grain rice is used in most of the recipes in this book, including the stuffings, soups and sweets. For the risotto-like dishes, Arborio is best.

SAFFRON: Saffron threads are the orange-red stigmas of the blue-purple crocus flower (*Crocus sativus*). It is the world's most expensive spice, because about 14,000 threads, which must be collected by hand, are needed for each ounce.

SALT COD: Salt cod, the cheapest fish available on the islands, is cooked in a variety of ways. Fished from the Atlantic and imported from Norway, Canada and Portugal, fresh cod is split in half and heavily salted and dried, so it keeps for more than a year. It needs to be soaked in several changes of water for at least 24 hours before using.

SAMOS SWEET WINE: See *Wines and Spirits.*

SAVORY: See *Herbs.*

SEA SALT: Sea salt is the only salt used in Greek cooking, but ordinary salt is fine. I suggest you use COARSE SEA SALT or KOSHER SALT in breads.

SEMOLINA: See *Flour.*

SORREL: A leafy green with a sour taste, sorrel is either foraged in the wild in Greece or cultivated. It is used in combination with other greens in pies and stews. It can occasionally be found in farmer's markets; see the individual recipes for substitutions.

TARAMA (ta-RAH-ma): This cured carp roe is mixed with soaked bread, scallions, olive oil and lemon juice to make a tasty dip called *taramosalata.* Tarama is sold in ethnic grocery stores, and although the artificially colored pink roe make a more attractive-looking dip, the best-tasting tarama is the natural beige-colored one.

THYME: See *Herbs.*

TRAHANA (tra-ha-NA): Also called *ksinhondros, trahana* is a traditional Greek homemade pasta. Coarsely ground whole wheat grains are cooked in, or simply soaked in, sour milk or a combination of milk and yogurt. *Trahana* is then dried in the sun and coarsely ground until it is about the size of large bread crumbs. Cooked in soups or added to stuffings and stews, *trahana* is a winter staple. It is occasionally imported into the United States (see page 285).

VEGETABLES: To duplicate the taste of the small and flavorful vegetables and fruits of Greece, buy seasonal organic vegetables from your local farmer's market. Walk around the market, select the best seasonal produce, and then choose your recipe on that basis, as Greek cooks most often do. If you decide to make, for example, stuffed tomatoes in January, don't expect good results.

VINEGAR, GREEK: Deep-flavored, with a taste similar to that of balsamic vinegar, this old-fashioned Greek vinegar is now available in the United States, imported from Kalamata, in the southern Peloponnese (see page 285). Balsamic vinegar is a good substitute.

WHEAT BERRIES: These wheat grains, which can be either whole or husked, look a bit

TRAHANA (CHIAN PASTA)

like fat brown rice. They need no soaking, but they must be simmered gently for about 1 hour before they become tender. Look for them in health-food stores and ethnic groceries.

WINES AND SPIRITS: Although most Greek wines are produced on the mainland, some very interesting wines are made on the islands from indigenous grapes. The Muscat of Samos is the most well known, while neighboring Limnos produces another good, lighter Muscat. The dry fruity white of Santorini and the fragrant Robola of Cephalonia are two more of the popular wines of the islands. The following wines and spirits are often used as flavorings:

BRANDY is an essential ingredient in most Greek sweets, cakes and syrups. Although Metaxa or other high-quality Greek brandy is the best, any brandy can be used.

COMMANDARIA (co-man-dar-EE-ah), a deep-flavored sweet red wine from Cyprus, is a wonderful and reasonably priced dessert wine and an invaluable ingredient in many desserts. It can be used interchangeably with Mavrodaphne. Sweet Marsala can be substituted.

MAVRODAPHNE (mav-ro-DAF-nee), a sweet dark red wine, is mainly used in cooking and baking. Sweet Marsala and Commandaria are good substitutes.

OUZO, the strong alcoholic anise-flavored Greek drink, is usually diluted with two parts water for each part ouzo. Slightly sweet and fragrant, ouzo is the perfect accompaniment to the often strongly flavored cured fish, cheese and other *meze* of the islands. Lesbos and Chios are the islands mostly associated with the ouzo culture, while on Crete, RAKI, a similarly strong drink that is unflavored, is usually consumed undiluted, in tiny glass tumblers.

SAMOS, from the island of the same name, is a Muscat with apricot- and peach-like aromas. An excellent and reasonably priced dessert wine, Samos is also used in sweets. Orange Muscat from California is a good substitute.

YELLOW SPLIT PEAS: These peeled and split dried peas cook fast and are often made into a puree called *fava*, replacing dried fava beans, which are more difficult to cook. Pureed yellow split peas are served cold, as a *meze*, flavored with olive oil, garlic and oregano (see page 24). Yellow split peas are sold in most supermarkets, Indian and other ethnic grocery stores; green split peas can be substituted.

YOGURT: Smooth and creamy Greek sheep's milk yogurt is now available in the United States (see page 286). Drained cow's milk yogurt (see page 266) is a good substitute.

ZANTE CURRANTS: See *Dried Fruit*.

SOURCES FOR
GREEK PRODUCTS

Most of the ingredients for the recipes in this book are readily available in supermarkets; others can be located in Greek and Middle Eastern grocery stores across the United States. The following sources can supply foods that may be difficult to find in your local supermarket.

ADRIANA'S BAZAAR

321 Grand Central Terminal
New York, NY 10017
(800) 316–0820

Aleppo pepper, salt-packed capers from Spain, a large variety of spices, mastic and bulgur. Catalog available.

ATHENS FOODS

13600 Snow Road
Cleveland, OH 44142
(216) 676–8500
Fax: (216) 676–0609

Manufacturer of frozen Apollo phyllo dough. Call to find the retail outlet nearest you.

BALDUCCI'S

424 6th Avenue
New York, NY 10011
(800) 225-3822
www.balducci.com

Greek olives, salt-packed capers (in store only). Catalog available.

THE COOK'S GARDEN

P.O. Box 535
Londonderry, VT 05148
(802) 824–5526
Fax: (802) 824–9556

Seeds for vegetables and exotic greens. Catalog available.

CYPRUS EMBASSY TRADE CENTER

13 East 40th Street
New York, NY 10016
(212) 213–9100
Fax: (212) 213–2918
www.cyprustradeny.org
e-mail: ctcny@aol.com

Cypriot cheeses and wines. Call to find the retail outlet nearest you.

DEAN & DELUCA

560 Broadway
New York, NY 10012
(800) 999–0306
www.deananddeluca.com

Greek oregano and other herbs from Crete, coarse (# 3) bulgur and Greek vinegar.
Catalog available.

EURO-USA
4 Hazel Drive
Pittsburgh, PA 15228
Fax: (412) 344–4599
Olive oil, olives, *trahana* and other Greek pastas.
Fax to find the retail outlet nearest you.

THE FILLO FACTORY INC.
74 Cortland Avenue
Dumont, NJ 07628
(800) 653–4566 , ext. 10 or 13
Fresh phyllo pastry.

FORMAGGIO KITCHEN
244 Huron Avenue
Cambridge, MA 02138
(888) 212–3224; (617) 354–4750
Fax: (617) 547–5680
Greek cheeses. Catalog available.

GERD STERN, ETC.
111 Madison Avenue
Cresskill, NJ 07626
(201) 816–9215
Greek cheeses. Call to find the retail outlet nearest you.

GREEK FOOD AND WINE INSTITUTE
825 8th Avenue
New York, NY 10019
(212) 474–5813
Fax: (212) 474–5196
Call for information on retail outlets for Greek olive oils, honey, olives and various other products.

GREENLEAF
1955 Jerrold Avenue
San Francisco, CA 94124
(415) 647–2991
Fax: (415) 647–2996
Wild greens.

HAIG'S DELICACIES
642 Clement Street
San Francisco, CA 94118
(415) 752–6283
Fax: (415) 752–6177
www.haigsdelicacies.com
e-mail: haigs@aol.com
Fresh phyllo pastry, bulgur, spices and *basturma*.

HELLAS INTERNATIONAL INC.
35 Congress Street
Salem, MA 01970
(800) 274–1233
Fax: (978) 744–3347
Olives, olive oil, Greek vinegar and Greek honey. Call to find the retail outlet nearest you.

INDIAN ROCK PRODUCE
530 California Road
Quakertown, PA 18951
(800) 882–0512; (215) 536–9600
Fax: (215) 529–9447
Fresh produce. Newsletter available.

JOHNNY'S SELECTED SEEDS
Foss Hill Road
Albion, ME 04910
(207) 437–9294
Amaranth seeds. Catalog available.

KALUSTYAN'S
123 Lexington Avenue
New York, NY 10016
(212) 685–3451
Fax: (212) 683–8458
www.kalustyans.com
Aleppo pepper, spices and coarse bulgur.
Catalog available.

KING ARTHUR FLOUR BAKER'S
CATALOGUE
P.O. Box 876
Norwich, VT 05055
(800) 827–6836
Barley flour. Catalog available.

KRINOS FOODS, INC.
47-00 Northern Blvd.
Long Island City, NY 11101
(718) 729–9000
Fax: (718) 361–9725
Frozen Krinos brand phyllo and many other
Greek products. Call to find the retail outlet
nearest you.

MOUNT VIKOS
477 Laurel Avenue
St. Paul, MN 55102
(651) 298–0864
Greek cheeses, olives and olive oil. Call to find
the retail outlet nearest you.

OLD CHATHAM SHEEP DAIRY
155 Shaker Road
Old Chatham, NY 12136
(518) 794–7726, ext. 9
Sheep's milk yogurt.

POSEIDON BAKERY
629 9th Avenue
New York, NY 10036
(212) 757–6173
Fresh phyllo pastry.

THE SPICE HUNTER
P.O. Box 8110
San Luis Obispo, CA 93403-8110
(800) 444–3061
Fax: (800) 444–3096
www.spicehunter.com
e-mail: consumerline@spicehunter.com
Greek oregano.

SULTAN'S DELIGHT
P.O. Box 090302
Brooklyn, NY 11209
(800) 852–5046
Mahlep, mastic and other Greek ingredients.
Catalog available.

TITAN FOODS
25-56 31st Street
Long Island City, NY 11102-1749
(718) 616–7771
Fax: (718) 626–2327
www.titanfood.com
Great selection of Greek foods, including *paxi-madia* (savory barley biscuits) from Crete, spices,
mastic, excellent olives and imported frozen pre-pared foods.

ZINGERMAN'S
1220 Jewett
Ann Arbor, MI 48104
(888) 636–8162
Salt-packed capers, olive oils, olives and Greek
cheeses. Catalog available.

WWW.ETHNICGROCER.COM
Coarse bulgur, spices, olive oils, olives and other
Greek products.

WWW.WORLDSPICE.COM
Aleppo pepper and all kinds of other spices.

INDEX

GREECE
Corfu
Thessaly
Aegea
Skiathos
Skopelos
Skyros
Ionian Sea
Lefkas
Ithaca
Evia
Cephalonia
ATHENS
PIRAEUS
Zakynthos
Aegina
Peloponnese
Poros
Kea
Hydra
Sifno
Kimolos
Milos
N
W
E
S
Kythera
Mediterranean Sea
Holmer 2000